Troilus and Criseyde

Geoffrey Chaucer

Contents

TROILUS AND CRISEYDE

BY

Geoffrey Chaucer

BOOK I. Incipit Liber Primus

The double sorwe of Troilus to tellen, 1
That was the king Priamus sone of Troye,
In lovinge, how his aventures fellen
Fro wo to wele, and after out of Ioye,
My purpos is, er that I parte fro ye. 5
Thesiphone, thou help me for tendyte
Thise woful vers, that wepen as I wryte!

To thee clepe I, thou goddesse of torment,
Thou cruel Furie, sorwing ever in peyne;
Help me, that am the sorwful instrument 10
That helpeth lovers, as I can, to pleyne!
For wel sit it, the sothe for to seyne,
A woful wight to han a drery fere,
And, to a sorwful tale, a sory chere.

For I, that god of Loves servaunts serve, 15
Ne dar to Love, for myn unlyklinesse,
Preyen for speed, al sholde I therfor sterve,
So fer am I fro his help in derknesse;
But nathelees, if this may doon gladnesse
To any lover, and his cause avayle, 20
Have he my thank, and myn be this travayle!

But ye loveres, that bathen in gladnesse,
If any drope of pitee in yow be,
Remembreth yow on passed hevinesse
That ye han felt, and on the adversitee 25
Of othere folk, and thenketh how that ye
Han felt that Love dorste yow displese;
Or ye han wonne hym with to greet an ese.

And preyeth for hem that ben in the cas
Of Troilus, as ye may after here, 30
That love hem bringe in hevene to solas,
And eek for me preyeth to god so dere,
That I have might to shewe, in som manere,
Swich peyne and wo as Loves folk endure,
In Troilus unsely aventure. 35

And biddeth eek for hem that been despeyred
In love, that never nil recovered be,
And eek for hem that falsly been apeyred
Thorugh wikked tonges, be it he or she;
Thus biddeth god, for his benignitee, 40
So graunte hem sone out of this world to pace,
That been despeyred out of Loves grace.

And biddeth eek for hem that been at ese,
That god hem graunte ay good perseveraunce,
And sende hem might hir ladies so to plese, 45
That it to Love be worship and plesaunce.
For so hope I my soule best avaunce,
To preye for hem that Loves servaunts be,
And wryte hir wo, and live in charitee.

And for to have of hem compassioun 50

As though I were hir owene brother dere.
Now herkeneth with a gode entencioun,
For now wol I gon streight to my matere,
In whiche ye may the double sorwes here
Of Troilus, in loving of Criseyde, 55
And how that she forsook him er she deyde.

  It is wel wist, how that the Grekes stronge
In armes with a thousand shippes wente
To Troyewardes, and the citee longe
Assegeden neigh ten yeer er they stente, 60
And, in diverse wyse and oon entente,
The ravisshing to wreken of Eleyne,
By Paris doon, they wroughten al hir peyne.

Now fil it so, that in the toun ther was
Dwellinge a lord of greet auctoritee, 65
A gret devyn that cleped was Calkas,
That in science so expert was, that he
Knew wel that Troye sholde destroyed be,
By answere of his god, that highte thus,
Daun Phebus or Apollo Delphicus. 70

So whan this Calkas knew by calculinge,
And eek by answere of this Appollo,
That Grekes sholden swich a peple bringe,
Thorugh which that Troye moste been for-do,
He caste anoon out of the toun to go; 75
For wel wiste he, by sort, that Troye sholde
Destroyed ben, ye, wolde who-so nolde.

For which, for to departen softely
Took purpos ful this forknowinge wyse,

And to the Grekes ost ful prively 80
He stal anoon; and they, in curteys wyse,
Hym deden bothe worship and servyse,
In trust that he hath conning hem to rede
In every peril which that is to drede.

The noyse up roos, whan it was first aspyed, 85
Thorugh al the toun, and generally was spoken,
That Calkas traytor fled was, and allyed
With hem of Grece; and casten to ben wroken
On him that falsly hadde his feith so broken;
And seyden, he and al his kin at ones 90
Ben worthy for to brennen, fel and bones.

Now hadde Calkas left, in this meschaunce,
Al unwist of this false and wikked dede,
His doughter, which that was in gret penaunce,
For of hir lyf she was ful sore in drede, 95
As she that niste what was best to rede;
For bothe a widowe was she, and allone
Of any freend to whom she dorste hir mone.

Criseyde was this lady name a-right;
As to my dome, in al Troyes citee 100
Nas noon so fair, for passing every wight
So aungellyk was hir natyf beautee,
That lyk a thing immortal semed she,
As doth an hevenish parfit creature,
That doun were sent in scorning of nature. 105

This lady, which that al-day herde at ere
Hir fadres shame, his falsnesse and tresoun,
Wel nigh out of hir wit for sorwe and fere,

In widewes habit large of samit broun,
On knees she fil biforn Ector a-doun; 110
With pitous voys, and tendrely wepinge,
His mercy bad, hir-selven excusinge.

Now was this Ector pitous of nature,
And saw that she was sorwfully bigoon,
And that she was so fair a creature; 115
Of his goodnesse he gladed hir anoon,
And seyde, `Lat your fadres treson goon
Forth with mischaunce, and ye your-self, in Ioye,
Dwelleth with us, whyl you good list, in Troye.

`And al thonour that men may doon yow have, 120
As ferforth as your fader dwelled here,
Ye shul han, and your body shal men save,
As fer as I may ought enquere or here.'
And she him thonked with ful humble chere,
And ofter wolde, and it hadde ben his wille, 125
And took hir leve, and hoom, and held hir stille.

And in hir hous she abood with swich meynee
As to hir honour nede was to holde;
And whyl she was dwellinge in that citee,
Kepte hir estat, and bothe of yonge and olde 130
Ful wel beloved, and wel men of hir tolde.
But whether that she children hadde or noon,
I rede it naught; therfore I late it goon.

The thinges fellen, as they doon of werre,
Bitwixen hem of Troye and Grekes ofte; 135
For som day boughten they of Troye it derre,
And eft the Grekes founden no thing softe

The folk of Troye; and thus fortune on-lofte,
And under eft, gan hem to wheelen bothe
After hir cours, ay whyl they were wrothe. 140

But how this toun com to destruccioun
Ne falleth nought to purpos me to telle;
For it were a long digressioun
Fro my matere, and yow to longe dwelle.
But the Troyane gestes, as they felle, 145
In Omer, or in Dares, or in Dyte,
Who-so that can, may rede hem as they wryte.

But though that Grekes hem of Troye shetten,
And hir citee bisegede al a-boute,
Hir olde usage wolde they not letten, 150
As for to honoure hir goddes ful devoute;
But aldermost in honour, out of doute,
They hadde a relik hight Palladion,
That was hir trist a-boven everichon.

And so bifel, whan comen was the tyme 155
Of Aperil, whan clothed is the mede
With newe grene, of lusty Ver the pryme,
And swote smellen floures whyte and rede,
In sondry wyses shewed, as I rede,
The folk of Troye hir observaunces olde, 160
Palladiones feste for to holde.

And to the temple, in al hir beste wyse,
In general, ther wente many a wight,
To herknen of Palladion servyse;
And namely, so many a lusty knight, 165
So many a lady fresh and mayden bright,

Ful wel arayed, bothe moste and leste,
Ye, bothe for the seson and the feste.

Among thise othere folk was Criseyda,
In widewes habite blak; but nathelees, 170
Right as our firste lettre is now an A,
In beautee first so stood she, makelees;
Hir godly looking gladede al the prees.
Nas never seyn thing to ben preysed derre,
Nor under cloude blak so bright a sterre 175

As was Criseyde, as folk seyde everichoon
That hir behelden in hir blake wede;
And yet she stood ful lowe and stille alloon,
Bihinden othere folk, in litel brede,
And neigh the dore, ay under shames drede, 180
Simple of a-tyr, and debonaire of chere,
With ful assured loking and manere.

This Troilus, as he was wont to gyde
His yonge knightes, ladde hem up and doun
In thilke large temple on every syde, 185
Biholding ay the ladyes of the toun,
Now here, now there, for no devocioun
Hadde he to noon, to reven him his reste,
But gan to preyse and lakken whom him leste.

And in his walk ful fast he gan to wayten 190
If knight or squyer of his companye
Gan for to syke, or lete his eyen bayten
On any woman that he coude aspye;
He wolde smyle, and holden it folye,
And seye him thus, `god wot, she slepeth softe 195

For love of thee, whan thou tornest ful ofte!

`I have herd told, pardieux, of your livinge,
Ye lovers, and your lewede observaunces,
And which a labour folk han in winninge
Of love, and, in the keping, which doutaunces; 200
And whan your preye is lost, wo and penaunces;
O verrey foles! nyce and blinde be ye;
Ther nis not oon can war by other be.'

And with that word he gan cast up the browe,
Ascaunces, `Lo! is this nought wysly spoken?' 205
At which the god of love gan loken rowe
Right for despyt, and shoop for to ben wroken;
He kidde anoon his bowe nas not broken;
For sodeynly he hit him at the fulle;
And yet as proud a pekok can he pulle. 210

O blinde world, O blinde entencioun!
How ofte falleth al theffect contraire
Of surquidrye and foul presumpcioun;
For caught is proud, and caught is debonaire.
This Troilus is clomben on the staire, 215
And litel weneth that he moot descenden.
But al-day falleth thing that foles ne wenden.

As proude Bayard ginneth for to skippe
Out of the wey, so priketh him his corn,
Til he a lash have of the longe whippe, 220
Than thenketh he, `Though I praunce al biforn
First in the trays, ful fat and newe shorn,
Yet am I but an hors, and horses lawe
I moot endure, and with my feres drawe.'

So ferde it by this fers and proude knight; 225
Though he a worthy kinges sone were,
And wende nothing hadde had swiche might
Ayens his wil that sholde his herte stere,
Yet with a look his herte wex a-fere,
That he, that now was most in pryde above, 230
Wex sodeynly most subget un-to love.

For-thy ensample taketh of this man,
Ye wyse, proude, and worthy folkes alle,
To scornen Love, which that so sone can
The freedom of your hertes to him thralle; 235
For ever it was, and ever it shal bifalle,
That Love is he that alle thing may binde;
For may no man for-do the lawe of kinde.

That this be sooth, hath preved and doth yet;
For this trowe I ye knowen, alle or some, 240
Men reden not that folk han gretter wit
Than they that han be most with love y-nome;
And strengest folk ben therwith overcome,
The worthiest and grettest of degree:
This was, and is, and yet men shal it see. 245

And trewelich it sit wel to be so;
For alderwysest han ther-with ben plesed;
And they that han ben aldermost in wo,
With love han ben conforted most and esed;
And ofte it hath the cruel herte apesed, 250
And worthy folk maad worthier of name,
And causeth most to dreden vyce and shame.

Now sith it may not goodly be withstonde,
And is a thing so vertuous in kinde,
Refuseth not to Love for to be bonde, 255
Sin, as him-selven list, he may yow binde.
The yerde is bet that bowen wole and winde
Than that that brest; and therfor I yow rede
To folwen him that so wel can yow lede.

But for to tellen forth in special 260
As of this kinges sone of which I tolde,
And leten other thing collateral,
Of him thenke I my tale for to holde,
Both of his Ioye, and of his cares colde;
And al his werk, as touching this matere, 265
For I it gan, I wol ther-to refere.

With-inne the temple he wente him forth pleyinge,
This Troilus, of every wight aboute,
On this lady and now on that lokinge,
Wher-so she were of toune, or of with-oute: 270
And up-on cas bifel, that thorugh a route
His eye perced, and so depe it wente,
Til on Criseyde it smoot, and ther it stente.

And sodeynly he wax ther-with astoned,
And gan hire bet biholde in thrifty wyse: 275
`O mercy, god!' thoughte he, `wher hastow woned,
That art so fair and goodly to devyse?'
Ther-with his herte gan to sprede and ryse,
And softe sighed, lest men mighte him here,
And caughte a-yein his firste pleyinge chere. 280

She nas nat with the leste of hir stature,

But alle hir limes so wel answeringe
Weren to womanhode, that creature
Was neuer lasse mannish in seminge.
And eek the pure wyse of here meninge 285
Shewede wel, that men might in hir gesse
Honour, estat, and wommanly noblesse.

To Troilus right wonder wel with-alle
Gan for to lyke hir meninge and hir chere,
Which somdel deynous was, for she leet falle 290
Hir look a lite a-side, in swich manere,
Ascaunces, `What! May I not stonden here?'
And after that hir loking gan she lighte,
That never thoughte him seen so good a sighte.

And of hir look in him ther gan to quiken 295
So greet desir, and swich affeccioun,
That in his herte botme gan to stiken
Of hir his fixe and depe impressioun:
And though he erst hadde poured up and doun,
He was tho glad his hornes in to shrinke; 300
Unnethes wiste he how to loke or winke.

Lo, he that leet him-selven so konninge,
And scorned hem that loves peynes dryen,
Was ful unwar that love hadde his dwellinge
With-inne the subtile stremes of hir yen; 305
That sodeynly him thoughte he felte dyen,
Right with hir look, the spirit in his herte;
Blissed be love, that thus can folk converte!

She, this in blak, likinge to Troylus,
Over alle thyng, he stood for to biholde; 310

Ne his desir, ne wherfor he stood thus,
He neither chere made, ne worde tolde;
But from a-fer, his maner for to holde,
On other thing his look som-tyme he caste,
And eft on hir, whyl that servyse laste. 315

And after this, not fulliche al awhaped,
Out of the temple al esiliche he wente,
Repentinge him that he hadde ever y-iaped
Of loves folk, lest fully the descente
Of scorn fille on him-self; but, what he mente, 320
Lest it were wist on any maner syde,
His wo he gan dissimulen and hyde.

Whan he was fro the temple thus departed,
He streyght anoon un-to his paleys torneth,
Right with hir look thurgh-shoten and thurgh-darted, 325
Al feyneth he in lust that he soiorneth;
And al his chere and speche also he borneth;
And ay, of loves servants every whyle,
Him-self to wrye, at hem he gan to smyle.

And seyde, `Lord, so ye live al in lest, 330
Ye loveres! For the conningest of yow,
That serveth most ententiflich and best,
Him tit as often harm ther-of as prow;
Your hyre is quit ayein, ye, god wot how!
Nought wel for wel, but scorn for good servyse; 335
In feith, your ordre is ruled in good wyse!

`In noun-certeyn ben alle your observaunces,
But it a sely fewe poyntes be;
Ne no-thing asketh so grete attendaunces

As doth youre lay, and that knowe alle ye; 340
But that is not the worste, as mote I thee;
But, tolde I yow the worste poynt, I leve,
Al seyde I sooth, ye wolden at me greve!

`But tak this, that ye loveres ofte eschuwe,
Or elles doon of good entencioun, 345
Ful ofte thy lady wole it misconstrue,
And deme it harm in hir opinioun;
And yet if she, for other enchesoun,
Be wrooth, than shalt thou han a groyn anoon:
Lord! wel is him that may be of yow oon!' 350

But for al this, whan that he say his tyme,
He held his pees, non other bote him gayned;
For love bigan his fetheres so to lyme,
That wel unnethe un-to his folk he fayned
That othere besye nedes him destrayned; 355
For wo was him, that what to doon he niste,
But bad his folk to goon wher that hem liste.

And whan that he in chaumbre was allone,
He doun up-on his beddes feet him sette,
And first be gan to syke, and eft to grone, 360
And thoughte ay on hir so, with-outen lette,
That, as he sat and wook, his spirit mette
That he hir saw a temple, and al the wyse
Right of hir loke, and gan it newe avyse.

Thus gan he make a mirour of his minde, 365
In which he saugh al hoolly hir figure;
And that he wel coude in his herte finde,
It was to him a right good aventure

To love swich oon, and if he dide his cure
To serven hir, yet mighte he falle in grace, 370
Or elles, for oon of hir servaunts pace.

Imagininge that travaille nor grame
Ne mighte, for so goodly oon, be lorn
As she, ne him for his desir ne shame,
Al were it wist, but in prys and up-born 375
Of alle lovers wel more than biforn;
Thus argumented he in his ginninge,
Ful unavysed of his wo cominge.

Thus took he purpos loves craft to suwe,
And thoughte he wolde werken prively, 380
First, to hyden his desir in muwe
From every wight y-born, al-outrely,
But he mighte ought recovered be therby;
Remembring him, that love to wyde y-blowe
Yelt bittre fruyt, though swete seed be sowe. 385

And over al this, yet muchel more he thoughte
What for to speke, and what to holden inne,
And what to arten hir to love he soughte,
And on a song anoon-right to biginne,
And gan loude on his sorwe for to winne; 390
For with good hope he gan fully assente
Criseyde for to love, and nought repente.

And of his song nought only the sentence,
As writ myn autour called Lollius,
But pleynly, save our tonges difference, 395
I dar wel sayn, in al that Troilus
Seyde in his song, lo! every word right thus

As I shal seyn; and who-so list it here,
Lo! next this vers, he may it finden here.

  Cantus Troili.

`If no love is, O god, what fele I so? 400
And if love is, what thing and whiche is he!
If love be good, from whennes comth my wo?
If it be wikke, a wonder thinketh me,
Whenne every torment and adversitee
That cometh of him, may to me savory thinke; 405
For ay thurst I, the more that I it drinke.

`And if that at myn owene lust I brenne,
Fro whennes cometh my wailing and my pleynte?
If harme agree me, wher-to pleyne I thenne?
I noot, ne why unwery that I feynte. 410
O quike deeth, O swete harm so queynte,
How may of thee in me swich quantitee,
But-if that I consente that it be?

`And if that I consente, I wrongfully
Compleyne, y-wis; thus possed to and fro, 415
Al sterelees with inne a boot am I
A-mid the see, by-twixen windes two,
That in contrarie stonden ever-mo.
Allas! what is this wonder maladye?
For hete of cold, for cold of hete, I deye.' 420

And to the god of love thus seyde he
With pitous voys, `O lord, now youres is
My spirit, which that oughte youres be.
Yow thanke I, lord, that han me brought to this;

But whether goddesse or womman, y-wis, 425
She be, I noot, which that ye do me serve;
But as hir man I wole ay live and sterve.

`Ye stonden in hire eyen mightily,
As in a place un-to youre vertu digne;
Wherfore, lord, if my servyse or I 430
May lyke yow, so beth to me benigne;
For myn estat royal here I resigne
In-to hir hond, and with ful humble chere
Bicome hir man, as to my lady dere.'

In him ne deyned sparen blood royal 435
The fyr of love, wher-fro god me blesse,
Ne him forbar in no degree, for al
His vertu or his excellent prowesse;
But held him as his thral lowe in distresse,
And brende him so in sondry wyse ay newe, 440
That sixty tyme a day he loste his hewe.

So muche, day by day, his owene thought,
For lust to hir, gan quiken and encrese,
That every other charge he sette at nought;
For-thy ful ofte, his hote fyr to cese, 445
To seen hir goodly look he gan to prese;
For ther-by to ben esed wel he wende,
And ay the ner he was, the more he brende.

For ay the ner the fyr, the hotter is,
This, trowe I, knoweth al this companye. 450
But were he fer or neer, I dar seye this,
By night or day, for wisdom or folye,
His herte, which that is his brestes ye,

Was ay on hir, that fairer was to sene
Than ever were Eleyne or Polixene. 455

Eek of the day ther passed nought an houre
That to him-self a thousand tyme he seyde,
`Good goodly, to whom serve I and laboure,
As I best can, now wolde god, Criseyde,
Ye wolden on me rewe er that I deyde! 460
My dere herte, allas! myn hele and hewe
And lyf is lost, but ye wole on me rewe.'

Alle othere dredes weren from him fledde,
Both of the assege and his savacioun;
Ne in him desyr noon othere fownes bredde 465
But argumentes to his conclusioun,
That she on him wolde han compassioun,
And he to be hir man, whyl he may dure;
Lo, here his lyf, and from the deeth his cure!
The sharpe shoures felle of armes preve, 470
That Ector or his othere bretheren diden,
Ne made him only ther-fore ones meve;
And yet was he, wher-so men wente or riden,
Founde oon the beste, and lengest tyme abiden
Ther peril was, and dide eek such travayle 475
In armes, that to thenke it was mervayle.

But for non hate he to the Grekes hadde,
Ne also for the rescous of the toun,
Ne made him thus in armes for to madde,
But only, lo, for this conclusioun, 480
To lyken hir the bet for his renoun;
Fro day to day in armes so he spedde,
That alle the Grekes as the deeth him dredde.

And fro this forth tho refte him love his sleep,
And made his mete his foo; and eek his sorwe 485
Gan multiplye, that, who-so toke keep,
It shewed in his hewe, bothe eve and morwe;
Therfor a title he gan him for to borwe
Of other syknesse, lest of him men wende
That the hote fyr of love him brende, 490

And seyde, he hadde a fever and ferde amis;
But how it was, certayn, can I not seye,
If that his lady understood not this,
Or feyned hir she niste, oon of the tweye;
But wel I rede that, by no maner weye, 495
Ne semed it as that she of him roughte,
Nor of his peyne, or what-so-ever he thoughte.

But than fel to this Troylus such wo,
That he was wel neigh wood; for ay his drede
Was this, that she som wight had loved so, 500
That never of him she wolde have taken hede;
For whiche him thoughte he felte his herte blede.
Ne of his wo ne dorste he not biginne
To tellen it, for al this world to winne.

But whanne he hadde a space fro his care, 505
Thus to him-self ful ofte he gan to pleyne;
He sayde, `O fool, now art thou in the snare,
That whilom Iapedest at loves peyne;
Now artow hent, now gnaw thyn owene cheyne;
Thou were ay wont eche lovere reprehende 510
Of thing fro which thou canst thee nat defende.

`What wol now every lover seyn of thee,
If this be wist, but ever in thyn absence
Laughen in scorn, and seyn, `Lo, ther gooth he,
That is the man of so gret sapience, 515
That held us lovers leest in reverence!
Now, thonked be god, he may goon in the daunce
Of hem that Love list febly for to avaunce!'
`But, O thou woful Troilus, god wolde,
Sin thou most loven thurgh thi destinee, 520
That thow beset were on swich oon that sholde
Knowe al thy wo, al lakkede hir pitee:
But al so cold in love, towardes thee,
Thy lady is, as frost in winter mone,
And thou fordoon, as snow in fyr is sone.' 525

`God wolde I were aryved in the port
Of deth, to which my sorwe wil me lede!
A, lord, to me it were a gret comfort;
Than were I quit of languisshing in drede.
For by myn hidde sorwe y-blowe on brede 530
I shal bi-Iaped been a thousand tyme
More than that fool of whos folye men ryme.

`But now help god, and ye, swete, for whom
I pleyne, y-caught, ye, never wight so faste!
O mercy, dere herte, and help me from 535
The deeth, for I, whyl that my lyf may laste,
More than my-self wol love yow to my laste.
And with som freendly look gladeth me, swete,
Though never more thing ye me bi-hete!'

This wordes and ful manye an-other to 540
He spak, and called ever in his compleynte

Hir name, for to tellen hir his wo,
Til neigh that he in salte teres dreynte.
Al was for nought, she herde nought his pleynte;
And whan that he bithoughte on that folye, 545
A thousand fold his wo gan multiplye.

Bi-wayling in his chambre thus allone,
A freend of his, that called was Pandare,
Com ones in unwar, and herde him grone,
And say his freend in swich distresse and care:
`Allas!' quod he, `who causeth al this fare? 551
O mercy, god! What unhap may this mene?
Han now thus sone Grekes maad yow lene?

`Or hastow som remors of conscience,
And art now falle in som devocioun, 555
And waylest for thy sinne and thyn offence,
And hast for ferde caught attricioun?
God save hem that bi-seged han our toun,
And so can leye our Iolyte on presse,
And bring our lusty folk to holinesse!' 560

These wordes seyde he for the nones alle,
That with swich thing he mighte him angry maken,
And with an angre don his sorwe falle,
As for the tyme, and his corage awaken;
But wel he wist, as fer as tonges spaken, 565
Ther nas a man of gretter hardinesse
Than he, ne more desired worthinesse.
`What cas,' quod Troilus, `or what aventure
Hath gyded thee to see my languisshinge,
That am refus of euery creature? 570
But for the love of god, at my preyinge,

Go henne a-way, for certes, my deyinge
Wol thee disese, and I mot nedes deye;
Ther-for go wey, ther is no more to seye.

`But if thou wene I be thus sik for drede, 575
It is not so, and ther-for scorne nought;
Ther is a-nother thing I take of hede
Wel more than ought the Grekes han y-wrought,
Which cause is of my deeth, for sorwe and thought.
But though that I now telle thee it ne leste, 580
Be thou nought wrooth; I hyde it for the beste.'

This Pandare, that neigh malt for wo and routhe,
Ful often seyde, `Allas! what may this be?
Now freend,' quod he, `if ever love or trouthe
Hath been, or is, bi-twixen thee and me, 585
Ne do thou never swiche a crueltee
To hyde fro thy freend so greet a care;
Wostow nought wel that it am I, Pandare?

`I wole parten with thee al thy peyne,
If it be so I do thee no comfort, 590
As it is freendes right, sooth for to seyne,
To entreparten wo, as glad desport.
I have, and shal, for trewe or fals report,
In wrong and right y-loved thee al my lyve;
Hyd not thy wo fro me, but telle it blyve.' 595

Than gan this sorwful Troilus to syke,
And seyde him thus, "God leve it be my beste
To telle it thee; for sith it may thee lyke,
Yet wole I telle it, though myn herte breste;
And wel wot I thou mayst do me no reste. 600

But lest thow deme I truste not to thee,
Now herkne, freend, for thus it stant with me.

` Love, a-yeins the which who-so defendeth
Him-selven most, him alder-lest avayleth,
With disespeir so sorwfully me offendeth, 605
That streyght un-to the deeth myn herte sayleth.
Ther-to desyr so brenningly me assaylleth,
That to ben slayn it were a gretter Ioye
To me than king of Grece been and Troye!

` Suffiseth this, my fulle freend Pandare, 610
That I have seyd, for now wostow my wo;
And for the love of god, my colde care
So hyd it wel, I telle it never to mo;
For harmes mighte folwen, mo than two,
If it were wist; but be thou in gladnesse, 615
And lat me sterve, unknowe, of my distresse.'
` How hastow thus unkindely and longe
Hid this fro me, thou fool?' quod Pandarus;
` Paraunter thou might after swich oon longe,
That myn avys anoon may helpen us.' 620
` This were a wonder thing,' quod Troylus,
` Thou coudest never in love thy-selven wisse;
How devel maystow bringen me to blisse?'

` Ye, Troilus, now herke,' quod Pandare,
` Though I be nyce; it happeth ofte so, 625
That oon that exces doth ful yvele fare,
By good counseyl can kepe his freend ther-fro.
I have my-self eek seyn a blind man go
Ther-as he fel that coude loke wyde;
A fool may eek a wys man ofte gyde. 630

`A whetston is no kerving instrument,
And yet it maketh sharpe kerving-tolis.
And ther thou woost that I have ought miswent,
Eschewe thou that, for swich thing to thee scole is;
Thus ofte wyse men ben war by folis. 635
If thou do so, thy wit is wel biwared;
By his contrarie is every thing declared.

`For how might ever sweetnesse have be knowe
To him that never tasted bitternesse?
Ne no man may be inly glad, I trowe, 640
That never was in sorwe or som distresse;
Eek whyt by blak, by shame eek worthinesse,
Ech set by other, more for other semeth;
As men may see; and so the wyse it demeth.

`Sith thus of two contraries is a lore, 645
I, that have in love so ofte assayed
Grevaunces, oughte conne, and wel the more
Counsayllen thee of that thou art amayed.
Eek thee ne oughte nat ben yvel apayed,
Though I desyre with thee for to bere 650
Thyn hevy charge; it shal the lasse dere.

`I woot wel that it fareth thus by me
As to thy brother Parys an herdesse,
Which that y-cleped was Oenone,
Wrot in a compleynte of hir hevinesse: 655
Ye say the lettre that she wroot, y gesse?'
`Nay, never yet, y-wis,' quod Troilus.
`Now,' quod Pandare, `herkneth, it was thus. --

"Phebus, that first fond art of medicyne,'
Quod she, `and coude in every wightes care 660
Remede and reed, by herbes he knew fyne,
Yet to him-self his conning was ful bare;
For love hadde him so bounden in a snare,
Al for the doughter of the kinge Admete,
That al his craft ne coude his sorwe bete." -- 665

`Right so fare I, unhappily for me;
I love oon best, and that me smerteth sore;
And yet, paraunter, can I rede thee,
And not my-self; repreve me no more.
I have no cause, I woot wel, for to sore 670
As doth an hauk that listeth for to pleye,
But to thyn help yet somwhat can I seye.

`And of o thing right siker maystow be,
That certayn, for to deyen in the peyne,
That I shal never-mo discoveren thee; 675
Ne, by my trouthe, I kepe nat restreyne
Thee fro thy love, thogh that it were Eleyne,
That is thy brotheres wif, if ich it wiste;
Be what she be, and love hir as thee liste.

`Therfore, as freend fullich in me assure, 680
And tel me plat what is thyn enchesoun,
And final cause of wo that ye endure;
For douteth no-thing, myn entencioun
Nis nought to yow of reprehencioun,
To speke as now, for no wight may bireve 685
A man to love, til that him list to leve.

`And witeth wel, that bothe two ben vyces,

Mistrusten alle, or elles alle leve;
But wel I woot, the mene of it no vyce is,
For to trusten sum wight is a preve 690
Of trouthe, and for-thy wolde I fayn remeve
Thy wrong conseyte, and do thee som wight triste,
Thy wo to telle; and tel me, if thee liste.

`The wyse seyth, "Wo him that is allone,
For, and he falle, he hath noon help to ryse;" 695
And sith thou hast a felawe, tel thy mone;
For this nis not, certeyn, the nexte wyse
To winnen love, as techen us the wyse,
To walwe and wepe as Niobe the quene,
Whos teres yet in marbel been y-sene. 700

`Lat be thy weping and thi drerinesse,
And lat us lissen wo with other speche;
So may thy woful tyme seme lesse.
Delyte not in wo thy wo to seche,
As doon thise foles that hir sorwes eche 705
With sorwe, whan they han misaventure,
And listen nought to seche hem other cure.

`Men seyn, "To wrecche is consolacioun
To have an-other felawe in his peyne;"
That oughte wel ben our opinioun, 710
For, bothe thou and I, of love we pleyne;
So ful of sorwe am I, soth for to seyne,
That certeynly no more harde grace
May sitte on me, for-why ther is no space.
`If god wole thou art not agast of me, 715
Lest I wolde of thy lady thee bigyle,
Thow wost thy-self whom that I love, pardee,

As I best can, gon sithen longe whyle.
And sith thou wost I do it for no wyle,
And sith I am he that thou tristest most, 720
Tel me sumwhat, sin al my wo thou wost.'

Yet Troilus, for al this, no word seyde,
But longe he ley as stille as he ded were;
And after this with sykinge he abreyde,
And to Pandarus voys he lente his ere, 725
And up his eyen caste he, that in fere
Was Pandarus, lest that in frenesye
He sholde falle, or elles sone dye;

And cryde `A-wake' ful wonderly and sharpe;
`What? Slombrestow as in a lytargye? 730
Or artow lyk an asse to the harpe,
That hereth soun, whan men the strenges plye,
But in his minde of that no melodye
May sinken, him to glade, for that he
So dul is of his bestialitee?' 735

And with that, Pandare of his wordes stente;
And Troilus yet him no word answerde,
For-why to telle nas not his entente
To never no man, for whom that he so ferde.
For it is seyd, `Man maketh ofte a yerde 740
With which the maker is him-self y-beten
In sondry maner,' as thise wyse treten,

And namely, in his counseyl tellinge
That toucheth love that oughte be secree;
For of him-self it wolde y-nough out-springe, 745
But-if that it the bet governed be.

Eek som-tyme it is craft to seme flee
Fro thing which in effect men hunte faste;
Al this gan Troilus in his herte caste.

But nathelees, whan he had herd him crye 750
`Awake!' he gan to syke wonder sore,
And seyde, `Freend, though that I stille lye,
I am not deef; now pees, and cry no more;
For I have herd thy wordes and thy lore;
But suffre me my mischef to biwayle, 755
For thy proverbes may me nought avayle.

`Nor other cure canstow noon for me.
Eek I nil not be cured, I wol deye;
What knowe I of the quene Niobe?
Lat be thyne olde ensaumples, I thee preye.' 760
`No,' quod tho Pandarus, `therfore I seye,
Swich is delyt of foles to biwepe
Hir wo, but seken bote they ne kepe.
`Now knowe I that ther reson in the fayleth.
But tel me, if I wiste what she were 765
For whom that thee al this misaunter ayleth?
Dorstestow that I tolde hir in hir ere
Thy wo, sith thou darst not thy-self for fere,
And hir bisoughte on thee to han som routhe?'
`Why, nay,' quod he, `by god and by my trouthe!' 770

`What, Not as bisily,' quod Pandarus,
`As though myn owene lyf lay on this nede?'
`No, certes, brother,' quod this Troilus,
`And why?' -- `For that thou sholdest never spede.'
`Wostow that wel?' -- `Ye, that is out of drede,' 775
Quod Troilus, `for al that ever ye conne,

She nil to noon swich wrecche as I be wonne.'

Quod Pandarus, `Allas! What may this be,
That thou dispeyred art thus causelees?
What? Liveth not thy lady? Benedicite! 780
How wostow so that thou art gracelees?
Swich yvel is nat alwey botelees.
Why, put not impossible thus thy cure,
Sin thing to come is ofte in aventure.

`I graunte wel that thou endurest wo 785
As sharp as doth he, Ticius, in helle,
Whos stomak foules tyren ever-mo
That highte volturis, as bokes telle.
But I may not endure that thou dwelle
In so unskilful an opinioun 790
That of thy wo is no curacioun.

`But ones niltow, for thy coward herte,
And for thyn ire and folish wilfulnesse,
For wantrust, tellen of thy sorwes smerte,
Ne to thyn owene help do bisinesse 795
As muche as speke a resoun more or lesse,
But lyest as he that list of no-thing recche.
What womman coude love swich a wrecche?

`What may she demen other of thy deeth,
If thou thus deye, and she not why it is, 800
But that for fere is yolden up thy breeth,
For Grekes han biseged us, y-wis?
Lord, which a thank than shaltow han of this!
Thus wol she seyn, and al the toun at ones,
"The wrecche is deed, the devel have his bones!" 805

`Thou mayst allone here wepe and crye and knele;
But, love a woman that she woot it nought,
And she wol quyte that thou shalt not fele;
Unknowe, unkist, and lost that is un-sought.
What! Many a man hath love ful dere y-bought 810
Twenty winter that his lady wiste,
That never yet his lady mouth he kiste.
`What? Shulde be therfor fallen in despeyr,
Or be recreaunt for his owene tene,
Or sleen him-self, al be his lady fayr? 815
Nay, nay, but ever in oon be fresh and grene
To serve and love his dere hertes quene,
And thenke it is a guerdoun hir to serve
A thousand-fold more than he can deserve.'

Of that word took hede Troilus, 820
And thoughte anoon what folye he was inne,
And how that sooth him seyde Pandarus,
That for to sleen him-self mighte he not winne,
But bothe doon unmanhod and a sinne,
And of his deeth his lady nought to wyte; 825
For of his wo, god woot, she knew ful lyte.

And with that thought he gan ful sore syke,
And seyde, `Allas! What is me best to do?'
To whom Pandare answered, `If thee lyke,
The best is that thou telle me thy wo; 830
And have my trouthe, but thou it finde so,
I be thy bote, or that it be ful longe,
To peces do me drawe, and sithen honge!'

`Ye, so thou seyst,' quod Troilus tho, `allas!

But, god wot, it is not the rather so; 835
Ful hard were it to helpen in this cas,
For wel finde I that Fortune is my fo,
Ne alle the men that ryden conne or go
May of hir cruel wheel the harm withstonde;
For, as hir list, she pleyeth with free and bonde.' 840

Quod Pandarus, `Than blamestow Fortune
For thou art wrooth, ye, now at erst I see;
Wostow nat wel that Fortune is commune
To every maner wight in som degree?
And yet thou hast this comfort, lo, pardee! 845
That, as hir Ioyes moten over-goon,
So mote hir sorwes passen everichoon.

`For if hir wheel stinte any-thing to torne,
Than cessed she Fortune anoon to be:
Now, sith hir wheel by no wey may soiorne, 850
What wostow if hir mutabilitee
Right as thy-selven list, wol doon by thee,
Or that she be not fer fro thyn helpinge?
Paraunter, thou hast cause for to singe!

`And therfor wostow what I thee beseche? 855
Lat be thy wo and turning to the grounde;
For who-so list have helping of his leche,
To him bihoveth first unwrye his wounde.
To Cerberus in helle ay be I bounde,
Were it for my suster, al thy sorwe, 860
By my wil, she sholde al be thyn to-morwe.
`Loke up, I seye, and tel me what she is
Anoon, that I may goon aboute thy nede;
Knowe ich hir ought? For my love, tel me this;

Than wolde I hopen rather for to spede.' 865
Tho gan the veyne of Troilus to blede,
For he was hit, and wex al reed for shame;
`A ha!' quod Pandare, `Here biginneth game!'
And with that word he gan him for to shake,
And seyde, `Theef, thou shalt hir name telle.' 870
But tho gan sely Troilus for to quake
As though men sholde han led him in-to helle,
And seyde, `Allas! Of al my wo the welle,
Than is my swete fo called Criseyde!'
And wel nigh with the word for fere he deyde. 875

And whan that Pandare herde hir name nevene,
Lord, he was glad, and seyde, `Freend so dere,
Now fare a-right, for Ioves name in hevene,
Love hath biset the wel, be of good chere;
For of good name and wysdom and manere 880
She hath y-nough, and eek of gentilesse;
If she be fayr, thou wost thy-self, I gesse,

`Ne I never saw a more bountevous
Of hir estat, ne a gladder, ne of speche
A freendlier, ne a more gracious 885
For to do wel, ne lasse hadde nede to seche
What for to doon; and al this bet to eche,
In honour, to as fer as she may strecche,
A kinges herte semeth by hirs a wrecche.

`And for-thy loke of good comfort thou be; 890
For certeinly, the firste poynt is this
Of noble corage and wel ordeyne,
A man to have pees with him-self, y-wis;
So oughtest thou, for nought but good it is

To loven wel, and in a worthy place; 895
Thee oghte not to clepe it hap, but grace.

`And also thenk, and ther-with glade thee,
That sith thy lady vertuous is al,
So folweth it that ther is som pitee
Amonges alle thise othere in general; 900
And for-thy see that thou, in special,
Requere nought that is ayein hir name;
For vertue streccheth not him-self to shame.

`But wel is me that ever that I was born,
That thou biset art in so good a place; 905
For by my trouthe, in love I dorste have sworn,
Thee sholde never han tid thus fayr a grace;
And wostow why? For thou were wont to chace
At Love in scorn, and for despyt him calle
"Seynt Idiot, lord of thise foles alle." 910

`How often hastow maad thy nyce Iapes,
And seyd, that loves servants everichone
Of nycetee been verray goddes apes;
And some wolde monche hir mete alone,
Ligging a-bedde, and make hem for to grone; 915
And som, thou seydest, hadde a blaunche fevere,
And preydest god he sholde never kevere.
`And som of hem tok on hem, for the colde,
More than y-nough, so seydestow ful ofte;
And som han feyned ofte tyme, and tolde 920
How that they wake, whan they slepen softe;
And thus they wolde han brought hem-self a-lofte,
And nathelees were under at the laste;
Thus seydestow, and Iapedest ful faste.

`Yet seydestow, that, for the more part, 925
These loveres wolden speke in general,
And thoughten that it was a siker art,
For fayling, for to assayen over-al.
Now may I iape of thee, if that I shal!
But nathelees, though that I sholde deye, 930
That thou art noon of tho, that dorste I seye.

`Now beet thy brest, and sey to god of love,
"Thy grace, lord! For now I me repente
If I mis spak, for now my-self I love:"
Thus sey with al thyn herte in good entente.' 935
Quod Troilus, `A! Lord! I me consente,
And prey to thee my Iapes thou foryive,
And I shal never-more whyl I live.'

`Thou seyst wel,' quod Pandare, `and now I hope
That thou the goddes wraththe hast al apesed; 940
And sithen thou hast wepen many a drope,
And seyd swich thing wher-with thy god is plesed,
Now wolde never god but thou were esed;
And think wel, she of whom rist al thy wo
Here-after may thy comfort been al-so. 945

`For thilke ground, that bereth the wedes wikke,
Bereth eek thise holsom herbes, as ful ofte
Next the foule netle, rough and thikke,
The rose waxeth swote and smothe and softe;
And next the valey is the hil a-lofte; 950
And next the derke night the glade morwe;
And also Ioye is next the fyn of sorwe.

`Now loke that atempre be thy brydel,
And, for the beste, ay suffre to the tyde,
Or elles al our labour is on ydel; 955
He hasteth wel that wysly can abyde;
Be diligent, and trewe, and ay wel hyde.
Be lusty, free, persevere in thy servyse,
And al is wel, if thou werke in this wyse.
`But he that parted is in every place 960
Is no-wher hool, as writen clerkes wyse;
What wonder is, though swich oon have no grace?
Eek wostow how it fareth of som servyse?
As plaunte a tre or herbe, in sondry wyse,
And on the morwe pulle it up as blyve, 965
No wonder is, though it may never thryve.

`And sith that god of love hath thee bistowed
In place digne un-to thy worthinesse,
Stond faste, for to good port hastow rowed;
And of thy-self, for any hevinesse, 970
Hope alwey wel; for, but-if drerinesse
Or over-haste our bothe labour shende,
I hope of this to maken a good ende.

`And wostow why I am the lasse a-fered
Of this matere with my nece trete? 975
For this have I herd seyd of wyse y-lered,
"Was never man ne woman yet bigete
That was unapt to suffren loves hete,
Celestial, or elles love of kinde;"
For-thy som grace I hope in hir to finde. 980

`And for to speke of hir in special,
Hir beautee to bithinken and hir youthe,

It sit hir nought to be celestial
As yet, though that hir liste bothe and couthe;
But trewely, it sete hir wel right nouthe 985
A worthy knight to loven and cheryce,
And but she do, I holde it for a vyce.

`Wherfore I am, and wol be, ay redy
To peyne me to do yow this servyse;
For bothe yow to plese thus hope I 990
Her-afterward; for ye beth bothe wyse,
And conne it counseyl kepe in swich a wyse
That no man shal the wyser of it be;
And so we may be gladed alle three.

`And, by my trouthe, I have right now of thee 995
A good conceyt in my wit, as I gesse,
And what it is, I wol now that thou see.
I thenke, sith that love, of his goodnesse,
Hath thee converted out of wikkednesse,
That thou shalt be the beste post, I leve, 1000
Of al his lay, and most his foos to-greve.

`Ensample why, see now these wyse clerkes,
That erren aldermost a-yein a lawe,
And ben converted from hir wikked werkes
Thorugh grace of god, that list hem to him drawe, 1005
Than arn they folk that han most god in awe,
And strengest-feythed been, I understonde,
And conne an errour alder-best withstonde.'
Whan Troilus had herd Pandare assented
To been his help in loving of Criseyde, 1010
Wex of his wo, as who seyth, untormented,
But hotter wex his love, and thus he seyde,

With sobre chere, al-though his herte pleyde,
`Now blisful Venus helpe, er that I sterve,
Of thee, Pandare, I may som thank deserve. 1015

`But, dere frend, how shal myn wo ben lesse
Til this be doon? And goode, eek tel me this,
How wiltow seyn of me and my destresse?
Lest she be wrooth, this drede I most, y-wys,
Or nil not here or trowen how it is. 1020
Al this drede I, and eek for the manere
Of thee, hir eem, she nil no swich thing here.'

Quod Pandarus, `Thou hast a ful gret care
Lest that the cherl may falle out of the mone!
Why, lord! I hate of the thy nyce fare! 1025
Why, entremete of that thou hast to done!
For goddes love, I bidde thee a bone,
So lat me alone, and it shal be thy beste.' --
`Why, freend,' quod he, `now do right as the leste.

`But herke, Pandare, o word, for I nolde 1030
That thou in me wendest so greet folye,
That to my lady I desiren sholde
That toucheth harm or any vilenye;
For dredelees, me were lever dye
Than she of me ought elles understode 1035
But that, that mighte sounen in-to gode.'

Tho lough this Pandare, and anoon answerde,
`And I thy borw? Fy! No wight dooth but so;
I roughte nought though that she stode and herde
How that thou seyst; but fare-wel, I wol go. 1040
A-dieu! Be glad! God spede us bothe two!

Yif me this labour and this besinesse,
And of my speed be thyn al that swetnesse.'

Tho Troilus gan doun on knees to falle,
And Pandare in his armes hente faste, 1045
And seyde, `Now, fy on the Grekes alle!
Yet, pardee, god shal helpe us at the laste;
And dredelees, if that my lyf may laste,
And god to-forn, lo, som of hem shal smerte;
And yet me athinketh that this avaunt me asterte! 1050

`Now, Pandare, I can no more seye,
But thou wys, thou wost, thou mayst, thou art al!
My lyf, my deeth, hool in thyn bonde I leye;
Help now,' Quod he, `Yis, by my trouthe, I shal.'
`God yelde thee, freend, and this in special,' 1055
Quod Troilus, `that thou me recomaunde
To hir that to the deeth me may comaunde.'
This Pandarus tho, desirous to serve
His fulle freend, than seyde in this manere, 1059
`Far-wel, and thenk I wol thy thank deserve;
Have here my trouthe, and that thou shalt wel here.' --
And wente his wey, thenking on this matere,
And how he best mighte hir beseche of grace,
And finde a tyme ther-to, and a place.

For every wight that hath an hous to founde 1065
Ne renneth nought the werk for to biginne
With rakel hond, but he wol byde a stounde,
And sende his hertes lyne out fro with-inne
Alderfirst his purpos for to winne.
Al this Pandare in his herte thoughte, 1070
And caste his werk ful wysly, or he wroughte.

But Troilus lay tho no lenger doun,
But up anoon up-on his stede bay,
And in the feld he pleyde tho leoun;
Wo was that Greek that with him mette that day. 1075
And in the toun his maner tho forth ay
So goodly was, and gat him so in grace,
That ech him lovede that loked on his face.

For he bicom the frendlyeste wight,
The gentileste, and eek the moste free, 1080
The thriftieste and oon the beste knight,
That in his tyme was, or mighte be.
Dede were his Iapes and his crueltee,
His heighe port and his manere estraunge,
And ech of tho gan for a vertu chaunge. 1085

Now lat us stinte of Troilus a stounde,
That fareth lyk a man that hurt is sore,
And is somdel of akinge of his wounde
Y-lissed wel, but heled no del more:
And, as an esy pacient, the lore 1090
Abit of him that gooth aboute his cure;
And thus he dryveth forth his aventure.

Explicit Liber Primus

BOOK II. Incipit Prohemium Secundi Libri.

Out of these blake wawes for to sayle,
O wind, O wind, the weder ginneth clere;
For in this see the boot hath swich travayle,
Of my conning, that unnethe I it stere:
This see clepe I the tempestous matere 5
Of desespeyr that Troilus was inne:
But now of hope the calendes biginne.
O lady myn, that called art Cleo,
Thou be my speed fro this forth, and my muse,
To ryme wel this book, til I have do; 10
Me nedeth here noon other art to use.
For-why to every lovere I me excuse,
That of no sentement I this endyte,
But out of Latin in my tonge it wryte.

Wherfore I nil have neither thank ne blame 15
Of al this werk, but prey yow mekely,
Disblameth me if any word be lame,
For as myn auctor seyde, so seye I.
Eek though I speke of love unfelingly,
No wondre is, for it no-thing of newe is; 20
A blind man can nat Iuggen wel in hewis.

Ye knowe eek, that in forme of speche is chaunge
With-inne a thousand yeer, and wordes tho

That hadden prys, now wonder nyce and straunge
Us thinketh hem; and yet they spake hem so, 25
And spedde as wel in love as men now do;
Eek for to winne love in sondry ages,
In sondry londes, sondry ben usages.

And for-thy if it happe in any wyse,
That here be any lovere in this place 30
That herkneth, as the storie wol devyse,
How Troilus com to his lady grace,
And thenketh, so nolde I nat love purchace,
Or wondreth on his speche or his doinge,
I noot; but it is me no wonderinge; 35

For every wight which that to Rome went,
Halt nat o path, or alwey o manere;
Eek in som lond were al the gamen shent,
If that they ferde in love as men don here,
As thus, in open doing or in chere, 40
In visitinge, in forme, or seyde hire sawes;
For-thy men seyn, ech contree hath his lawes.

Eek scarsly been ther in this place three
That han in love seid lyk and doon in al;
For to thy purpos this may lyken thee, 45
And thee right nought, yet al is seyd or shal;
Eek som men grave in tree, som in stoon wal,
As it bitit; but sin I have begonne,
Myn auctor shal I folwen, if I conne.

Exclipit prohemium Secundi Libri.

Incipit Liber Secundus.

In May, that moder is of monthes glade, 50
That fresshe floures, blewe, and whyte, and rede,
Ben quike agayn, that winter dede made,
And ful of bawme is fleting every mede;
Whan Phebus doth his brighte bemes sprede
Right in the whyte Bole, it so bitidde 55
As I shal singe, on Mayes day the thridde,

That Pandarus, for al his wyse speche,
Felt eek his part of loves shottes kene,
That, coude he never so wel of loving preche,
It made his hewe a-day ful ofte grene; 60
So shoop it, that hym fil that day a tene
In love, for which in wo to bedde he wente,
And made, er it was day, ful many a wente.

The swalwe Proigne, with a sorwful lay,
Whan morwe com, gan make hir waymentinge, 65
Why she forshapen was; and ever lay
Pandare a-bedde, half in a slomeringe,
Til she so neigh him made hir chiteringe
How Tereus gan forth hir suster take,
That with the noyse of hir he gan a-wake; 70

And gan to calle, and dresse him up to ryse,
Remembringe him his erand was to done
From Troilus, and eek his greet empryse;
And caste and knew in good plyt was the mone
To doon viage, and took his wey ful sone 75
Un-to his neces paleys ther bi-syde;
Now Ianus, god of entree, thou him gyde!

Whan he was come un-to his neces place,
`Wher is my lady?' to hir folk seyde he;
And they him tolde; and he forth in gan pace, 80
And fond, two othere ladyes sete and she,
With-inne a paved parlour; and they three
Herden a mayden reden hem the geste
Of the Sege of Thebes, whyl hem leste.

Quod Pandarus, `Ma dame, god yow see, 85
With al your book and al the companye!'
`Ey, uncle myn, welcome y-wis,' quod she,
And up she roos, and by the hond in hye
She took him faste, and seyde, `This night thrye,
To goode mote it turne, of yow I mette!' 90
And with that word she doun on bench him sette.

`Ye, nece, ye shal fare wel the bet,
If god wole, al this yeer,' quod Pandarus;
`But I am sory that I have yow let
To herknen of your book ye preysen thus; 95
For goddes love, what seith it? tel it us.
Is it of love? O, som good ye me lere!'
`Uncle,' quod she, `your maistresse is not here!'

With that they gonnen laughe, and tho she seyde,
`This romaunce is of Thebes, that we rede; 100
And we han herd how that king Laius deyde
Thurgh Edippus his sone, and al that dede;
And here we stenten at these lettres rede,
How the bisshop, as the book can telle,
Amphiorax, fil thurgh the ground to helle.' 105

Quod Pandarus, `Al this knowe I my-selve,
And al the assege of Thebes and the care;
For her-of been ther maked bokes twelve: --
But lat be this, and tel me how ye fare;
Do wey your barbe, and shew your face bare; 110
Do wey your book, rys up, and lat us daunce,
And lat us don to May som observaunce.'

`A! God forbede!' quod she. `Be ye mad?
Is that a widewes lyf, so god you save?
By god, ye maken me right sore a-drad, 115
Ye ben so wilde, it semeth as ye rave!
It sete me wel bet ay in a cave
To bidde, and rede on holy seyntes lyves;
Lat maydens gon to daunce, and yonge wyves.'

`As ever thryve I,' quod this Pandarus, 120
`Yet coude I telle a thing to doon you pleye.'
`Now, uncle dere,' quod she, `tel it us
For goddes love; is than the assege aweye?
I am of Grekes so ferd that I deye.'
`Nay, nay,' quod he, `as ever mote I thryve! 125
It is a thing wel bet than swiche fyve.'

`Ye, holy god,' quod she, `what thing is that?
What! Bet than swiche fyve? Ey, nay, y-wis!
For al this world ne can I reden what
It sholde been; som Iape, I trowe, is this; 130
And but your-selven telle us what it is,
My wit is for to arede it al to lene;
As help me god, I noot nat what ye meene.'

`And I your borow, ne never shal, for me,

This thing be told to yow, as mote I thryve!' 135
`And why so, uncle myn? Why so?' quod she.
`By god,' quod he, `that wole I telle as blyve;
For prouder womman were ther noon on-lyve,
And ye it wiste, in al the toun of Troye;
I iape nought, as ever have I Ioye!' 140

Tho gan she wondren more than biforn
A thousand fold, and doun hir eyen caste;
For never, sith the tyme that she was born,
To knowe thing desired she so faste;
And with a syk she seyde him at the laste, 145
`Now, uncle myn, I nil yow nought displese,
Nor axen more, that may do yow disese.'

So after this, with many wordes glade,
And freendly tales, and with mery chere,
Of this and that they pleyde, and gunnen wade 150
In many an unkouth glad and deep matere,
As freendes doon, whan they ben met y-fere;
Til she gan axen him how Ector ferde,
That was the tounes wal and Grekes yerde.

`Ful wel, I thanke it god,' quod Pandarus, 155
`Save in his arm he hath a litel wounde;
And eek his fresshe brother Troilus,
The wyse worthy Ector the secounde,
In whom that ever vertu list abounde,
As alle trouthe and alle gentillesse, 160
Wysdom, honour, fredom, and worthinesse.'

`In good feith, eem,' quod she, `that lyketh me;
They faren wel, god save hem bothe two!

For trewely I holde it greet deyntee
A kinges sone in armes wel to do, 165
And been of good condiciouns ther-to;
For greet power and moral vertu here
Is selde y-seye in o persone y-fere.'

`In good feith, that is sooth,' quod Pandarus;
`But, by my trouthe, the king hath sones tweye, 170
That is to mene, Ector and Troilus,
That certainly, though that I sholde deye,
They been as voyde of vyces, dar I seye,
As any men that liveth under the sonne,
Hir might is wyde y-knowe, and what they conne. 175

`Of Ector nedeth it nought for to telle:
In al this world ther nis a bettre knight
Than he, that is of worthinesse welle;
And he wel more vertu hath than might.
This knoweth many a wys and worthy wight. 180
The same prys of Troilus I seye,
God help me so, I knowe not swiche tweye.'

`By god,' quod she, `of Ector that is sooth;
Of Troilus the same thing trowe I;
For, dredelees, men tellen that he dooth 185
In armes day by day so worthily,
And bereth him here at hoom so gentilly
To every wight, that al the prys hath he
Of hem that me were levest preysed be.'

`Ye sey right sooth, y-wis,' quod Pandarus; 190
`For yesterday, who-so hadde with him been,
He might have wondred up-on Troilus;

For never yet so thikke a swarm of been
Ne fleigh, as Grekes fro him gonne fleen;
And thorugh the feld, in everi wightes ere, 195
Ther nas no cry but "Troilus is there!"

`Now here, now there, he hunted hem so faste,
Ther nas but Grekes blood; and Troilus,
Now hem he hurte, and hem alle doun he caste;
Ay where he wente, it was arayed thus: 200
He was hir deeth, and sheld and lyf for us;
That as that day ther dorste noon with-stonde,
Whyl that he held his blody swerd in honde.

`Therto he is the freendlieste man
Of grete estat, that ever I saw my lyve; 205
And wher him list, best felawshipe can
To suche as him thinketh able for to thryve.'
And with that word tho Pandarus, as blyve,
He took his leve, and seyde, `I wol go henne.'
`Nay, blame have I, myn uncle,' quod she thenne. 210

`What eyleth yow to be thus wery sone,
And namelich of wommen? Wol ye so?
Nay, sitteth down; by god, I have to done
With yow, to speke of wisdom er ye go.'
And every wight that was a-boute hem tho, 215
That herde that, gan fer a-wey to stonde,
Whyl they two hadde al that hem liste in honde.

Whan that hir tale al brought was to an ende,
Of hire estat and of hir governaunce,
Quod Pandarus, `Now is it tyme I wende; 220
But yet, I seye, aryseth, lat us daunce,

And cast your widwes habit to mischaunce:
What list yow thus your-self to disfigure,
Sith yow is tid thus fair an aventure?'

`A! Wel bithought! For love of god,' quod she, 225
`Shal I not witen what ye mene of this?'
`No, this thing axeth layser,' tho quod he,
`And eek me wolde muche greve, y-wis,
If I it tolde, and ye it toke amis.
Yet were it bet my tonge for to stille 230
Than seye a sooth that were ayeins your wille.

`For, nece, by the goddesse Minerve,
And Iuppiter, that maketh the thonder ringe,
And by the blisful Venus that I serve,
Ye been the womman in this world livinge, 235
With-oute paramours, to my wittinge,
That I best love, and lothest am to greve,
And that ye witen wel your-self, I leve.'

`Y-wis, myn uncle,' quod she, `grant mercy;
Your freendship have I founden ever yit; 240
I am to no man holden trewely,
So muche as yow, and have so litel quit;
And, with the grace of god, emforth my wit,
As in my gilt I shal you never offende;
And if I have er this, I wol amende. 245

`But, for the love of god, I yow beseche,
As ye ben he that I love most and triste,
Lat be to me your fremde manere speche,
And sey to me, your nece, what yow liste:'
And with that word hir uncle anoon hir kiste, 250

And seyde, `Gladly, leve nece dere,
Tak it for good that I shal seye yow here.'

With that she gan hir eiyen doun to caste,
And Pandarus to coghe gan a lyte,
And seyde, `Nece, alwey, lo! To the laste, 255
How-so it be that som men hem delyte
With subtil art hir tales for to endyte,
Yet for al that, in hir entencioun
Hir tale is al for som conclusioun.

`And sithen thende is every tales strengthe, 260
And this matere is so bihovely,
What sholde I peynte or drawen it on lengthe
To yow, that been my freend so feithfully?'
And with that word he gan right inwardly
Biholden hir, and loken on hir face, 265
And seyde, `On suche a mirour goode grace!'

Than thoughte he thus: `If I my tale endyte
Ought hard, or make a proces any whyle,
She shal no savour han ther-in but lyte,
And trowe I wolde hir in my wil bigyle. 270
For tendre wittes wenen al be wyle
Ther-as they can nat pleynly understonde;
For-thy hir wit to serven wol I fonde --'

And loked on hir in a besy wyse,
And she was war that he byheld hir so, 275
And seyde, `Lord! So faste ye me avyse!
Sey ye me never er now? What sey ye, no?'
`Yes, yes,' quod he, `and bet wole er I go;
But, by my trouthe, I thoughte now if ye

Be fortunat, for now men shal it see. 280

`For to every wight som goodly aventure
Som tyme is shape, if he it can receyven;
And if that he wol take of it no cure,
Whan that it commeth, but wilfully it weyven,
Lo, neither cas nor fortune him deceyven, 285
But right his verray slouthe and wrecchednesse;
And swich a wight is for to blame, I gesse.

`Good aventure, O bele nece, have ye
Ful lightly founden, and ye conne it take;
And, for the love of god, and eek of me, 290
Cacche it anoon, lest aventure slake.
What sholde I lenger proces of it make?
Yif me your hond, for in this world is noon,
If that yow list, a wight so wel begoon.

`And sith I speke of good entencioun, 295
As I to yow have told wel here-biforn,
And love as wel your honour and renoun
As creature in al this world y-born;
By alle the othes that I have yow sworn,
And ye be wrooth therfore, or wene I lye, 300
Ne shal I never seen yow eft with ye.

`Beth nought agast, ne quaketh nat; wher-to?
Ne chaungeth nat for fere so your hewe;
For hardely the werste of this is do;
And though my tale as now be to yow newe, 305
Yet trist alwey, ye shal me finde trewe;
And were it thing that me thoughte unsittinge,
To yow nolde I no swiche tales bringe.'

`Now, my good eem, for goddes love, I preye,'
Quod she, `com of, and tel me what it is; 310
For bothe I am agast what ye wol seye,
And eek me longeth it to wite, y-wis.
For whether it be wel or be amis,
Say on, lat me not in this fere dwelle:'
`So wol I doon; now herkneth, I shal telle: 315

`Now, nece myn, the kinges dere sone,
The goode, wyse, worthy, fresshe, and free,
Which alwey for to do wel is his wone,
The noble Troilus, so loveth thee,
That, bot ye helpe, it wol his bane be. 320
Lo, here is al, what sholde I more seye?
Doth what yow list, to make him live or deye.

`But if ye lete him deye, I wol sterve;
Have her my trouthe, nece, I nil not lyen;
Al sholde I with this knyf my throte kerve --' 325
With that the teres braste out of his yen,
And seyde, `If that ye doon us bothe dyen,
Thus giltelees, than have ye fisshed faire;
What mende ye, though that we bothe apeyre?

`Allas! He which that is my lord so dere, 330
That trewe man, that noble gentil knight,
That nought desireth but your freendly chere,
I see him deye, ther he goth up-right,
And hasteth him, with al his fulle might,
For to be slayn, if fortune wol assente; 335
Allas! That god yow swich a beautee sente!

`If it be so that ye so cruel be,
That of his deeth yow liste nought to recche,
That is so trewe and worthy, as ye see,
No more than of a Iapere or a wrecche, 340
If ye be swich, your beautee may not strecche
To make amendes of so cruel a dede;
Avysement is good bifore the nede.

`Wo worth the faire gemme vertulees!
Wo worth that herbe also that dooth no bote! 345
Wo worth that beautee that is routhelees!
Wo worth that wight that tret ech under fote!
And ye, that been of beautee crop and rote,
If therwith-al in you ther be no routhe,
Than is it harm ye liven, by my trouthe! 350

`And also thenk wel that this is no gaude;
For me were lever, thou and I and he
Were hanged, than I sholde been his baude,
As heyghe, as men mighte on us alle y-see:
I am thyn eem, the shame were to me, 355
As wel as thee, if that I sholde assente,
Thorugh myn abet, that he thyn honour shente.

`Now understond, for I yow nought requere,
To binde yow to him thorugh no beheste,
But only that ye make him bettre chere 360
Than ye han doon er this, and more feste,
So that his lyf be saved, at the leste;
This al and som, and playnly our entente;
God help me so, I never other mente.

`Lo, this request is not but skile, y-wis, 365

Ne doute of reson, pardee, is ther noon.
I sette the worste that ye dredden this,
Men wolden wondren seen him come or goon:
Ther-ayeins answere I thus a-noon,
That every wight, but he be fool of kinde, 370
Wol deme it love of freendship in his minde.

`What? Who wol deme, though he see a man
To temple go, that he the images eteth?
Thenk eek how wel and wysly that he can
Governe him-self, that he no-thing foryeteth, 375
That, wher he cometh, he prys and thank him geteth;
And eek ther-to, he shal come here so selde,
What fors were it though al the toun behelde?

`Swich love of freendes regneth al this toun;
And wrye yow in that mantel ever-mo; 380
And god so wis be my savacioun,
As I have seyd, your beste is to do so.
But alwey, goode nece, to stinte his wo,
So lat your daunger sucred ben a lyte,
That of his deeth ye be nought for to wyte.' 385

Criseyde, which that herde him in this wyse,
Thoughte, `I shal fele what he meneth, y-wis.'
`Now, eem,' quod she, `what wolde ye devyse?
What is your reed I sholde doon of this?'
`That is wel seyd,' quod he. `certayn, best is 390
That ye him love ayein for his lovinge,
As love for love is skilful guerdoninge.

`Thenk eek, how elde wasteth every houre
In eche of yow a party of beautee;

And therfore, er that age thee devoure, 395
Go love, for, olde, ther wol no wight of thee.
Lat this proverbe a lore un-to yow be;
"To late y-war, quod Beautee, whan it paste;"
And elde daunteth daunger at the laste.

`The kinges fool is woned to cryen loude, 400
Whan that him thinketh a womman bereth hir hye,
"So longe mote ye live, and alle proude,
Til crowes feet be growe under your ye,
And sende yow thanne a mirour in to prye
In whiche that ye may see your face a-morwe!" 405
Nece, I bidde wisshe yow no more sorwe.'

With this he stente, and caste adoun the heed,
And she bigan to breste a-wepe anoon,
And seyde, `Allas, for wo! Why nere I deed?
For of this world the feith is al agoon! 410
Allas! What sholden straunge to me doon,
Whan he, that for my beste freend I wende,
Ret me to love, and sholde it me defende?

`Allas! I wolde han trusted, doutelees,
That if that I, thurgh my disaventure, 415
Had loved other him or Achilles,
Ector, or any mannes creature,
Ye nolde han had no mercy ne mesure
On me, but alwey had me in repreve;
This false world, allas! Who may it leve? 420

`What? Is this al the Ioye and al the feste?
Is this your reed, is this my blisful cas?
Is this the verray mede of your beheste?

Is al this peynted proces seyd, allas!
Right for this fyn? O lady myn, Pallas! 425
Thou in this dredful cas for me purveye;
For so astonied am I that I deye!'

With that she gan ful sorwfully to syke;
`A! May it be no bet?' quod Pandarus;
`By god, I shal no-more come here this wyke, 430
And god to-forn, that am mistrusted thus;
I see ful wel that ye sette lyte of us,
Or of our deeth! Allas! I woful wrecche!
Mighte he yet live, of me is nought to recche.

`O cruel god, O dispitouse Marte, 435
O Furies three of helle, on yow I crye!
So lat me never out of this hous departe,
If that I mente harm or vilanye!
But sith I see my lord mot nedes dye,
And I with him, here I me shryve, and seye 440
That wikkedly ye doon us bothe deye.

`But sith it lyketh yow that I be deed,
By Neptunus, that god is of the see,
Fro this forth shal I never eten breed
Til I myn owene herte blood may see; 445
For certayn, I wole deye as sone as he --'
And up he sterte, and on his wey he raughte,
Til she agayn him by the lappe caughte.

Criseyde, which that wel neigh starf for fere,
So as she was the ferfulleste wight 450
That mighte be, and herde eek with hir ere,
And saw the sorwful ernest of the knight,

And in his preyere eek saw noon unright,
And for the harm that mighte eek fallen more,
She gan to rewe and dredde hir wonder sore; 455

And thoughte thus, `Unhappes fallen thikke
Alday for love, and in swich maner cas,
As men ben cruel in hem-self and wikke;
And if this man slee here him-self, allas!
In my presence, it wol be no solas. 460
What men wolde of hit deme I can nat seye;
It nedeth me ful sleyly for to pleye.'

And with a sorwful syk she seyde thrye,
`A! Lord! What me is tid a sory chaunce!
For myn estat lyth in Iupartye, 465
And eek myn emes lyf lyth in balaunce;
But nathelees, with goddes governaunce,
I shal so doon, myn honour shal I kepe,
And eek his lyf;' and stinte for to wepe.

`Of harmes two, the lesse is for to chese; 470
Yet have I lever maken him good chere
In honour, than myn emes lyf to lese;
Ye seyn, ye no-thing elles me requere?'
`No, wis,' quod he, `myn owene nece dere.'
`Now wel,' quod she, `and I wol doon my peyne; 475
I shal myn herte ayeins my lust constreyne.

`But that I nil not holden him in honde,
Ne love a man, ne can I not, ne may
Ayeins my wil; but elles wol I fonde,
Myn honour sauf, plese him fro day to day; 480
Ther-to nolde I nought ones have seyd nay,

But that I dredde, as in my fantasye;
But cesse cause, ay cesseth maladye.

`And here I make a protestacioun,
That in this proces if ye depper go, 485
That certaynly, for no savacioun
Of yow, though that ye sterve bothe two,
Though al the world on o day be my fo,
Ne shal I never on him han other routhe. --'
`I graunte wel,' quod Pandare, `by my trouthe. 490

`But may I truste wel ther-to,' quod he,
`That of this thing that ye han hight me here,
Ye wol it holden trewly un-to me?'
`Ye, doutelees,' quod she, `myn uncle dere.'
`Ne that I shal han cause in this matere,' 495
Quod he, `to pleyne, or after yow to preche?'
`Why, no, parde; what nedeth more speche?'

Tho fillen they in othere tales glade,
Til at the laste, `O good eem,' quod she tho,
`For love of god, which that us bothe made, 500
Tel me how first ye wisten of his wo:
Wot noon of hit but ye?' He seyde, `No.'
`Can he wel speke of love?' quod she, `I preye,
Tel me, for I the bet me shal purveye.'

Tho Pandarus a litel gan to smyle, 505
And seyde, `By my trouthe, I shal yow telle.
This other day, nought gon ful longe whyle,
In-with the paleys-gardyn, by a welle,
Gan he and I wel half a day to dwelle,
Right for to speken of an ordenaunce, 510

How we the Grekes myghte disavaunce.

`Sone after that bigonne we to lepe,
And casten with our dartes to and fro,
Til at the laste he seyde he wolde slepe,
And on the gres a-doun he leyde him tho; 515
And I after gan rome to and fro
Til that I herde, as that I welk allone,
How he bigan ful wofully to grone.

`Tho gan I stalke him softely bihinde,
And sikerly, the sothe for to seyne, 520
As I can clepe ayein now to my minde,
Right thus to Love he gan him for to pleyne;
He seyde, "Lord! Have routhe up-on my peyne,
Al have I been rebel in myn entente;
Now, MEA CULPA, lord! I me repente. 525

`"O god, that at thy disposicioun
Ledest the fyn by Iuste purveyaunce,
Of every wight, my lowe confessioun
Accepte in gree, and send me swich penaunce
As lyketh thee, but from desesperaunce, 530
That may my goost departe awey fro thee,
Thou be my sheld, for thy benignitee.

`"For certes, lord, so soore hath she me wounded,
That stod in blak, with loking of hir yen,
That to myn hertes botme it is y-sounded, 535
Thorugh which I woot that I mot nedes dyen;
This is the worste, I dar me not bi-wryen;
And wel the hotter been the gledes rede,
That men hem wryen with asshen pale and dede."

`With that he smoot his heed adoun anoon, 540
And gan to motre, I noot what, trewely.
And I with that gan stille awey to goon,
And leet ther-of as no-thing wist hadde I,
And come ayein anoon and stood him by,
And seyde, "A-wake, ye slepen al to longe; 545
It semeth nat that love dooth yow longe,

`"That slepen so that no man may yow wake.
Who sey ever or this so dul a man?"
"Ye, freend," quod he, "do ye your hedes ake
For love, and lat me liven as I can." 550
But though that he for wo was pale and wan,
Yet made he tho as freshe a countenaunce
As though he shulde have led the newe daunce.

`This passed forth, til now, this other day,
It fel that I com roming al allone 555
Into his chaumbre, and fond how that he lay
Up-on his bed; but man so sore grone
Ne herde I never, and what that was his mone,
Ne wist I nought; for, as I was cominge,
Al sodeynly he lefte his compleyninge. 560

`Of which I took somwat suspecioun,
And neer I com, and fond he wepte sore;
And god so wis be my savacioun,
As never of thing hadde I no routhe more.
For neither with engyn, ne with no lore, 565
Unethes mighte I fro the deeth him kepe;
That yet fele I myn herte for him wepe.

`And god wot, never, sith that I was born,
Was I so bisy no man for to preche,
Ne never was to wight so depe y-sworn, 570
Or he me tolde who mighte been his leche.
But now to yow rehersen al his speche,
Or alle his woful wordes for to soune,
Ne bid me not, but ye wol see me swowne.

`But for to save his lyf, and elles nought, 575
And to non harm of yow, thus am I driven;
And for the love of god that us hath wrought,
Swich chere him dooth, that he and I may liven.
Now have I plat to yow myn herte shriven;
And sin ye woot that myn entente is clene, 580
Tak hede ther-of, for I non yvel mene.

`And right good thrift, I prey to god, have ye,
That han swich oon y-caught with-oute net;
And be ye wys, as ye ben fair to see,
Wel in the ring than is the ruby set. 585
Ther were never two so wel y-met,
Whan ye ben his al hool, as he is youre:
Ther mighty god yet graunte us see that houre!'

`Nay, therof spak I not, a, ha!' quod she,
`As helpe me god, ye shenden every deel!' 590
`O mercy, dere nece,' anoon quod he,
`What-so I spak, I mente nought but weel,
By Mars the god, that helmed is of steel;
Now beth nought wrooth, my blood, my nece dere.'
`Now wel,' quod she, `foryeven be it here!' 595

With this he took his leve, and hoom he wente;

And lord, he was glad and wel bigoon!
Criseyde aroos, no lenger she ne stente,
But straught in-to hir closet wente anoon,
And sette here doun as stille as any stoon, 600
And every word gan up and doun to winde,
That he hadde seyd, as it com hir to minde;

And wex somdel astonied in hir thought,
Right for the newe cas; but whan that she
Was ful avysed, tho fond she right nought 605
Of peril, why she oughte afered be.
For man may love, of possibilitee,
A womman so, his herte may to-breste,
And she nought love ayein, but-if hir leste.

But as she sat allone and thoughte thus, 610
Thascry aroos at skarmish al with-oute,
And men cryde in the strete, `See, Troilus
Hath right now put to flight the Grekes route!'
With that gan al hir meynee for to shoute,
`A! Go we see, caste up the latis wyde; 615
For thurgh this strete he moot to palays ryde;

`For other wey is fro the yate noon
Of Dardanus, ther open is the cheyne.'
With that com he and al his folk anoon
An esy pas rydinge, in routes tweyne, 620
Right as his happy day was, sooth to seyne,
For which, men say, may nought disturbed be
That shal bityden of necessitee.

This Troilus sat on his baye stede,
Al armed, save his heed, ful richely, 625

And wounded was his hors, and gan to blede,
On whiche he rood a pas, ful softely;
But swych a knightly sighte, trewely,
As was on him, was nought, with-outen faile,
To loke on Mars, that god is of batayle. 630

So lyk a man of armes and a knight
He was to seen, fulfild of heigh prowesse;
For bothe he hadde a body and a might
To doon that thing, as wel as hardinesse;
And eek to seen him in his gere him dresse, 635
So fresh, so yong, so weldy semed he,
It was an heven up-on him for to see.

His helm to-hewen was in twenty places,
That by a tissew heng, his bak bihinde,
His sheld to-dasshed was with swerdes and maces, 640
In which men mighte many an arwe finde
That thirled hadde horn and nerf and rinde;
And ay the peple cryde, `Here cometh our Ioye,
And, next his brother, holdere up of Troye!'

For which he wex a litel reed for shame, 645
Whan he the peple up-on him herde cryen,
That to biholde it was a noble game,
How sobreliche he caste doun his yen.
Cryseyda gan al his chere aspyen,
And leet so softe it in hir herte sinke, 650
That to hir-self she seyde, `Who yaf me drinke?'

For of hir owene thought she wex al reed,
Remembringe hir right thus, `Lo, this is he
Which that myn uncle swereth he moot be deed,

But I on him have mercy and pitee;' 655
And with that thought, for pure a-shamed, she
Gan in hir heed to pulle, and that as faste,
Whyl he and al the peple for-by paste,

And gan to caste and rollen up and doun
With-inne hir thought his excellent prowesse, 660
And his estat, and also his renoun,
His wit, his shap, and eek his gentillesse;
But most hir favour was, for his distresse
Was al for hir, and thoughte it was a routhe
To sleen swich oon, if that he mente trouthe. 665

Now mighte som envyous Iangle thus,
`This was a sodeyn love; how mighte it be
That she so lightly lovede Troilus
Right for the firste sighte; ye, pardee?'
Now who-so seyth so, mote he never thee! 670
For every thing, a ginning hath it nede
Er al be wrought, with-outen any drede.

For I sey nought that she so sodeynly
Yaf him hir love, but that she gan enclyne
To lyke him first, and I have told yow why; 675
And after that, his manhod and his pyne
Made love with-inne hir for to myne,
For which, by proces and by good servyse,
He gat hir love, and in no sodeyn wyse.

And also blisful Venus, wel arayed, 680
Sat in hir seventhe hous of hevene tho,
Disposed wel, and with aspectes payed,
To helpen sely Troilus of his wo.

And, sooth to seyn, she nas not al a fo
To Troilus in his nativitee; 685
God woot that wel the soner spedde he.

Now lat us stinte of Troilus a throwe,
That rydeth forth, and lat us tourne faste
Un-to Criseyde, that heng hir heed ful lowe,
Ther-as she sat allone, and gan to caste 690
Wher-on she wolde apoynte hir at the laste,
If it so were hir eem ne wolde cesse,
For Troilus, up-on hir for to presse.

And, lord! So she gan in hir thought argue
In this matere of which I have yow told, 695
And what to doon best were, and what eschue,
That plyted she ful ofte in many fold.
Now was hir herte warm, now was it cold,
And what she thoughte somwhat shal I wryte,
As to myn auctor listeth for to endyte. 700

She thoughte wel that Troilus persone
She knew by sighte and eek his gentillesse,
And thus she seyde, `Al were it nought to done,
To graunte him love, yet, for his worthinesse,
It were honour, with pley and with gladnesse, 705
In honestee, with swich a lord to dele,
For myn estat, and also for his hele.

`Eek, wel wot I my kinges sone is he;
And sith he hath to see me swich delyt,
If I wolde utterly his sighte flee, 710
Peraunter he mighte have me in dispyt,
Thurgh which I mighte stonde in worse plyt;

Now were I wys, me hate to purchace,
With-outen nede, ther I may stonde in grace?

`In every thing, I woot, ther lyth mesure. 715
For though a man forbede dronkenesse,
He nought for-bet that every creature
Be drinkelees for alwey, as I gesse;
Eek sith I woot for me is his distresse,
I ne oughte not for that thing him despyse, 720
Sith it is so, he meneth in good wyse.

`And eek I knowe, of longe tyme agoon,
His thewes goode, and that he is not nyce.
Ne avauntour, seyth men, certein, he is noon;
To wys is he to do so gret a vyce; 725
Ne als I nel him never so cheryce,
That he may make avaunt, by Iuste cause;
He shal me never binde in swiche a clause.

`Now set a cas, the hardest is, y-wis,
Men mighten deme that he loveth me; 730
What dishonour were it un-to me, this?
May I him lette of that? Why nay, pardee!
I knowe also, and alday here and see,
Men loven wommen al this toun aboute;
Be they the wers? Why, nay, with-outen doute. 735

`I thenk eek how he able is for to have
Of al this noble toun the thriftieste,
To been his love, so she hir honour save;
For out and out he is the worthieste,
Save only Ector, which that is the beste. 740
And yet his lyf al lyth now in my cure,

But swich is love, and eek myn aventure.

`Ne me to love, a wonder is it nought;
For wel wot I my-self, so god me spede,
Al wolde I that noon wiste of this thought, 745
I am oon the fayreste, out of drede,
And goodlieste, who-so taketh hede;
And so men seyn in al the toun of Troye.
What wonder is it though he of me have Ioye?

`I am myn owene woman, wel at ese, 750
I thank it god, as after myn estat;
Right yong, and stonde unteyd in lusty lese,
With-outen Ialousye or swich debat;
Shal noon housbonde seyn to me "Chekmat!"
For either they ben ful of Ialousye, 755
Or maisterful, or loven novelrye.

`What shal I doon? To what fyn live I thus?
Shal I nat loven, in cas if that me leste?
What, par dieux! I am nought religious!
And though that I myn herte sette at reste 760
Upon this knight, that is the worthieste,
And kepe alwey myn honour and my name,
By alle right, it may do me no shame.'

But right as whan the sonne shyneth brighte,
In March, that chaungeth ofte tyme his face, 765
And that a cloud is put with wind to flighte
Which over-sprat the sonne as for a space,
A cloudy thought gan thorugh hir soule pace,
That over-spradde hir brighte thoughtes alle,
So that for fere almost she gan to falle. 770

That thought was this: `Allas! Sin I am free,
Sholde I now love, and putte in Iupartye
My sikernesse, and thrallen libertee?
Allas! How dorste I thenken that folye?
May I nought wel in other folk aspye 775
Hir dredful Ioye, hir constreynt, and hir peyne?
Ther loveth noon, that she nath why to pleyne.

`For love is yet the moste stormy lyf,
Right of him-self, that ever was bigonne;
For ever som mistrust, or nyce stryf, 780
Ther is in love, som cloud is over that sonne:
Ther-to we wrecched wommen no-thing conne,
Whan us is wo, but wepe and sitte and thinke;
Our wreche is this, our owene wo to drinke.

`Also these wikked tonges been so prest 785
To speke us harm, eek men be so untrewe,
That, right anoon as cessed is hir lest,
So cesseth love, and forth to love a newe:
But harm y-doon, is doon, who-so it rewe.
For though these men for love hem first to-rende, 790
Ful sharp biginning breketh ofte at ende.

`How ofte tyme hath it y-knowen be,
The treson, that to womman hath be do?
To what fyn is swich love, I can nat see,
Or wher bicometh it, whan it is ago; 795
Ther is no wight that woot, I trowe so,
Wher it bycomth; lo, no wight on it sporneth;
That erst was no-thing, in-to nought it torneth.

`How bisy, if I love, eek moste I be
To plesen hem that Iangle of love, and demen, 800
And coye hem, that they sey non harm of me?
For though ther be no cause, yet hem semen
Al be for harm that folk hir freendes quemen;
And who may stoppen every wikked tonge,
Or soun of belles whyl that they be ronge?' 805

And after that, hir thought bigan to clere,
And seyde, `He which that no-thing under-taketh,
No thing ne acheveth, be him looth or dere.'
And with an other thought hir herte quaketh;
Than slepeth hope, and after dreed awaketh; 810
Now hoot, now cold; but thus, bi-twixen tweye,
She rist hir up, and went hir for to pleye.

Adoun the steyre anoon-right tho she wente
In-to the gardin, with hir neces three,
And up and doun ther made many a wente, 815
Flexippe, she, Tharbe, and Antigone,
To pleyen, that it Ioye was to see;
And othere of hir wommen, a gret route,
hir folwede in the gardin al aboute.

This yerd was large, and rayled alle the aleyes, 820
And shadwed wel with blosmy bowes grene,
And benched newe, and sonded alle the weyes,
In which she walketh arm in arm bi-twene;
Til at the laste Antigone the shene
Gan on a Troian song to singe clere, 825
That it an heven was hir voys to here. --

She seyde, `O love, to whom I have and shal

Ben humble subgit, trewe in myn entente,
As I best can, to yow, lord, yeve ich al
For ever-more, myn hertes lust to rente. 830
For never yet thy grace no wight sente
So blisful cause as me, my lyf to lede
In alle Ioye and seurtee, out of drede.

`Ye, blisful god, han me so wel beset
In love, y-wis, that al that bereth lyf 835
Imaginen ne cowde how to ben bet;
For, lord, with-outen Ialousye or stryf,
I love oon which that is most ententyf
To serven wel, unwery or unfeyned,
That ever was, and leest with harm distreyned. 840

`As he that is the welle of worthinesse,
Of trouthe ground, mirour of goodliheed,
Of wit Appollo, stoon of sikernesse,
Of vertu rote, of lust findere and heed,
Thurgh which is alle sorwe fro me deed, 845
Y-wis, I love him best, so doth he me;
Now good thrift have he, wher-so that he be!

`Whom sholde I thanke but yow, god of love,
Of al this blisse, in which to bathe I ginne?
And thanked be ye, lord, for that I love! 850
This is the righte lyf that I am inne,
To flemen alle manere vyce and sinne:
This doth me so to vertu for to entende,
That day by day I in my wil amende.

`And who-so seyth that for to love is vyce, 855
Or thraldom, though he fele in it distresse,

He outher is envyous, or right nyce,
Or is unmighty, for his shrewednesse,
To loven; for swich maner folk, I gesse,
Defamen love, as no-thing of him knowe; 860
Thei speken, but they bente never his bowe.

`What is the sonne wers, of kinde righte,
Though that a man, for feblesse of his yen,
May nought endure on it to see for brighte?
Or love the wers, though wrecches on it cryen? 865
No wele is worth, that may no sorwe dryen.
And for-thy, who that hath an heed of verre,
Fro cast of stones war him in the werre!

`But I with al myn herte and al my might,
As I have seyd, wol love, un-to my laste, 870
My dere herte, and al myn owene knight,
In which myn herte growen is so faste,
And his in me, that it shal ever laste.
Al dredde I first to love him to biginne,
Now woot I wel, ther is no peril inne.' 875

And of hir song right with that word she stente,
And therwith-al, `Now, nece,' quod Criseyde,
`Who made this song with so good entente?'
Antigone answerde anoon, and seyde,
`Ma dame, y-wis, the goodlieste mayde 880
Of greet estat in al the toun of Troye;
And let hir lyf in most honour and Ioye.'

`Forsothe, so it semeth by hir song,'
Quod tho Criseyde, and gan ther-with to syke,
And seyde, `Lord, is there swich blisse among 885

These lovers, as they conne faire endyte?'
`Ye, wis,' quod freshe Antigone the whyte,
`For alle the folk that han or been on lyve
Ne conne wel the blisse of love discryve.

`But wene ye that every wrecche woot 890
The parfit blisse of love? Why, nay, y-wis;
They wenen al be love, if oon be hoot;
Do wey, do wey, they woot no-thing of this!
Men mosten axe at seyntes if it is
Aught fair in hevene; Why? For they conne telle; 895
And axen fendes, is it foul in helle.'

Criseyde un-to that purpos nought answerde,
But seyde, `Y-wis, it wol be night as faste.'
But every word which that she of hir herde,
She gan to prenten in hir herte faste; 900
And ay gan love hir lasse for to agaste
Than it dide erst, and sinken in hir herte,
That she wex somwhat able to converte.

The dayes honour, and the hevenes ye,
The nightes fo, al this clepe I the sonne, 905
Gan westren faste, and dounward for to wrye,
As he that hadde his dayes cours y-ronne;
And whyte thinges wexen dimme and donne
For lak of light, and sterres for to appere,
That she and al hir folk in wente y-fere. 910

So whan it lyked hir to goon to reste,
And voyded weren they that voyden oughte,
She seyde, that to slepe wel hir leste.
Hir wommen sone til hir bed hir broughte.

Whan al was hust, than lay she stille, and thoughte 915
Of al this thing the manere and the wyse.
Reherce it nedeth nought, for ye ben wyse.

A nightingale, upon a cedre grene,
Under the chambre-wal ther as she lay,
Ful loude sang ayein the mone shene, 920
Paraunter, in his briddes wyse, a lay
Of love, that made hir herte fresh and gay.
That herkned she so longe in good entente,
Til at the laste the dede sleep hir hente.

And as she sleep, anoon-right tho hir mette, 925
How that an egle, fethered whyt as boon,
Under hir brest his longe clawes sette,
And out hir herte he rente, and that a-noon,
And dide his herte in-to hir brest to goon,
Of which she nought agroos, ne no-thing smerte, 930
And forth he fleigh, with herte left for herte.

Now lat hir slepe, and we our tales holde
Of Troilus, that is to paleys riden,
Fro the scarmuch, of the whiche I tolde,
And in his chaumbre sit, and hath abiden 935
Til two or three of his messages yeden
For Pandarus, and soughten him ful faste,
Til they him founde and broughte him at the laste.

This Pandarus com leping in at ones,
And seiyde thus: `Who hath ben wel y-bete 940
To-day with swerdes, and with slinge-stones,
But Troilus, that hath caught him an hete?'
And gan to Iape, and seyde, `Lord, so ye swete!

But rys, and lat us soupe and go to reste;' 944
And he answerde him, `Do we as thee leste.'

With al the haste goodly that they mighte,
They spedde hem fro the souper un-to bedde;
And every wight out at the dore him dighte,
And wher him liste upon his wey him spedde;
But Troilus, that thoughte his herte bledde 950
For wo, til that he herde som tydinge,
He seyde, `Freend, shal I now wepe or singe?'

Quod Pandarus, `Ly stille and lat me slepe,
And don thyn hood, thy nedes spedde be;
And chese, if thou wolt singe or daunce or lepe; 955
At shorte wordes, thow shal trowe me. --
Sire, my nece wol do wel by thee,
And love thee best, by god and by my trouthe,
But lak of pursuit make it in thy slouthe.

`For thus ferforth I have thy work bigonne, 960
Fro day to day, til this day, by the morwe,
Hir love of freendship have I to thee wonne,
And also hath she leyd hir feyth to borwe.
Algate a foot is hameled of thy sorwe.'
What sholde I lenger sermon of it holde? 965
As ye han herd bifore, al he him tolde.

But right as floures, thorugh the colde of night
Y-closed, stoupen on hir stalke lowe,
Redressen hem a-yein the sonne bright,
And spreden on hir kinde cours by rowe, 970
Right so gan tho his eyen up to throwe
This Troilus, and seyde, `O Venus dere,

Thy might, thy grace, y-heried be it here!'

And to Pandare he held up bothe his hondes,
And seyde, `Lord, al thyn be that I have; 975
For I am hool, al brosten been my bondes;
A thousand Troians who so that me yave,
Eche after other, god so wis me save,
Ne mighte me so gladen; lo, myn herte,
It spredeth so for Ioye, it wol to-sterte! 980

`But Lord, how shal I doon, how shal I liven?
Whan shal I next my dere herte see?
How shal this longe tyme a-wey be driven,
Til that thou be ayein at hir fro me?
Thou mayst answere, "A-byd, a-byd," but he 985
That hangeth by the nekke, sooth to seyne,
In grete disese abydeth for the peyne.'

`Al esily, now, for the love of Marte,'
Quod Pandarus, `for every thing hath tyme;
So longe abyd til that the night departe; 990
For al so siker as thow lyst here by me,
And god toforn, I wol be there at pryme,
And for thy werk somwhat as I shal seye,
Or on som other wight this charge leye.

`For pardee, god wot, I have ever yit 995
Ben redy thee to serve, and to this night
Have I nought fayned, but emforth my wit
Don al thy lust, and shal with al my might.
Do now as I shal seye, and fare a-right;
And if thou nilt, wyte al thy-self thy care, 1000
On me is nought along thyn yvel fare.

`I woot wel that thow wyser art than I
A thousand fold, but if I were as thou,
God help me so, as I wolde outrely,
Right of myn owene hond, wryte hir right now 1005
A lettre, in which I wolde hir tellen how
I ferde amis, and hir beseche of routhe;
Now help thy-self, and leve it not for slouthe.

`And I my-self shal ther-with to hir goon;
And whan thou wost that I am with hir there, 1010
Worth thou up-on a courser right anoon,
Ye, hardily, right in thy beste gere,
And ryd forth by the place, as nought ne were,
And thou shalt finde us, if I may, sittinge
At som windowe, in-to the strete lokinge. 1015

`And if thee list, than maystow us saluwe,
And up-on me make thy contenaunce;
But, by thy lyf, be war and faste eschuwe
To tarien ought, god shilde us fro mischaunce!
Ryd forth thy wey, and hold thy governaunce; 1020
And we shal speke of thee som-what, I trowe,
Whan Thou art goon, to do thyne eres glowe!

`Touching thy lettre, thou art wys y-nough,
I woot thow nilt it digneliche endyte;
As make it with thise argumentes tough; 1025
Ne scrivenish or craftily thou it wryte;
Beblotte it with thy teres eek a lyte;
And if thou wryte a goodly word al softe,
Though it be good, reherce it not to ofte.

`For though the beste harpour upon lyve 1030
Wolde on the beste souned Ioly harpe
That ever was, with alle his fingres fyve,
Touche ay o streng, or ay o werbul harpe,
Were his nayles poynted never so sharpe,
It shulde maken every wight to dulle, 1035
To here his glee, and of his strokes fulle.

`Ne Iompre eek no discordaunt thing y-fere,
As thus, to usen termes of phisyk;
In loves termes, hold of thy matere
The forme alwey, and do that it be lyk; 1040
For if a peyntour wolde peynte a pyk
With asses feet, and hede it as an ape,
It cordeth nought; so nere it but a Iape.'

This counseyl lyked wel to Troilus;
But, as a dreedful lover, he seyde this: -- 1045
`Allas, my dere brother Pandarus,
I am ashamed for to wryte, y-wis,
Lest of myn innocence I seyde a-mis,
Or that she nolde it for despyt receyve;
Thanne were I deed, ther mighte it no-thing weyve.' 1050

To that Pandare answerde, `If thee lest,
Do that I seye, and lat me therwith goon;
For by that lord that formed est and west,
I hope of it to bringe answere anoon
Right of hir hond, and if that thou nilt noon, 1055
Lat be; and sory mote he been his lyve,
Ayeins thy lust that helpeth thee to thryve.'

Quod Troilus, `Depardieux, I assente;

Sin that thee list, I will aryse and wryte;
And blisful god preye ich, with good entente, 1060
The vyage, and the lettre I shal endyte,
So spede it; and thou, Minerva, the whyte,
Yif thou me wit my lettre to devyse:'
And sette him doun, and wroot right in this wyse. --

First he gan hir his righte lady calle, 1065
His hertes lyf, his lust, his sorwes leche,
His blisse, and eek these othere termes alle,
That in swich cas these loveres alle seche;
And in ful humble wyse, as in his speche,
He gan him recomaunde un-to hir grace; 1070
To telle al how, it axeth muchel space.

And after this, ful lowly he hir prayde
To be nought wrooth, though he, of his folye,
So hardy was to hir to wryte, and seyde,
That love it made, or elles moste he dye, 1075
And pitously gan mercy for to crye;
And after that he seyde, and ley ful loude,
Him-self was litel worth, and lesse he coude;

And that she sholde han his conning excused,
That litel was, and eek he dredde hir so, 1080
And his unworthinesse he ay acused;
And after that, than gan he telle his woo;
But that was endeles, with-outen ho;
And seyde, he wolde in trouthe alwey him holde; --
And radde it over, and gan the lettre folde. 1085

And with his salte teres gan he bathe
The ruby in his signet, and it sette

Upon the wex deliverliche and rathe;
Ther-with a thousand tymes, er he lette,
He kiste tho the lettre that he shette, 1090
And seyde, `Lettre, a blisful destenee
Thee shapen is, my lady shal thee see.'

This Pandare took the lettre, and that by tyme
A-morwe, and to his neces paleys sterte,
And faste he swoor, that it was passed pryme, 1095
And gan to Iape, and seyde, `Y-wis, myn herte,
So fresh it is, al-though it sore smerte,
I may not slepe never a Mayes morwe;
I have a Ioly wo, a lusty sorwe.'

Criseyde, whan that she hir uncle herde, 1100
With dreedful herte, and desirous to here
The cause of his cominge, thus answerde:
`Now by your feyth, myn uncle,' quod she, `dere,
What maner windes gydeth yow now here?
Tel us your Ioly wo and your penaunce, 1105
How ferforth be ye put in loves daunce.'

`By god,' quod he, `I hoppe alwey bihinde!'
And she to-laugh, it thoughte hir herte breste.
Quod Pandarus, `Loke alwey that ye finde
Game in myn hood, but herkneth, if yow leste; 1110
Ther is right now come in-to toune a geste,
A Greek espye, and telleth newe thinges,
For which I come to telle yow tydinges.

`Into the gardin go we, and we shal here,
Al prevely, of this a long sermoun.' 1115
With that they wenten arm in arm y-fere

In-to the gardin from the chaumbre doun.
And whan that he so fer was that the soun
Of that he speke, no man here mighte,
He seyde hir thus, and out the lettre plighte, 1120

`Lo, he that is al hoolly youres free
Him recomaundeth lowly to your grace,
And sent to you this lettre here by me;
Avyseth you on it, whan ye han space,
And of som goodly answere yow purchace; 1125
Or, helpe me god, so pleynly for to seyne,
He may not longe liven for his peyne.'

Ful dredfully tho gan she stonde stille,
And took it nought, but al hir humble chere
Gan for to chaunge, and seyde, `Scrit ne bille, 1130
For love of god, that toucheth swich matere,
Ne bring me noon; and also, uncle dere,
To myn estat have more reward, I preye,
Than to his lust; what sholde I more seye?

`And loketh now if this be resonable, 1135
And letteth nought, for favour ne for slouthe,
To seyn a sooth; now were it covenable
To myn estat, by god, and by your trouthe,
To taken it, or to han of him routhe,
In harming of my-self or in repreve? 1140
Ber it a-yein, for him that ye on leve!'

This Pandarus gan on hir for to stare,
And seyde, `Now is this the grettest wonder
That ever I sey! Lat be this nyce fare!
To deethe mote I smiten be with thonder, 1145

If, for the citee which that stondeth yonder,
Wolde I a lettre un-to yow bringe or take
To harm of yow; what list yow thus it make?

`But thus ye faren, wel neigh alle and some,
That he that most desireth yow to serve, 1150
Of him ye recche leest wher he bicome,
And whether that he live or elles sterve.
But for al that that ever I may deserve,
Refuse it nought,' quod he, and hente hir faste,
And in hir bosom the lettre doun he thraste, 1155

And seyde hire, `Now cast it awey anoon,
That folk may seen and gauren on us tweye.'
Quod she, `I can abyde til they be goon,'
And gan to smyle, and seyde hym, `Eem, I preye,
Swich answere as yow list, your-self purveye, 1160
For trewely I nil no lettre wryte.'
`No? than wol I,' quod he, `so ye endyte.'

Therwith she lough, and seyde, `Go we dyne.'
And he gan at him-self to iape faste,
And seyde, `Nece, I have so greet a pyne 1165
For love, that every other day I faste' --
And gan his beste Iapes forth to caste;
And made hir so to laughe at his folye,
That she for laughter wende for to dye.

And whan that she was comen in-to halle, 1170
`Now, eem,' quod she, `we wol go dine anoon;'
And gan some of hir women to hir calle,
And streyght in-to hir chaumbre gan she goon;
But of hir besinesses, this was oon

A-monges othere thinges, out of drede, 1175
Ful prively this lettre for to rede;

Avysed word by word in every lyne,
And fond no lak, she thoughte he coude good;
And up it putte, and went hir in to dyne.
But Pandarus, that in a study stood, 1180
Er he was war, she took him by the hood,
And seyde, `Ye were caught er that ye wiste;'
`I vouche sauf,' quod he. `do what yow liste.'

Tho wesshen they, and sette hem doun and ete;
And after noon ful sleyly Pandarus 1185
Gan drawe him to the window next the strete,
And seyde, `Nece, who hath arayed thus
The yonder hous, that stant afor-yeyn us?'
`Which hous?' quod she, and gan for to biholde,
And knew it wel, and whos it was him tolde, 1190

And fillen forth in speche of thinges smale,
And seten in the window bothe tweye.
Whan Pandarus saw tyme un-to his tale,
And saw wel that hir folk were alle aweye,
`Now, nece myn, tel on,' quod he; `I seye, 1195
How liketh yow the lettre that ye woot?
Can he ther-on? For, by my trouthe, I noot.'

Therwith al rosy hewed tho wex she,
And gan to humme, and seyde, `So I trowe.'
`Aquyte him wel, for goddes love,' quod he; 1200
`My-self to medes wol the lettre sowe.'
And held his hondes up, and sat on knowe,
`Now, goode nece, be it never so lyte,

Yif me the labour, it to sowe and plyte.'

`Ye, for I can so wryte,' quod she tho; 1205
`And eek I noot what I sholde to him seye.'
`Nay, nece,' quod Pandare, `sey nat so;
Yet at the leste thanketh him, I preye,
Of his good wil, and doth him not to deye.
Now for the love of me, my nece dere, 1210
Refuseth not at this tyme my preyere.'

`Depar-dieux,' quod she, `God leve al be wel!
God help me so, this is the firste lettre
That ever I wroot, ye, al or any del.'
And in-to a closet, for to avyse hir bettre, 1215
She wente allone, and gan hir herte unfettre
Out of disdaynes prison but a lyte;
And sette hir doun, and gan a lettre wryte,

Of which to telle in short is myn entente
Theffect, as fer as I can understonde: -- 1220
She thonked him of al that he wel mente
Towardes hir, but holden him in honde
She nolde nought, ne make hir-selven bonde
In love, but as his suster, him to plese,
She wolde fayn to doon his herte an ese. 1225

She shette it, and to Pandarus in gan goon,
There as he sat and loked in-to the strete,
And doun she sette hir by him on a stoon
Of Iaspre, up-on a quisshin gold y-bete,
And seyde, `As wisly helpe me god the grete, 1230
I never dide a thing with more peyne
Than wryte this, to which ye me constreyne;'

And took it him: He thonked hir and seyde,
`God woot, of thing ful ofte looth bigonne
Cometh ende good; and nece myn, Criseyde, 1235
That ye to him of hard now ben y-wonne
Oughte he be glad, by god and yonder sonne!
For-why men seyth, "Impressiounes lighte
Ful lightly been ay redy to the flighte.'

`But ye han pleyed tyraunt neigh to longe, 1240
And hard was it your herte for to grave;
Now stint, that ye no longer on it honge,
Al wolde ye the forme of daunger save.
But hasteth yow to doon him Ioye have;
For trusteth wel, to longe y-doon hardnesse 1245
Causeth despyt ful often, for destresse.'

And right as they declamed this matere,
Lo, Troilus, right at the stretes ende,
Com ryding with his tenthe some y-fere,
Al softely, and thiderward gan bende 1250
Ther-as they sete, as was his way to wende
To paleys-ward; and Pandare him aspyde,
And seyde, `Nece, y-see who cometh here ryde!

`O flee not in, he seeth us, I suppose;
Lest he may thinke that ye him eschuwe.' 1255
`Nay, nay,' quod she, and wex as reed as rose.
With that he gan hir humbly to saluwe
With dreedful chere, and oft his hewes muwe;
And up his look debonairly he caste,
And bekked on Pandare, and forth he paste. 1260

God woot if he sat on his hors a-right,
Or goodly was beseyn, that ilke day!
God woot wher he was lyk a manly knight!
What sholde I drecche, or telle of his aray?
Criseyde, which that alle these thinges say, 1265
To telle in short, hir lyked al y-fere,
His persone, his aray, his look, his chere,

His goodly manere, and his gentillesse,
So wel, that never, sith that she was born,
Ne hadde she swich routhe of his distresse; 1270
And how-so she hath hard ben her-biforn,
To god hope I, she hath now caught a thorn,
She shal not pulle it out this nexte wyke;
God sende mo swich thornes on to pyke!

Pandare, which that stood hir faste by, 1275
Felte iren hoot, and he bigan to smyte,
And seyde, `Nece, I pray yow hertely,
Tel me that I shal axen yow a lyte:
A womman, that were of his deeth to wyte,
With-outen his gilt, but for hir lakked routhe, 1280
Were it wel doon?' Quod she, `Nay, by my trouthe!'

`God help me so,' quod he, `ye sey me sooth.
Ye felen wel your-self that I not lye;
Lo, yond he rit!' Quod she, `Ye, so he dooth!'
`Wel,' quod Pandare, `as I have told yow thrye, 1285
Lat be youre nyce shame and youre folye,
And spek with him in esing of his herte;
Lat nycetee not do yow bothe smerte.'

But ther-on was to heven and to done;

Considered al thing, it may not be; 1290
And why, for shame; and it were eek to sone
To graunten him so greet a libertee.
`For playnly hir entente,' as seyde she,
`Was for to love him unwist, if she mighte,
And guerdon him with no-thing but with sighte.' 1295

But Pandarus thoughte, `It shal not be so,
If that I may; this nyce opinioun
Shal not be holden fully yeres two.'
What sholde I make of this a long sermoun?
He moste assente on that conclusioun, 1300
As for the tyme; and whan that it was eve,
And al was wel, he roos and took his leve.

And on his wey ful faste homward he spedde,
And right for Ioye he felte his herte daunce;
And Troilus he fond alone a-bedde, 1305
That lay as dooth these loveres, in a traunce,
Bitwixen hope and derk desesperaunce.
But Pandarus, right at his in-cominge,
He song, as who seyth, `Lo! Sumwhat I bringe,'

And seyde, `Who is in his bed so sone 1310
Y-buried thus?' `It am I, freend,' quod he.
`Who, Troilus? Nay, helpe me so the mone,'
Quod Pandarus, `Thou shalt aryse and see
A charme that was sent right now to thee,
The which can helen thee of thyn accesse, 1315
If thou do forth-with al thy besinesse.'

`Ye, through the might of god!' quod Troilus.
And Pandarus gan him the lettre take,

And seyde, `Pardee, god hath holpen us;
Have here a light, and loke on al this blake.' 1320
But ofte gan the herte glade and quake
Of Troilus, whyl that he gan it rede,
So as the wordes yave him hope or drede.

But fynally, he took al for the beste
That she him wroot, for somwhat he biheld 1325
On which, him thoughte, he mighte his herte reste,
Al covered she the wordes under sheld.
Thus to the more worthy part he held,
That, what for hope and Pandarus biheste,
His grete wo for-yede he at the leste. 1330

But as we may alday our-selven see,
Through more wode or col, the more fyr;
Right so encrees hope, of what it be,
Therwith ful ofte encreseth eek desyr;
Or, as an ook cometh of a litel spyr, 1335
So through this lettre, which that she him sente,
Encresen gan desyr, of which he brente.

Wherfore I seye alwey, that day and night
This Troilus gan to desiren more
Than he dide erst, thurgh hope, and dide his might 1340
To pressen on, as by Pandarus lore,
And wryten to hir of his sorwes sore
Fro day to day; he leet it not refreyde,
That by Pandare he wroot somwhat or seyde;

And dide also his othere observaunces 1345
That to a lovere longeth in this cas;
And, after that these dees turnede on chaunces,

So was he outher glad or seyde `Allas!'
And held after his gestes ay his pas;
And aftir swiche answeres as he hadde, 1350
So were his dayes sory outher gladde.

But to Pandare alwey was his recours,
And pitously gan ay til him to pleyne,
And him bisoughte of rede and som socours;
And Pandarus, that sey his wode peyne, 1355
Wex wel neigh deed for routhe, sooth to seyne,
And bisily with al his herte caste
Som of his wo to sleen, and that as faste;

And seyde, `Lord, and freend, and brother dere,
God woot that thy disese dooth me wo. 1360
But woltow stinten al this woful chere,
And, by my trouthe, or it be dayes two,
And god to-forn, yet shal I shape it so,
That thou shalt come in-to a certayn place,
Ther-as thou mayst thy-self hir preye of grace. 1365

`And certainly, I noot if thou it wost,
But tho that been expert in love it seye,
It is oon of the thinges that furthereth most,
A man to have a leyser for to preye,
And siker place his wo for to biwreye; 1370
For in good herte it moot som routhe impresse,
To here and see the giltles in distresse.

`Paraunter thenkestow: though it be so
That kinde wolde doon hir to biginne
To han a maner routhe up-on my wo, 1375
Seyth Daunger, "Nay, thou shalt me never winne;

So reuleth hir hir hertes goost with-inne,
That, though she bende, yet she stant on rote;
What in effect is this un-to my bote?"

`Thenk here-ayeins, whan that the sturdy ook,   1380
On which men hakketh ofte, for the nones,
Receyved hath the happy falling strook,
The grete sweigh doth it come al at ones,
As doon these rokkes or these milne-stones.
For swifter cours cometh thing that is of wighte,   1385
Whan it descendeth, than don thinges lighte.

`And reed that boweth doun for every blast,
Ful lightly, cesse wind, it wol aryse;
But so nil not an ook whan it is cast;
It nedeth me nought thee longe to forbyse.   1390
Men shal reioysen of a greet empryse
Acheved wel, and stant with-outen doute,
Al han men been the lenger ther-aboute.

`But, Troilus, yet tel me, if thee lest,
A thing now which that I shal axen thee;   1395
Which is thy brother that thou lovest best
As in thy verray hertes privetee?'
`Y-wis, my brother Deiphebus,' quod he.
`Now,' quod Pandare, `er houres twyes twelve,
He shal thee ese, unwist of it him-selve.   1400

`Now lat me allone, and werken as I may,'
Quod he; and to Deiphebus wente he tho
Which hadde his lord and grete freend ben ay;
Save Troilus, no man he lovede so.
To telle in short, with-outen wordes mo,   1405

Quod Pandarus, `I pray yow that ye be
Freend to a cause which that toucheth me.'

`Yis, pardee,' quod Deiphebus, `wel thow wost,
In al that ever I may, and god to-fore,
Al nere it but for man I love most, 1410
My brother Troilus; but sey wherfore
It is; for sith that day that I was bore,
I nas, ne never-mo to been I thinke,
Ayeins a thing that mighte thee for-thinke.'

Pandare gan him thonke, and to him seyde, 1415
`Lo, sire, I have a lady in this toun,
That is my nece, and called is Criseyde,
Which some men wolden doon oppressioun,
And wrongfully have hir possessioun:
Wherfor I of your lordship yow biseche 1420
To been our freend, with-oute more speche.'

Deiphebus him answerde, `O, is not this,
That thow spekest of to me thus straungely,
Criseyda, my freend?' He seyde, `Yis.'
`Than nedeth,' quod Deiphebus, `hardely, 1425
Na-more to speke, for trusteth wel, that I
Wol be hir champioun with spore and yerde;
I roughte nought though alle hir foos it herde.

`But tel me how, thou that woost al this matere,
How I might best avaylen? Now lat see.' 1430
Quod Pandarus; `If ye, my lord so dere,
Wolden as now don this honour to me,
To preyen hir to-morwe, lo, that she
Come un-to yow hir pleyntes to devyse,

Hir adversaries wolde of it agryse. 1435

`And if I more dorste preye as now,
And chargen yow to have so greet travayle,
To han som of your bretheren here with yow,
That mighten to hir cause bet avayle,
Than, woot I wel, she mighte never fayle 1440
For to be holpen, what at your instaunce,
What with hir othere freendes governaunce.'

Deiphebus, which that comen was, of kinde,
To al honour and bountee to consente,
Answerde, `It shal be doon; and I can finde 1445
Yet gretter help to this in myn entente.
What wolt thow seyn, if I for Eleyne sente
To speke of this? I trowe it be the beste;
For she may leden Paris as hir leste.

`Of Ector, which that is my lord, my brother, 1450
It nedeth nought to preye him freend to be;
For I have herd him, o tyme and eek other,
Speke of Criseyde swich honour, that he
May seyn no bet, swich hap to him hath she.
It nedeth nought his helpes for to crave; 1455
He shal be swich, right as we wole him have.

`Spek thou thy-self also to Troilus
On my bihalve, and pray him with us dyne.'
`Sire, al this shal be doon,' quod Pandarus;
And took his leve, and never gan to fyne, 1460
But to his neces hous, as streyt as lyne,
He com; and fond hir fro the mete aryse;
And sette him doun, and spak right in this wyse.

He seyde, `O veray god, so have I ronne!
Lo, nece myn, see ye nought how I swete? 1465
I noot whether ye the more thank me conne.
Be ye nought war how that fals Poliphete
Is now aboute eft-sones for to plete,
And bringe on yow advocacyes newe?'
`I? No,' quod she, and chaunged al hir hewe. 1470

`What is he more aboute, me to drecche
And doon me wrong? What shal I do, allas?
Yet of him-self no-thing ne wolde I recche,
Nere it for Antenor and Eneas,
That been his freendes in swich maner cas; 1475
But, for the love of god, myn uncle dere,
No fors of that; lat him have al y-fere;

`With-outen that I have ynough for us.'
`Nay,' quod Pandare, `it shal no-thing be so.
For I have been right now at Deiphebus, 1480
And Ector, and myne othere lordes mo,
And shortly maked eche of hem his fo;
That, by my thrift, he shal it never winne
For ought he can, whan that so he biginne.'

And as they casten what was best to done, 1485
Deiphebus, of his owene curtasye,
Com hir to preye, in his propre persone,
To holde him on the morwe companye
At diner, which she nolde not denye,
But goodly gan to his preyere obeye. 1490
He thonked hir, and wente up-on his weye.

Whanne this was doon, this Pandare up a-noon,
To telle in short, and forth gan for to wende
To Troilus, as stille as any stoon;
And al this thing he tolde him, word and ende; 1495
And how that he Deiphebus gan to blende;
And seyde him, `Now is tyme, if that thou conne,
To bere thee wel to-morwe, and al is wonne.

`Now spek, now prey, now pitously compleyne;
Lat not for nyce shame, or drede, or slouthe; 1500
Som-tyme a man mot telle his owene peyne;
Bileve it, and she shal han on thee routhe;
Thou shalt be saved by thy feyth, in trouthe.
But wel wot I, thou art now in a drede;
And what it is, I leye, I can arede. 1505

`Thow thinkest now, "How sholde I doon al this?
For by my cheres mosten folk aspye,
That for hir love is that I fare a-mis;
Yet hadde I lever unwist for sorwe dye."
Now thenk not so, for thou dost greet folye. 1510
For I right now have founden o manere
Of sleighte, for to coveren al thy chere.

`Thow shalt gon over night, and that as blyve,
Un-to Deiphebus hous, as thee to pleye,
Thy maladye a-wey the bet to dryve, 1515
For-why thou semest syk, soth for to seye.
Sone after that, doun in thy bed thee leye,
And sey, thow mayst no lenger up endure,
And ly right there, and byde thyn aventure.

`Sey that thy fever is wont thee for to take 1520

The same tyme, and lasten til a-morwe;
And lat see now how wel thou canst it make,
For, par-dee, syk is he that is in sorwe.
Go now, farwel! And, Venus here to borwe,
I hope, and thou this purpos holde ferme, 1525
Thy grace she shal fully ther conferme.'

Quod Troilus, `Y-wis, thou nedelees
Conseylest me, that sykliche I me feyne,
For I am syk in ernest, doutelees,
So that wel neigh I sterve for the peyne.' 1530
Quod Pandarus, `Thou shalt the bettre pleyne,
And hast the lasse need to countrefete;
For him men demen hoot that men seen swete.

`Lo, holde thee at thy triste cloos, and I
Shal wel the deer un-to thy bowe dryve.' 1535
Therwith he took his leve al softely,
And Troilus to paleys wente blyve.
So glad ne was he never in al his lyve;
And to Pandarus reed gan al assente,
And to Deiphebus hous at night he wente. 1540

What nedeth yow to tellen al the chere
That Deiphebus un-to his brother made,
Or his accesse, or his siklych manere,
How men gan him with clothes for to lade,
Whan he was leyd, and how men wolde him glade? 1545
But al for nought; he held forth ay the wyse
That ye han herd Pandare er this devyse.

But certeyn is, er Troilus him leyde,
Deiphebus had him prayed, over night,

To been a freend and helping to Criseyde. 1550
God woot, that he it grauntede anon-right,
To been hir fulle freend with al his might.
But swich a nede was to preye him thenne,
As for to bidde a wood man for to renne.

The morwen com, and neighen gan the tyme 1555
Of meel-tyd, that the faire quene Eleyne
Shoop hir to been, an houre after the pryme,
With Deiphebus, to whom she nolde feyne;
But as his suster, hoomly, sooth to seyne,
She com to diner in hir playn entente. 1560
But god and Pandare wiste al what this mente.

Com eek Criseyde, al innocent of this,
Antigone, hir sister Tarbe also;
But flee we now prolixitee best is,
For love of god, and lat us faste go 1565
Right to the effect, with-oute tales mo,
Why al this folk assembled in this place;
And lat us of hir saluinges pace.

Gret honour dide hem Deiphebus, certeyn,
And fedde hem wel with al that mighte lyke. 1570
But ever-more, `Allas!' was his refreyn,
`My goode brother Troilus, the syke,
Lyth yet"--and therwith-al he gan to syke;
And after that, he peyned him to glade
Hem as he mighte, and chere good he made. 1575

Compleyned eek Eleyne of his syknesse
So feithfully, that pitee was to here,
And every wight gan waxen for accesse

A leche anoon, and seyde, `In this manere
Men curen folk; this charme I wol yow lere.' 1580
But ther sat oon, al list hir nought to teche,
That thoughte, best coude I yet been his leche.

After compleynt, him gonnen they to preyse,
As folk don yet, whan som wight hath bigonne
To preyse a man, and up with prys him reyse 1585
A thousand fold yet hyer than the sonne: --
`He is, he can, that fewe lordes conne.'
And Pandarus, of that they wolde afferme,
He not for-gat hir preysing to conferme.

Herde al this thing Criseyde wel y-nough, 1590
And every word gan for to notifye;
For which with sobre chere hir herte lough;
For who is that ne wolde hir glorifye,
To mowen swich a knight don live or dye?
But al passe I, lest ye to longe dwelle; 1595
For for o fyn is al that ever I telle.

The tyme com, fro diner for to ryse,
And, as hem oughte, arisen everychoon,
And gonne a while of this and that devyse.
But Pandarus brak al this speche anoon, 1600
And seyde to Deiphebus, `Wole ye goon,
If youre wille be, as I yow preyde,
To speke here of the nedes of Criseyde?'

Eleyne, which that by the hond hir held,
Took first the tale, and seyde, `Go we blyve;' 1605
And goodly on Criseyde she biheld,
And seyde, `Ioves lat him never thryve,

That dooth yow harm, and bringe him sone of lyve!
And yeve me sorwe, but he shal it rewe,
If that I may, and alle folk be trewe.' 1610

`Tel thou thy neces cas,' quod Deiphebus
To Pandarus, `for thou canst best it telle.' --
`My lordes and my ladyes, it stant thus;
What sholde I lenger,' quod he, `do yow dwelle?'
He rong hem out a proces lyk a belle, 1615
Up-on hir fo, that highte Poliphete,
So heynous, that men mighte on it spete.

Answerde of this ech worse of hem than other,
And Poliphete they gonnen thus to warien,
`An-honged be swich oon, were he my brother; 1620
And so he shal, for it ne may not varien.'
What sholde I lenger in this tale tarien?
Pleynly, alle at ones, they hir highten
To been hir helpe in al that ever they mighten.

Spak than Eleyne, and seyde, `Pandarus, 1625
Woot ought my lord, my brother, this matere,
I mene, Ector? Or woot it Troilus?'
He seyde, `Ye, but wole ye now me here?
Me thinketh this, sith Troilus is here,
It were good, if that ye wolde assente, 1630
She tolde hir-self him al this, er she wente.

`For he wole have the more hir grief at herte,
By cause, lo, that she a lady is;
And, by your leve, I wol but right in sterte,
And do yow wite, and that anoon, y-wis, 1635
If that he slepe, or wole ought here of this.'

And in he lepte, and seyde him in his ere,
`God have thy soule, y-brought have I thy bere!'

To smylen of this gan tho Troilus,
And Pandarus, with-oute rekeninge, 1640
Out wente anoon to Eleyne and Deiphebus,
And seyde hem, `So there be no taryinge,
Ne more pres, he wol wel that ye bringe
Criseyda, my lady, that is here;
And as he may enduren, he wole here. 1645

`But wel ye woot, the chaumbre is but lyte,
And fewe folk may lightly make it warm;
Now loketh ye, (for I wol have no wyte,
To bringe in prees that mighte doon him harm
Or him disesen, for my bettre arm), 1650
Wher it be bet she byde til eft-sones;
Now loketh ye, that knowen what to doon is.

`I sey for me, best is, as I can knowe,
That no wight in ne wente but ye tweye,
But it were I, for I can, in a throwe, 1655
Reherce hir cas unlyk that she can seye;
And after this, she may him ones preye
To ben good lord, in short, and take hir leve;
This may not muchel of his ese him reve.

`And eek, for she is straunge, he wol forbere 1660
His ese, which that him thar nought for yow;
Eek other thing that toucheth not to here,
He wol me telle, I woot it wel right now,
That secret is, and for the tounes prow.'
And they, that no-thing knewe of his entente, 1665

With-oute more, to Troilus in they wente.

Eleyne, in al hir goodly softe wyse,
Gan him saluwe, and womanly to pleye,
And seyde, `Ywis, ye moste alweyes aryse!
Now fayre brother, beth al hool, I preye!' 1670
And gan hir arm right over his sholder leye,
And him with al hir wit to recomforte;
As she best coude, she gan him to disporte.

So after this quod she, `We yow biseke,
My dere brother, Deiphebus and I, 1675
For love of god, and so doth Pandare eke,
To been good lord and freend, right hertely,
Un-to Criseyde, which that certeinly
Receyveth wrong, as woot wel here Pandare,
That can hir cas wel bet than I declare.' 1680

This Pandarus gan newe his tunge affyle,
And al hir cas reherce, and that anoon;
Whan it was seyd, sone after, in a whyle,
Quod Troilus, `As sone as I may goon,
I wol right fayn with al my might ben oon, 1685
Have god my trouthe, hir cause to sustene.'
`Good thrift have ye,' quod Eleyne the quene.

Quod Pandarus, `And it your wille be
That she may take hir leve, er that she go?'
`O, elles god for-bede,' tho quod he, 1690
`If that she vouche sauf for to do so.'
And with that word quod Troilus, `Ye two,
Deiphebus, and my suster leef and dere,
To yow have I to speke of o matere,

`To been avysed by your reed the bettre': -- 1695
And fond, as hap was, at his beddes heed,
The copie of a tretis and a lettre,
That Ector hadde him sent to axen reed,
If swich a man was worthy to ben deed,
Woot I nought who; but in a grisly wyse 1700
He preyede hem anoon on it avyse.

Deiphebus gan this lettre to unfolde
In ernest greet; so did Eleyne the quene;
And rominge outward, fast it gan biholde,
Downward a steyre, in-to an herber grene. 1705
This ilke thing they redden hem bi-twene;
And largely, the mountaunce of an houre,
Thei gonne on it to reden and to poure.

Now lat hem rede, and turne we anoon
To Pandarus, that gan ful faste prye 1710
That al was wel, and out he gan to goon
In-to the grete chambre, and that in hye,
And seyde, `God save al this companye!
Com, nece myn; my lady quene Eleyne
Abydeth yow, and eek my lordes tweyne. 1715

`Rys, take with yow your nece Antigone,
Or whom yow list, or no fors, hardily;
The lesse prees, the bet; com forth with me,
And loke that ye thonke humblely
Hem alle three, and, whan ye may goodly 1720
Your tyme y-see, taketh of hem your leve,
Lest we to longe his restes him bireve.'

Al innocent of Pandarus entente,
Quod tho Criseyde, `Go we, uncle dere';
And arm in arm inward with him she wente, 1725
Avysed wel hir wordes and hir chere;
And Pandarus, in ernestful manere,
Seyde, `Alle folk, for goddes love, I preye,
Stinteth right here, and softely yow pleye.

`Aviseth yow what folk ben here with-inne, 1730
And in what plyt oon is, god him amende!
And inward thus ful softely biginne;
Nece, I conjure and heighly yow defende,
On his half, which that sowle us alle sende,
And in the vertue of corounes tweyne, 1735
Slee nought this man, that hath for yow this peyne!

`Fy on the devel! Thenk which oon he is,
And in what plyt he lyth; com of anoon;
Thenk al swich taried tyd, but lost it nis!
That wol ye bothe seyn, whan ye ben oon. 1740
Secoundelich, ther yet devyneth noon
Up-on yow two; come of now, if ye conne;
Whyl folk is blent, lo, al the tyme is wonne!

`In titering, and pursuite, and delayes,
The folk devyne at wagginge of a stree; 1745
And though ye wolde han after merye dayes,
Than dar ye nought, and why? For she, and she
Spak swich a word; thus loked he, and he;
Lest tyme I loste, I dar not with yow dele;
Com of therfore, and bringeth him to hele.' 1750

But now to yow, ye lovers that ben here,

Was Troilus nought in a cankedort,
That lay, and mighte whispringe of hem here,
And thoughte, `O lord, right now renneth my sort
Fully to dye, or han anoon comfort'; 1755
And was the firste tyme he shulde hir preye
Of love; O mighty god, what shal he seye?

Explicit Secundus Liber.

BOOK III. Incipit prohemium tercii libri.

O blisful light of whiche the bemes clere 1
Adorneth al the thridde hevene faire!
O sonnes lief, O Ioves doughter dere,
Plesaunce of love, O goodly debonaire,
In gentil hertes ay redy to repaire! 5
O verray cause of hele and of gladnesse,
Y-heried be thy might and thy goodnesse!

In hevene and helle, in erthe and salte see
Is felt thy might, if that I wel descerne;
As man, brid, best, fish, herbe and grene tree 10
Thee fele in tymes with vapour eterne.
God loveth, and to love wol nought werne;
And in this world no lyves creature,
With-outen love, is worth, or may endure.

Ye Ioves first to thilke effectes glade, 15
Thorugh which that thinges liven alle and be,
Comeveden, and amorous him made
On mortal thing, and as yow list, ay ye
Yeve him in love ese or adversitee;
And in a thousand formes doun him sente 20
For love in erthe, and whom yow liste, he hente.

Ye fierse Mars apeysen of his ire,

And, as yow list, ye maken hertes digne;
Algates, hem that ye wol sette a-fyre,
They dreden shame, and vices they resigne; 25
Ye do hem corteys be, fresshe and benigne,
And hye or lowe, after a wight entendeth;
The Ioyes that he hath, your might him sendeth.

Ye holden regne and hous in unitee;
Ye soothfast cause of frendship been also; 30
Ye knowe al thilke covered qualitee
Of thinges which that folk on wondren so,
Whan they can not construe how it may io,
She loveth him, or why he loveth here;
As why this fish, and nought that, comth to were. 35

Ye folk a lawe han set in universe,
And this knowe I by hem that loveres be,
That who-so stryveth with yow hath the werse:
Now, lady bright, for thy benignitee,
At reverence of hem that serven thee, 40
Whos clerk I am, so techeth me devyse
Som Ioye of that is felt in thy servyse.

Ye in my naked herte sentement
Inhelde, and do me shewe of thy swetnesse. --
Caliope, thy vois be now present, 45
For now is nede; sestow not my destresse,
How I mot telle anon-right the gladnesse
Of Troilus, to Venus heryinge?
To which gladnes, who nede hath, god him bringe!

Explicit prohemium Tercii Libri.

Incipit Liber Tercius.

 Lay al this mene whyle Troilus, 50
Recordinge his lessoun in this manere,
`Ma fey!' thought he, `Thus wole I seye and thus;
Thus wole I pleyne unto my lady dere;
That word is good, and this shal be my chere;
This nil I not foryeten in no wyse.' 55
God leve him werken as he can devyse!

And, lord, so that his herte gan to quappe,
Heringe hir come, and shorte for to syke!
And Pandarus, that ledde hir by the lappe,
Com ner, and gan in at the curtin pyke, 60
And seyde, `God do bote on alle syke!
See, who is here yow comen to visyte;
Lo, here is she that is your deeth to wyte.'

Ther-with it semed as he wepte almost;
`A ha,' quod Troilus so rewfully, 65
`Wher me be wo, O mighty god, thow wost!
Who is al there? I se nought trewely.'
`Sire,' quod Criseyde, `it is Pandare and I.'
`Ye, swete herte? Allas, I may nought ryse
To knele, and do yow honour in som wyse.' 70

And dressede him upward, and she right tho
Gan bothe here hondes softe upon him leye,
`O, for the love of god, do ye not so
To me,' quod she, `Ey! What is this to seye?
Sire, come am I to yow for causes tweye; 75
First, yow to thonke, and of your lordshipe eke

Continuance I wolde yow biseke.'

This Troilus, that herde his lady preye
Of lordship him, wex neither quik ne deed,
Ne mighte a word for shame to it seye, 80
Al-though men sholde smyten of his heed.
But lord, so he wex sodeinliche reed,
And sire, his lesson, that he wende conne,
To preyen hir, is thurgh his wit y-ronne.

Cryseyde al this aspyede wel y-nough, 85
For she was wys, and lovede him never-the-lasse,
Al nere he malapert, or made it tough,
Or was to bold, to singe a fool a masse.
But whan his shame gan somwhat to passe,
His resons, as I may my rymes holde, 90
I yow wole telle, as techen bokes olde.

In chaunged vois, right for his verray drede,
Which vois eek quook, and ther-to his manere
Goodly abayst, and now his hewes rede,
Now pale, un-to Criseyde, his lady dere, 95
With look doun cast and humble yolden chere,
Lo, the alderfirste word that him asterte
Was, twyes, 'Mercy, mercy, swete herte!'

And stinte a whyl, and whan he mighte out-bringe,
The nexte word was, 'God wot, for I have, 100
As feyfully as I have had konninge,
Ben youres, also god so my sowle save;
And shal til that I, woful wight, be grave.
And though I dar ne can un-to yow pleyne,
Y-wis, I suffre nought the lasse peyne. 105

`Thus muche as now, O wommanliche wyf,
I may out-bringe, and if this yow displese,
That shal I wreke upon myn owne lyf
Right sone, I trowe, and doon your herte an ese,
If with my deeth your herte I may apese. 110
But sin that ye han herd me som-what seye,
Now recche I never how sone that I deye.'

Ther-with his manly sorwe to biholde,
It mighte han maad an herte of stoon to rewe;
And Pandare weep as he to watre wolde, 115
And poked ever his nece newe and newe,
And seyde, `Wo bigon ben hertes trewe!
For love of god, make of this thing an ende,
Or slee us bothe at ones, er that ye wende.'

`I? What?' quod she, `By god and by my trouthe, 120
I noot nought what ye wilne that I seye.'
`I? What?' quod he, `That ye han on him routhe,
For goddes love, and doth him nought to deye.'
`Now thanne thus,' quod she, `I wolde him preye
To telle me the fyn of his entente; 125
Yet wist I never wel what that he mente.'

`What that I mene, O swete herte dere?'
Quod Troilus, `O goodly, fresshe free!
That, with the stremes of your eyen clere,
Ye wolde som-tyme freendly on me see, 130
And thanne agreen that I may ben he,
With-oute braunche of vyce on any wyse,
In trouthe alwey to doon yow my servyse,

`As to my lady right and chief resort,
With al my wit and al my diligence, 135
And I to han, right as yow list, comfort,
Under your yerde, egal to myn offence,
As deeth, if that I breke your defence;
And that ye deigne me so muche honoure,
Me to comaunden ought in any houre. 140

`And I to ben your verray humble trewe,
Secret, and in my paynes pacient,
And ever-mo desire freshly newe,
To serven, and been y-lyke ay diligent,
And, with good herte, al holly your talent 145
Receyven wel, how sore that me smerte,
Lo, this mene I, myn owene swete herte.'

Quod Pandarus, `Lo, here an hard request,
And resonable, a lady for to werne!
Now, nece myn, by natal Ioves fest, 150
Were I a god, ye sholde sterve as yerne,
That heren wel, this man wol no-thing yerne
But your honour, and seen him almost sterve,
And been so looth to suffren him yow serve.'

With that she gan hir eyen on him caste 155
Ful esily, and ful debonairly,
Avysing hir, and hyed not to faste
With never a word, but seyde him softely,
`Myn honour sauf, I wol wel trewely,
And in swich forme as he can now devyse, 160
Receyven him fully to my servyse,

`Biseching him, for goddes love, that he

Wolde, in honour of trouthe and gentilesse,
As I wel mene, eek mene wel to me,
And myn honour, with wit and besinesse 165
Ay kepe; and if I may don him gladnesse,
From hennes-forth, y-wis, I nil not feyne:
Now beeth al hool; no lenger ye ne pleyne.

`But nathelees, this warne I yow,' quod she,
`A kinges sone al-though ye be, y-wis, 170
Ye shal na-more have soverainetee
Of me in love, than right in that cas is;
Ne I nil forbere, if that ye doon a-mis,
To wrathen yow; and whyl that ye me serve,
Cherycen yow right after ye deserve. 175

`And shortly, dere herte and al my knight,
Beth glad, and draweth yow to lustinesse,
And I shal trewely, with al my might,
Your bittre tornen al in-to swetenesse.
If I be she that may yow do gladnesse, 180
For every wo ye shal recovere a blisse';
And him in armes took, and gan him kisse.

Fil Pandarus on knees, and up his eyen
To hevene threw, and held his hondes hye,
`Immortal god!' quod he, `That mayst nought dyen, 185
Cupide I mene, of this mayst glorifye;
And Venus, thou mayst maken melodye;
With-outen hond, me semeth that in the towne,
For this merveyle, I here ech belle sowne.

`But ho! No more as now of this matere, 190
For-why this folk wol comen up anoon,

That han the lettre red; lo, I hem here.
But I coniure thee, Criseyde, and oon,
And two, thou Troilus, whan thow mayst goon,
That at myn hous ye been at my warninge, 195
For I ful wel shal shape youre cominge;

`And eseth ther your hertes right y-nough;
And lat see which of yow shal bere the belle
To speke of love a-right!' ther-with he lough,
`For ther have ye a layser for to telle.' 200
Quod Troilus, `How longe shal I dwelle
Er this be doon?' Quod he, `Whan thou mayst ryse,
This thing shal be right as I yow devyse.'

With that Eleyne and also Deiphebus
Tho comen upward, right at the steyres ende; 205
And Lord, so than gan grone Troilus,
His brother and his suster for to blende.
Quod Pandarus, `It tyme is that we wende;
Tak, nece myn, your leve at alle three,
And lat hem speke, and cometh forth with me.' 210

She took hir leve at hem ful thriftily,
As she wel coude, and they hir reverence
Un-to the fulle diden hardely,
And speken wonder wel, in hir absence,
Of hir, in preysing of hir excellence, 215
Hir governaunce, hir wit; and hir manere
Commendeden, it Ioye was to here.

Now lat hir wende un-to hir owne place,
And torne we to Troilus a-yein,
That gan ful lightly of the lettre passe 220

That Deiphebus hadde in the gardin seyn.
And of Eleyne and him he wolde fayn
Delivered been, and seyde that him leste
To slepe, and after tales have reste.

Eleyne him kiste, and took hir leve blyve, 225
Deiphebus eek, and hoom wente every wight;
And Pandarus, as faste as he may dryve,
To Troilus tho com, as lyne right;
And on a paillet, al that glade night,
By Troilus he lay, with mery chere, 230
To tale; and wel was hem they were y-fere.

Whan every wight was voided but they two,
And alle the dores were faste y-shette,
To telle in short, with-oute wordes mo,
This Pandarus, with-outen any lette, 235
Up roos, and on his beddes syde him sette,
And gan to speken in a sobre wyse
To Troilus, as I shal yow devyse:

`Myn alderlevest lord, and brother dere,
God woot, and thou, that it sat me so sore, 240
When I thee saw so languisshing to-yere,
For love, of which thy wo wex alwey more;
That I, with al my might and al my lore,
Have ever sithen doon my bisinesse
To bringe thee to Ioye out of distresse, 245

`And have it brought to swich plyt as thou wost,
So that, thorugh me, thow stondest now in weye
To fare wel, I seye it for no bost,
And wostow which? For shame it is to seye,

For thee have I bigonne a gamen pleye 250
Which that I never doon shal eft for other,
Al-though he were a thousand fold my brother.

`That is to seye, for thee am I bicomen,
Bitwixen game and ernest, swich a mene
As maken wommen un-to men to comen; 255
Al sey I nought, thou wost wel what I mene.
For thee have I my nece, of vyces clene,
So fully maad thy gentilesse triste,
That al shal been right as thy-selve liste.

`But god, that al wot, take I to witnesse, 260
That never I this for coveityse wroughte,
But only for to abregge that distresse,
For which wel nygh thou deydest, as me thoughte.
But, gode brother, do now as thee oughte,
For goddes love, and kep hir out of blame, 265
Sin thou art wys, and save alwey hir name.

`For wel thou wost, the name as yet of here
Among the peple, as who seyth, halwed is;
For that man is unbore, I dar wel swere,
That ever wiste that she dide amis. 270
But wo is me, that I, that cause al this,
May thenken that she is my nece dere,
And I hir eem, and trattor eek y-fere!

`And were it wist that I, through myn engyn,
Hadde in my nece y-put this fantasye, 275
To do thy lust, and hoolly to be thyn,
Why, al the world up-on it wolde crye,
And seye, that I the worste trecherye

Dide in this cas, that ever was bigonne,
And she for-lost, and thou right nought y-wonne. 280

`Wher-fore, er I wol ferther goon a pas,
Yet eft I thee biseche and fully seye,
That privetee go with us in this cas;
That is to seye, that thou us never wreye;
And be nought wrooth, though I thee ofte preye 285
To holden secree swich an heigh matere;
For skilful is, thow wost wel, my preyere.

`And thenk what wo ther hath bitid er this,
For makinge of avantes, as men rede;
And what mischaunce in this world yet ther is, 290
Fro day to day, right for that wikked dede;
For which these wyse clerkes that ben dede
Han ever yet proverbed to us yonge,
That "Firste vertu is to kepe tonge."

`And, nere it that I wilne as now tabregge 295
Diffusioun of speche, I coude almost
A thousand olde stories thee alegge
Of wommen lost, thorugh fals and foles bost;
Proverbes canst thy-self y-nowe, and wost,
Ayeins that vyce, for to been a labbe, 300
Al seyde men sooth as often as they gabbe.

`O tonge, allas! So often here-biforn
Hastow made many a lady bright of hewe
Seyd, "Welawey! The day that I was born!"
And many a maydes sorwes for to newe; 305
And, for the more part, al is untrewe
That men of yelpe, and it were brought to preve;

Of kinde non avauntour is to leve.

`Avauntour and a lyere, al is on;
As thus: I pose, a womman graunte me 310
Hir love, and seyth that other wol she non,
And I am sworn to holden it secree,
And after I go telle it two or three;
Y-wis, I am avauntour at the leste,
And lyere, for I breke my biheste. 315

`Now loke thanne, if they be nought to blame,
Swich maner folk; what shal I clepe hem, what,
That hem avaunte of wommen, and by name,
That never yet bihighte hem this ne that,
Ne knewe hem more than myn olde hat? 320
No wonder is, so god me sende hele,
Though wommen drede with us men to dele.

`I sey not this for no mistrust of yow,
Ne for no wys man, but for foles nyce,
And for the harm that in the world is now, 325
As wel for foly ofte as for malyce;
For wel wot I, in wyse folk, that vyce
No womman drat, if she be wel avysed;
For wyse ben by foles harm chastysed.

`But now to purpos; leve brother dere, 330
Have al this thing that I have seyd in minde,
And keep thee clos, and be now of good chere,
For at thy day thou shalt me trewe finde.
I shal thy proces sette in swich a kinde,
And god to-forn, that it shall thee suffyse, 335
For it shal been right as thou wolt devyse.

`For wel I woot, thou menest wel, parde;
Therfore I dar this fully undertake.
Thou wost eek what thy lady grauntED thee,
And day is set, the chartres up to make. 340
Have now good night, I may no lenger wake;
And bid for me, sin thou art now in blisse,
That god me sende deeth or sone lisse.'

Who mighte telle half the Ioye or feste
Which that the sowle of Troilus tho felte, 345
Heringe theffect of Pandarus biheste?
His olde wo, that made his herte swelte,
Gan tho for Ioye wasten and to-melte,
And al the richesse of his sykes sore
At ones fledde, he felte of hem no more. 350

But right so as these holtes and these hayes,
That han in winter dede been and dreye,
Revesten hem in grene, whan that May is,
Whan every lusty lyketh best to pleye;
Right in that selve wyse, sooth to seye, 355
Wax sodeynliche his herte ful of Ioye,
That gladder was ther never man in Troye.

And gan his look on Pandarus up caste
Ful sobrely, and frendly for to see,
And seyde, `Freend, in Aprille the laste, 360
As wel thou wost, if it remembre thee,
How neigh the deeth for wo thou founde me;
And how thou didest al thy bisinesse
To knowe of me the cause of my distresse.

`Thou wost how longe I it for-bar to seye 365
To thee, that art the man that I best triste;
And peril was it noon to thee by-wreye,
That wiste I wel; but tel me, if thee liste,
Sith I so looth was that thy-self it wiste,
How dorst I mo tellen of this matere, 370
That quake now, and no wight may us here?

`But natheles, by that god I thee swere,
That, as him list, may al this world governe,
And, if I lye, Achilles with his spere
Myn herte cleve, al were my lyf eterne, 375
As I am mortal, if I late or yerne
Wolde it biwreye, or dorste, or sholde conne,
For al the good that god made under sonne;

`That rather deye I wolde, and determyne,
As thinketh me, now stokked in presoun, 380
In wrecchednesse, in filthe, and in vermyne,
Caytif to cruel king Agamenoun;
And this, in alle the temples of this toun
Upon the goddes alle, I wol thee swere,
To-morwe day, if that thee lyketh here. 385

`And that thou hast so muche y-doon for me,
That I ne may it never-more deserve,
This knowe I wel, al mighte I now for thee
A thousand tymes on a morwen sterve.
I can no more, but that I wol thee serve 390
Right as thy sclave, whider-so thou wende,
For ever-more, un-to my lyves ende!

`But here, with al myn herte, I thee biseche,

That never in me thou deme swich folye
As I shal seyn; me thoughte, by thy speche, 395
That this, which thou me dost for companye,
I sholde wene it were a bauderye;
I am nought wood, al-if I lewed be;
It is not so, that woot I wel, pardee.

`But he that goth, for gold or for richesse, 400
On swich message, calle him what thee list;
And this that thou dost, calle it gentilesse,
Compassioun, and felawship, and trist;
Departe it so, for wyde-where is wist
How that there is dyversitee requered 405
Bitwixen thinges lyke, as I have lered.

`And, that thou knowe I thenke nought ne wene
That this servyse a shame be or Iape,
I have my faire suster Polixene,
Cassandre, Eleyne, or any of the frape; 410
Be she never so faire or wel y-shape,
Tel me, which thou wilt of everichone,
To han for thyn, and lat me thanne allone.

`But, sith that thou hast don me this servyse
My lyf to save, and for noon hope of mede, 415
So, for the love of god, this grete empryse
Performe it out; for now is moste nede.
For high and low, with-outen any drede,
I wol alwey thyne hestes alle kepe;
Have now good night, and lat us bothe slepe.' 420

Thus held him ech of other wel apayed,
That al the world ne mighte it bet amende;

And, on the morwe, whan they were arayed,
Ech to his owene nedes gan entende.
But Troilus, though as the fyr he brende 425
For sharp desyr of hope and of plesaunce,
He not for-gat his gode governaunce.

But in him-self with manhod gan restreyne
Ech rakel dede and ech unbrydled chere,
That alle tho that liven, sooth to seyne, 430
Ne sholde han wist, by word or by manere,
What that he mente, as touching this matere.
From every wight as fer as is the cloude
He was, so wel dissimulen he coude.

And al the whyl which that I yow devyse, 435
This was his lyf; with al his fulle might,
By day he was in Martes high servyse,
This is to seyn, in armes as a knight;
And for the more part, the longe night
He lay, and thoughte how that he mighte serve 440
His lady best, hir thank for to deserve.

Nil I nought swere, al-though he lay softe,
That in his thought he nas sumwhat disesed,
Ne that he tornede on his pilwes ofte,
And wolde of that him missed han ben sesed; 445
But in swich cas men is nought alwey plesed,
For ought I wot, no more than was he;
That can I deme of possibilitee.

But certeyn is, to purpos for to go,
That in this whyle, as writen is in geste, 450
He say his lady som-tyme; and also

She with him spak, whan that she dorste or leste,
And by hir bothe avys, as was the beste,
Apoynteden ful warly in this nede,
So as they dorste, how they wolde procede. 455

But it was spoken in so short a wyse,
In swich awayt alwey, and in swich fere,
Lest any wyght devynen or devyse
Wolde of hem two, or to it leye an ere,
That al this world so leef to hem ne were 460
As that Cupido wolde hem grace sende
To maken of hir speche aright an ende.

But thilke litel that they spake or wroughte,
His wyse goost took ay of al swich hede,
It semed hir, he wiste what she thoughte 465
With-outen word, so that it was no nede
To bidde him ought to done, or ought for-bede;
For which she thought that love, al come it late,
Of alle Ioye hadde opned hir the yate.

And shortly of this proces for to pace, 470
So wel his werk and wordes he bisette,
That he so ful stood in his lady grace,
That twenty thousand tymes, or she lette,
She thonked god she ever with him mette;
So coude he him governe in swich servyse, 475
That al the world ne might it bet devyse.

For-why she fond him so discreet in al,
So secret, and of swich obeisaunce,
That wel she felte he was to hir a wal
Of steel, and sheld from every displesaunce; 480

That, to ben in his gode governaunce,
So wys he was, she was no more afered,
I mene, as fer as oughte ben requered.

And Pandarus, to quike alwey the fyr,
Was evere y-lyke prest and diligent; 485
To ese his frend was set al his desyr.
He shof ay on, he to and fro was sent;
He lettres bar whan Troilus was absent.
That never man, as in his freendes nede,
Ne bar him bet than he, with-outen drede. 490

But now, paraunter, som man wayten wolde
That every word, or sonde, or look, or chere
Of Troilus that I rehersen sholde,
In al this whyle un-to his lady dere;
I trowe it were a long thing for to here; 495
Or of what wight that stant in swich disioynte,
His wordes alle, or every look, to poynte.

For sothe, I have not herd it doon er this,
In storye noon, ne no man here, I wene;
And though I wolde I coude not, y-wis; 500
For ther was som epistel hem bitwene,
That wolde, as seyth myn auctor, wel contene
Neigh half this book, of which him list not wryte;
How sholde I thanne a lyne of it endyte?

But to the grete effect: than sey I thus, 505
That stonding in concord and in quiete,
Thise ilke two, Criseyde and Troilus,
As I have told, and in this tyme swete,
Save only often mighte they not mete,

Ne layser have hir speches to fulfelle, 510
That it befel right as I shal yow telle.

That Pandarus, that ever dide his might
Right for the fyn that I shal speke of here,
As for to bringe to his hous som night
His faire nece, and Troilus y-fere, 515
Wher-as at leyser al this heigh matere,
Touching hir love, were at the fulle up-bounde,
Hadde out of doute a tyme to it founde.

For he with greet deliberacioun
Hadde every thing that her-to mighte avayle 520
Forn-cast, and put in execucioun.
And neither laft, for cost ne for travayle;
Come if hem list, hem sholde no-thing fayle;
And for to been in ought espyed there,
That, wiste he wel, an inpossible were. 525

Dredelees, it cleer was in the wind
Of every pye and every lette-game;
Now al is wel, for al the world is blind
In this matere, bothe fremed and tame.
This timbur is al redy up to frame; 530
Us lakketh nought but that we witen wolde
A certein houre, in which she comen sholde.

And Troilus, that al this purveyaunce
Knew at the fulle, and waytede on it ay,
Hadde here-up-on eek made gret ordenaunce, 535
And founde his cause, and ther-to his aray,
If that he were missed, night or day,
Ther-whyle he was aboute this servyse,

That he was goon to doon his sacrifyse,

And moste at swich a temple alone wake, 540
Answered of Appollo for to be;
And first to seen the holy laurer quake,
Er that Apollo spak out of the tree,
To telle him next whan Grekes sholden flee,
And forthy lette him no man, god forbede, 545
But preye Apollo helpen in this nede.

Now is ther litel more for to doone,
But Pandare up, and shortly for to seyne,
Right sone upon the chaunging of the mone,
Whan lightles is the world a night or tweyne, 550
And that the welken shoop him for to reyne,
He streight a-morwe un-to his nece wente;
Ye han wel herd the fyn of his entente.

Whan he was come, he gan anoon to pleye
As he was wont, and of him-self to Iape; 555
And fynally, he swor and gan hir seye,
By this and that, she sholde him not escape,
Ne lengere doon him after hir to gape;
But certeynly she moste, by hir leve,
Come soupen in his hous with him at eve. 560

At whiche she lough, and gan hir faste excuse,
And seyde, `It rayneth; lo, how sholde I goon?'
`Lat be,' quod he, `ne stond not thus to muse;
This moot be doon, ye shal be ther anoon.'
So at the laste her-of they felle at oon, 565
Or elles, softe he swor hir in hir ere,
He nolde never come ther she were.

Sone after this, to him she gan to rowne,
And asked him if Troilus were there?
He swor hir, `Nay, for he was out of towne,' 570
And seyde, `Nece, I pose that he were,
Yow thurfte never have the more fere.
For rather than men mighte him ther aspye,
Me were lever a thousand-fold to dye.'

Nought list myn auctor fully to declare 575
What that she thoughte whan he seyde so,
That Troilus was out of town y-fare,
As if he seyde ther-of sooth or no;
But that, with-outen awayt, with him to go,
She graunted him, sith he hir that bisoughte 580
And, as his nece, obeyed as hir oughte.

But nathelees, yet gan she him biseche,
Al-though with him to goon it was no fere,
For to be war of goosish peples speche,
That dremen thinges whiche that never were, 585
And wel avyse him whom he broughte there;
And seyde him, `Eem, sin I mot on yow triste,
Loke al be wel, and do now as yow liste.'

He swor hire, `Yis, by stokkes and by stones,
And by the goddes that in hevene dwelle, 590
Or elles were him levere, soule and bones,
With Pluto king as depe been in helle
As Tantalus!' What sholde I more telle?
Whan al was wel, he roos and took his leve,
And she to souper com, whan it was eve, 595

With a certayn of hir owene men,
And with hir faire nece Antigone,
And othere of hir wommen nyne or ten;
But who was glad now, who, as trowe ye,
But Troilus, that stood and mighte it see 600
Thurgh-out a litel windowe in a stewe,
Ther he bishet, sin midnight, was in mewe,

Unwist of every wight but of Pandare?
But to the poynt; now whan that she was y-come
With alle Ioye, and alle frendes fare, 605
Hir em anoon in armes hath hir nome,
And after to the souper, alle and some,
Whan tyme was, ful softe they hem sette;
God wot, ther was no deyntee for to fette.

And after souper gonnen they to ryse, 610
At ese wel, with hertes fresshe and glade,
And wel was him that coude best devyse
To lyken hir, or that hir laughen made.
He song; she pleyde; he tolde tale of Wade.
But at the laste, as every thing hath ende, 615
She took hir leve, and nedes wolde wende.

But O, Fortune, executrice of wierdes,
O influences of thise hevenes hye!
Soth is, that, under god, ye ben our hierdes,
Though to us bestes been the causes wrye. 620
This mene I now, for she gan hoomward hye,
But execut was al bisyde hir leve,
At the goddes wil, for which she moste bleve.

The bente mone with hir hornes pale,

Saturne, and Iove, in Cancro ioyned were, 625
That swich a rayn from hevene gan avale
That every maner womman that was there
Hadde of that smoky reyn a verray fere;
At which Pandare tho lough, and seyde thenne,
`Now were it tyme a lady to go henne! 630

`But goode nece, if I mighte ever plese
Yow any-thing, than prey I yow,' quod he,
`To doon myn herte as now so greet an ese
As for to dwelle here al this night with me,
For-why this is your owene hous, pardee. 635
For, by my trouthe, I sey it nought a-game,
To wende as now, it were to me a shame.'

Criseyde, which that coude as muche good
As half a world, tok hede of his preyere;
And sin it ron, and al was on a flood, 640
She thoughte, as good chep may I dwellen here,
And graunte it gladly with a freendes chere,
And have a thank, as grucche and thanne abyde;
For hoom to goon, it may nought wel bityde.'

`I wol,' quod she, `myn uncle leef and dere, 645
Sin that yow list, it skile is to be so;
I am right glad with yow to dwellen here;
I seyde but a-game, I wolde go.'
`Y-wis, graunt mercy, nece!' quod he tho;
`Were it a game or no, soth for to telle, 650
Now am I glad, sin that yow list to dwelle.'

Thus al is wel; but tho bigan aright
The newe Ioye, and al the feste agayn;

But Pandarus, if goodly hadde he might,
He wolde han hyed hir to bedde fayn,　655
And seyde, `Lord, this is an huge rayn!
This were a weder for to slepen inne;
And that I rede us sonE to biginne.

`And nece, woot ye wher I wol yow leye,
For that we shul not liggen fer asonder,　660
And for ye neither shullen, dar I seye,
Heren noise of reynes nor of thondre?
By god, right in my lyte closet yonder.
And I wol in that outer hous allone
Be wardeyn of your wommen everichone.　665

`And in this middel chaumbre that ye see
Shal youre wommen slepen wel and softe;
And ther I seyde shal your-selve be;
And if ye liggen wel to-night, com ofte,
And careth not what weder is on-lofte.　670
The wyn anon, and whan so that yow leste,
So go we slepe, I trowe it be the beste.'

Ther nis no more, but here-after sone,
The voyde dronke, and travers drawe anon,
Gan every wight, that hadde nought to done　675
More in the place, out of the chaumber gon.
And ever-mo so sternelich it ron,
And blew ther-with so wonderliche loude,
That wel neigh no man heren other coude.

Tho Pandarus, hir eem, right as him oughte,　680
With women swiche as were hir most aboute,
Ful glad un-to hir beddes syde hir broughte,

And toke his leve, and gan ful lowe loute,
And seyde, `Here at this closet-dore with-oute,
Right over-thwart, your wommen liggen alle, 685
That, whom yow list of hem, ye may here calle.'

So whan that she was in the closet leyd,
And alle hir wommen forth by ordenaunce
A-bedde weren, ther as I have seyd,
There was no more to skippen nor to traunce, 690
But boden go to bedde, with mischaunce,
If any wight was steringe any-where,
And late hem slepe that a-bedde were.

But Pandarus, that wel coude eche a del
The olde daunce, and every poynt ther-inne, 695
Whan that he sey that alle thing was wel,
He thoughte he wolde up-on his werk biginne,
And gan the stewe-dore al softe un-pinne;
And stille as stoon, with-outen lenger lette,
By Troilus a-doun right he him sette. 700

And, shortly to the poynt right for to gon,
Of al this werk he tolde him word and ende,
And seyde, `Make thee redy right anon,
For thou shalt in-to hevene blisse wende.'
`Now blisful Venus, thou me grace sende,' 705
Quod Troilus, `for never yet no nede
Hadde I er now, ne halvendel the drede.'

Quod Pandarus, `Ne drede thee never a del,
For it shal been right as thou wilt desyre;
So thryve I, this night shal I make it wel, 710
Or casten al the gruwel in the fyre.'

`Yit blisful Venus, this night thou me enspyre,'
Quod Troilus, `as wis as I thee serve,
And ever bet and bet shal, til I sterve.

`And if I hadde, O Venus ful of murthe, 715
Aspectes badde of Mars or of Saturne,
Or thou combust or let were in my birthe,
Thy fader prey al thilke harm disturne
Of grace, and that I glad ayein may turne,
For love of him thou lovedest in the shawe, 720
I mene Adoon, that with the boor was slawe.

`O Iove eek, for the love of faire Europe,
The whiche in forme of bole awey thou fette;
Now help, O Mars, thou with thy blody cope,
For love of Cipris, thou me nought ne lette; 725
O Phebus, thenk whan Dane hir-selven shette
Under the bark, and laurer wex for drede,
Yet for hir love, O help now at this nede!

`Mercurie, for the love of Hierse eke,
For which Pallas was with Aglauros wrooth, 730
Now help, and eek Diane, I thee biseke
That this viage be not to thee looth.
O fatal sustren, which, er any clooth
Me shapen was, my destene me sponne,
So helpeth to this werk that is bi-gonne!' 735

Quod Pandarus, `Thou wrecched mouses herte,
Art thou agast so that she wol thee byte?
Why, don this furred cloke up-on thy sherte,
And folowe me, for I wol have the wyte;
But byd, and lat me go bifore a lyte.' 740

And with that word he gan un-do a trappe,
And Troilus he broughte in by the lappe.

The sterne wind so loude gan to route
That no wight other noyse mighte here;
And they that layen at the dore with-oute, 745
Ful sykerly they slepten alle y-fere;
And Pandarus, with a ful sobre chere,
Goth to the dore anon with-outen lette,
Ther-as they laye, and softely it shette.

And as he com ayeinward prively, 750
His nece awook, and asked, `Who goth there?'
`My dere nece,' quod he, `it am I;
Ne wondreth not, ne have of it no fere;'
And ner he com, and seyde hir in hir ere,
`No word, for love of god I yow biseche; 755
Lat no wight ryse and heren of oure speche.'

`What! Which wey be ye comen, benedicite?'
Quod she; `And how thus unwist of hem alle?'
`Here at this secre trappe-dore,' quod he.
Quod tho Criseyde, `Lat me som wight calle.' 760
`Ey! God forbede that it sholde falle,'
Quod Pandarus, `that ye swich foly wroughte!
They mighte deme thing they never er thoughte!

`It is nought good a sleping hound to wake,
Ne yeve a wight a cause to devyne; 765
Your wommen slepen alle, I under-take,
So that, for hem, the hous men mighte myne;
And slepen wolen til the sonne shyne.
And whan my tale al brought is to an ende,

Unwist, right as I com, so wol I wende. 770

'Now, nece myn, ye shul wel understonde,'
Quod he, 'so as ye wommen demen alle,
That for to holde in love a man in honde,
And him hir "leef" and "dere herte" calle,
And maken him an howve above a calle, 775
I mene, as love an other in this whyle,
She doth hir-self a shame, and him a gyle.

'Now wherby that I telle yow al this?
Ye woot your-self, as wel as any wight,
How that your love al fully graunted is 780
To Troilus, the worthieste knight,
Oon of this world, and ther-to trouthe plyght,
That, but it were on him along, ye nolde
Him never falsen, whyle ye liven sholde.

'Now stant it thus, that sith I fro yow wente, 785
This Troilus, right platly for to seyn,
Is thurgh a goter, by a prive wente,
In-to my chaumbre come in al this reyn,
Unwist of every maner wight, certeyn,
Save of my-self, as wisly have I Ioye, 790
And by that feith I shal Pryam of Troye!

'And he is come in swich peyne and distresse
That, but he be al fully wood by this,
He sodeynly mot falle in-to wodnesse,
But-if god helpe; and cause why this is, 795
He seyth him told is, of a freend of his,
How that ye sholde love oon that hatte Horaste,
For sorwe of which this night shalt been his laste.'

Criseyde, which that al this wonder herde,
Gan sodeynly aboute hir herte colde, 800
And with a syk she sorwfully answerde,
`Allas! I wende, who-so tales tolde,
My dere herte wolde me not holde
So lightly fals! Allas! Conceytes wronge,
What harm they doon, for now live I to longe! 805

`Horaste! Allas! And falsen Troilus?
I knowe him not, god helpe me so,' quod she;
`Allas! What wikked spirit tolde him thus?
Now certes, eem, to-morwe, and I him see,
I shal ther-of as ful excusen me 810
As ever dide womman, if him lyke';
And with that word she gan ful sore syke.

`O god!' quod she, `So worldly selinesse,
Which clerkes callen fals felicitee,
Y-medled is with many a bitternesse! 815
Ful anguisshous than is, god woot,' quod she,
`Condicioun of veyn prosperitee;
For either Ioyes comen nought y-fere,
Or elles no wight hath hem alwey here.

`O brotel wele of mannes Ioye unstable! 820
With what wight so thou be, or how thou pleye,
Either he woot that thou, Ioye, art muable,
Or woot it not, it moot ben oon of tweye;
Now if he woot it not, how may he seye
That he hath verray Ioye and selinesse, 825
That is of ignoraunce ay in derknesse?

`Now if he woot that Ioye is transitorie,
As every Ioye of worldly thing mot flee,
Than every tyme he that hath in memorie,
The drede of lesing maketh him that he 830
May in no perfit selinesse be.
And if to lese his Ioye he set a myte,
Than semeth it that Ioye is worth ful lyte.

`Wherfore I wol deffyne in this matere,
That trewely, for ought I can espye, 835
Ther is no verray wele in this world here.
But O, thou wikked serpent, Ialousye,
Thou misbeleved and envious folye,
Why hastow Troilus me mad untriste,
That never yet agilte him, that I wiste?' 840

Quod Pandarus, `Thus fallen is this cas.'
`Why, uncle myn,' quod she, `who tolde him this?
Why doth my dere herte thus, allas?'
`Ye woot, ye nece myn,' quod he, `what is;
I hope al shal be wel that is amis, 845
For ye may quenche al this, if that yow leste,
And doth right so, for I holde it the beste.'

`So shal I do to-morwe, y-wis,' quod she,
`And god to-forn, so that it shal suffyse.'
`To-morwe? Allas, that were a fair!' quod he, 850
`Nay, nay, it may not stonden in this wyse;
For, nece myn, thus wryten clerkes wyse,
That peril is with drecching in y-drawe;
Nay, swich abodes been nought worth an hawe.

`Nece, al thing hath tyme, I dar avowe; 855

For whan a chaumber a-fyr is, or an halle,
Wel more nede is, it sodeynly rescowe
Than to dispute, and axe amonges alle
How is this candele in the straw y-falle?
A! Benedicite! For al among that fare 860
The harm is doon, and fare-wel feldefare!

`And, nece myn, ne take it not a-greef,
If that ye suffre him al night in this wo,
God help me so, ye hadde him never leef,
That dar I seyn, now there is but we two; 865
But wel I woot, that ye wol not do so;
Ye been to wys to do so gret folye,
To putte his lyf al night in Iupertye.

`Hadde I him never leef? By god, I wene
Ye hadde never thing so leef,' quod she. 870
`Now by my thrift,' quod he, `that shal be sene;
For, sin ye make this ensample of me,
If I al night wolde him in sorwe see
For al the tresour in the toun of Troye,
I bidde god, I never mote have Ioye! 875

`Now loke thanne, if ye, that been his love,
Shul putte al night his lyf in Iupartye
For thing of nought! Now, by that god above,
Nought only this delay comth of folye,
But of malyce, if that I shal nought lye. 880
What, platly, and ye suffre him in distresse,
Ye neither bountee doon ne gentilesse!'

Quod tho Criseyde, `Wole ye doon o thing,
And ye therwith shal stinte al his disese?

Have here, and bereth him this blewe ringe, 885
For ther is no-thing mighte him bettre plese,
Save I my-self, ne more his herte apese;
And sey my dere herte, that his sorwe
Is causeles, that shal be seen to-morwe.'

`A ring?' quod he, `Ye, hasel-wodes shaken! 890
Ye nece myn, that ring moste han a stoon
That mighte dede men alyve maken;
And swich a ring trowe I that ye have noon.
Discrecioun out of your heed is goon;
That fele I now,' quod he, `and that is routhe; 895
O tyme y-lost, wel maystow cursen slouthe!

`Wot ye not wel that noble and heigh corage
Ne sorweth not, ne stinteth eek for lyte?
But if a fool were in a Ialous rage,
I nolde setten at his sorwe a myte, 900
But feffe him with a fewe wordes whyte
Another day, whan that I mighte him finde;
But this thing stant al in another kinde.

`This is so gentil and so tendre of herte,
That with his deeth he wol his sorwes wreke; 905
For trusteth wel, how sore that him smerte,
He wol to yow no Ialouse wordes speke.
And for-thy, nece, er that his herte breke,
So spek your-self to him of this matere;
For with o word ye may his herte stere. 910

`Now have I told what peril he is inne,
And his coming unwist is to every wight;
Ne, pardee, harm may ther be noon, ne sinne;

I wol my-self be with yow al this night.
Ye knowe eek how it is your owne knight, 915
And that, by right, ye moste upon him triste,
And I al prest to fecche him whan yow liste.'

This accident so pitous was to here,
And eek so lyk a sooth, at pryme face,
And Troilus hir knight to hir so dere, 920
His prive coming, and the siker place,
That, though that she dide him as thanne a grace,
Considered alle thinges as they stode,
No wonder is, sin she dide al for gode.

Cryseyde answerde, `As wisly god at reste 925
My sowle bringe, as me is for him wo!
And eem, y-wis, fayn wolde I doon the beste,
If that I hadde grace to do so.
But whether that ye dwelle or for him go,
I am, til god me bettre minde sende, 930
At dulcarnon, right at my wittes ende.'

Quod Pandarus, `Ye, nece, wol ye here?
Dulcarnon called is "fleminge of wrecches";
It semeth hard, for wrecches wol not lere
For verray slouthe or othere wilful tecches; 935
This seyd by hem that be not worth two fecches.
But ye ben wys, and that we han on honde
Nis neither hard, ne skilful to withstonde.'

`Thanne, eem,' quod she, `doth her-of as yow list;
But er he come, I wil up first aryse; 940
And, for the love of god, sin al my trist
Is on yow two, and ye ben bothe wyse,

So wircheth now in so discreet a wyse,
That I honour may have, and he plesaunce;
For I am here al in your governaunce.' 945

'That is wel seyd,' quod he, 'my nece dere'
Ther good thrift on that wyse gentil herte!
But liggeth stille, and taketh him right here,
It nedeth not no ferther for him sterte;
And ech of yow ese otheres sorwes smerte, 950
For love of god; and, Venus, I the herie;
For sone hope I we shulle ben alle merie.'

This Troilus ful sone on knees him sette
Ful sobrely, right be hir beddes heed,
And in his beste wyse his lady grette; 955
But lord, so she wex sodeynliche reed!
Ne, though men sholden smyten of hir heed,
She coude nought a word a-right out-bringe
So sodeynly, for his sodeyn cominge.

But Pandarus, that so wel coude fele 960
In every thing, to pleye anoon bigan,
And seyde, 'Nece, see how this lord can knele!
Now, for your trouthe, seeth this gentil man!'
And with that word he for a quisshen ran,
And seyde, 'Kneleth now, whyl that yow leste, 965
Ther god your hertes bringe sone at reste!'

Can I not seyn, for she bad him not ryse,
If sorwe it putte out of hir remembraunce,
Or elles that she toke it in the wyse
Of duetee, as for his observaunce; 970
But wel finde I she dide him this plesaunce,

That she him kiste, al-though she syked sore;
And bad him sitte a-doun with-outen more.

Quod Pandarus, `Now wol ye wel biginne;
Now doth him sitte, gode nece dere, 975
Upon your beddes syde al there with-inne,
That ech of yow the bet may other here.'
And with that word he drow him to the fere,
And took a light, and fond his contenaunce,
As for to loke up-on an old romaunce. 980

Criseyde, that was Troilus lady right,
And cleer stood on a ground of sikernesse,
Al thoughte she, hir servaunt and hir knight
Ne sholde of right non untrouthe in hir gesse,
Yet nathelees, considered his distresse, 985
And that love is in cause of swich folye,
Thus to him spak she of his Ialousye:

`Lo, herte myn, as wolde the excellence
Of love, ayeins the which that no man may,
Ne oughte eek goodly maken resistence 990
And eek bycause I felte wel and say
Youre grete trouthe, and servyse every day;
And that your herte al myn was, sooth to seyne,
This droof me for to rewe up-on your peyne.

`And your goodnesse have I founde alwey yit, 995
Of whiche, my dere herte and al my knight,
I thonke it yow, as fer as I have wit,
Al can I nought as muche as it were right;
And I, emforth my conninge and my might,
Have and ay shal, how sore that me smerte, 1000

Ben to yow trewe and hool, with a myn herte;

`And dredelees, that shal be founde at preve. --
But, herte myn, what al this is to seyne
Shal wel be told, so that ye noght yow greve,
Though I to yow right on your-self compleyne. 1005
For ther-with mene I fynally the peyne,
That halt your herte and myn in hevinesse,
Fully to sleen, and every wrong redresse.

`My goode, myn, not I for-why ne how
That Ialousye, allas! That wikked wivere, 1010
Thus causelees is cropen in-to yow;
The harm of which I wolde fayn delivere!
Allas! That he, al hool, or of him slivere,
Shuld have his refut in so digne a place,
Ther Iove him sone out of your herte arace! 1015

`But O, thou Iove, O auctor of nature,
Is this an honour to thy deitee,
That folk ungiltif suffren here iniure,
And who that giltif is, al quit goth he?
O were it leful for to pleyne on thee, 1020
That undeserved suffrest Ialousye,
Of that I wolde up-on thee pleyne and crye!

`Eek al my wo is this, that folk now usen
To seyn right thus, "Ye, Ialousye is love!"
And wolde a busshel venim al excusen, 1025
For that o greyn of love is on it shove!
But that wot heighe god that sit above,
If it be lyker love, or hate, or grame;
And after that, it oughte bere his name.

`But certeyn is, som maner Ialousye 1030
Is excusable more than som, y-wis.
As whan cause is, and som swich fantasye
With pietee so wel repressed is,
That it unnethe dooth or seyth amis,
But goodly drinketh up al his distresse; 1035
And that excuse I, for the gentilesse.

`And som so ful of furie is and despyt
That it sourmounteth his repressioun;
But herte myn, ye be not in that plyt,
That thanke I god, for whiche your passioun 1040
I wol not calle it but illusioun,
Of habundaunce of love and bisy cure,
That dooth your herte this disese endure.

`Of which I am right sory but not wrooth;
But, for my devoir and your hertes reste, 1045
Wher-so yow list, by ordal or by ooth,
By sort, or in what wyse so yow leste,
For love of god, lat preve it for the beste!
And if that I be giltif, do me deye,
Allas! What mighte I more doon or seye?' 1050

With that a fewe brighte teres newe
Owt of hir eyen fille, and thus she seyde,
`Now god, thou wost, in thought ne dede untrewe
To Troilus was never yet Criseyde.'
With that hir heed doun in the bed she leyde, 1055
And with the shete it wreigh, and syghed sore,
And held hir pees; not o word spak she more.

But now help god to quenchen al this sorwe,
So hope I that he shal, for he best may;
For I have seyn, of a ful misty morwe 1060
Folwen ful ofte a mery someres day;
And after winter folweth grene May.
Men seen alday, and reden eek in stories,
That after sharpe shoures been victories.

This Troilus, whan he hir wordes herde, 1065
Have ye no care, him liste not to slepe;
For it thoughte him no strokes of a yerde
To here or seen Criseyde, his lady wepe;
But wel he felte aboute his herte crepe,
For every teer which that Criseyde asterte, 1070
The crampe of deeth, to streyne him by the herte.

And in his minde he gan the tyme acurse
That he cam there, and that that he was born;
For now is wikke y-turned in-to worse,
And al that labour he hath doon biforn, 1075
He wende it lost, he thoughte he nas but lorn.
`O Pandarus,' thoughte he, `allas! Thy wyle
Serveth of nought, so weylaway the whyle!'

And therwithal he heng a-doun the heed,
And fil on knees, and sorwfully he sighte; 1080
What mighte he seyn? He felte he nas but deed,
For wrooth was she that shulde his sorwes lighte.
But nathelees, whan that he speken mighte,
Than seyde he thus, `God woot, that of this game,
Whan al is wist, than am I not to blame!' 1085

Ther-with the sorwe so his herte shette,

That from his eyen fil there not a tere,
And every spirit his vigour in-knette,
So they astoned or oppressed were.
The feling of his sorwe, or of his fere, 1090
Or of ought elles, fled was out of towne;
And doun he fel al sodeynly a-swowne.

This was no litel sorwe for to see;
But al was hust, and Pandare up as faste,
`O nece, pees, or we be lost,' quod he, 1095
`Beth nought agast;' But certeyn, at the laste,
For this or that, he in-to bedde him caste,
And seyde, `O theef, is this a mannes herte?'
And of he rente al to his bare sherte;

And seyde, `Nece, but ye helpe us now, 1100
Allas, your owne Troilus is lorn!'
`Y-wis, so wolde I, and I wiste how,
Ful fayn,' quod she; `Allas! That I was born!'
`Ye, nece, wole ye pullen out the thorn
That stiketh in his herte?' quod Pandare; 1105
`Sey "Al foryeve," and stint is al this fare!'

`Ye, that to me,' quod she, `ful lever were
Than al the good the sonne aboute gooth';
And therwith-al she swoor him in his ere,
`Y-wis, my dere herte, I am nought wrooth, 1110
Have here my trouthe and many another ooth;
Now speek to me, for it am I, Cryseyde!'
But al for nought; yet mighte he not a-breyde.

Therwith his pous and pawmes of his hondes
They gan to frote, and wete his temples tweyne, 1115

And, to deliveren him from bittre bondes,
She ofte him kiste; and, shortly for to seyne,
Him to revoken she dide al hir peyne.
And at the laste, he gan his breeth to drawe,
And of his swough sone after that adawe, 1120

And gan bet minde and reson to him take,
But wonder sore he was abayst, y-wis.
And with a syk, whan he gan bet a-wake,
He seyde, `O mercy, god, what thing is this?'
`Why do ye with your-selven thus amis?' 1125
Quod tho Criseyde, `Is this a mannes game?
What, Troilus! Wol ye do thus, for shame?'

And therwith-al hir arm over him she leyde,
And al foryaf, and ofte tyme him keste.
He thonked hir, and to hir spak, and seyde 1130
As fil to purpos for his herte reste.
And she to that answerde him as hir leste;
And with hir goodly wordes him disporte
She gan, and ofte his sorwes to comforte.

Quod Pandarus, `For ought I can espyen, 1135
This light, nor I ne serven here of nought;
Light is not good for syke folkes yen.
But for the love of god, sin ye be brought
In thus good plyt, lat now non hevy thought
Ben hanginge in the hertes of yow tweye:' 1140
And bar the candele to the chimeneye.

Sone after this, though it no nede were,
Whan she swich othes as hir list devyse
Hadde of him take, hir thoughte tho no fere,

Ne cause eek non, to bidde him thennes ryse. 1145
Yet lesse thing than othes may suffyse
In many a cas; for every wight, I gesse,
That loveth wel meneth but gentilesse.

But in effect she wolde wite anoon
Of what man, and eek where, and also why 1150
He Ielous was, sin ther was cause noon;
And eek the signe, that he took it by,
She bad him that to telle hir bisily,
Or elles, certeyn, she bar him on honde,
That this was doon of malis, hir to fonde. 1155

With-outen more, shortly for to seyne,
He moste obeye un-to his lady heste;
And for the lasse harm, he moste feyne.
He seyde hir, whan she was at swiche a feste,
She mighte on him han loked at the leste; 1160
Not I not what, al dere y-nough a risshe,
As he that nedes moste a cause fisshe.

And she answerde, `Swete, al were it so,
What harm was that, sin I non yvel mene?
For, by that god that boughte us bothe two, 1165
In alle thinge is myn entente clene.
Swich arguments ne been not worth a bene;
Wol ye the childish Ialous contrefete?
Now were it worthy that ye were y-bete.'

Tho Troilus gan sorwfully to syke, 1170
Lest she be wrooth, him thoughte his herte deyde;
And seyde, `Allas! Up-on my sorwes syke
Have mercy, swete herte myn, Cryseyde!

And if that, in tho wordes that I seyde,
Be any wrong, I wol no more trespace; 1175
Do what yow list, I am al in your grace.'

And she answerde, `Of gilt misericorde!
That is to seyn, that I foryeve al this;
And ever-more on this night yow recorde,
And beth wel war ye do no more amis.' 1180
`Nay, dere herte myn,' quod he, `y-wis.'
`And now,' quod she, `that I have do yow smerte,
Foryeve it me, myn owene swete herte.'

This Troilus, with blisse of that supprysed,
Put al in goddes hond, as he that mente 1185
No-thing but wel; and, sodeynly avysed,
He hir in armes faste to him hente.
And Pandarus, with a ful good entente,
Leyde him to slepe, and seyde, `If ye ben wyse,
Swowneth not now, lest more folk aryse.' 1190

What mighte or may the sely larke seye,
Whan that the sperhauk hath it in his foot?
I can no more, but of thise ilke tweye,
To whom this tale sucre be or soot,
Though that I tarie a yeer, som-tyme I moot, 1195
After myn auctor, tellen hir gladnesse,
As wel as I have told hir hevinesse.

Criseyde, which that felte hir thus y-take,
As writen clerkes in hir bokes olde,
Right as an aspes leef she gan to quake, 1200
Whan she him felte hir in his armes folde.
But Troilus, al hool of cares colde,

Gan thanken tho the blisful goddes sevene;
Thus sondry peynes bringen folk in hevene.

This Troilus in armes gan hir streyne, 1205
And seyde, `O swete, as ever mote I goon,
Now be ye caught, now is ther but we tweyne;
Now yeldeth yow, for other boot is noon.'
To that Criseyde answerde thus anoon,
`Ne hadde I er now, my swete herte dere, 1210
Ben yolde, y-wis, I were now not here!'

O! Sooth is seyd, that heled for to be
As of a fevre or othere greet syknesse,
Men moste drinke, as men may often see,
Ful bittre drink; and for to han gladnesse, 1215
Men drinken often peyne and greet distresse;
I mene it here, as for this aventure,
That thourgh a peyne hath founden al his cure.

And now swetnesse semeth more sweet,
That bitternesse assayed was biforn; 1220
For out of wo in blisse now they flete;
Non swich they felten, sith they were born;
Now is this bet, than bothe two be lorn!
For love of god, take every womman hede
To werken thus, if it comth to the nede. 1225

Criseyde, al quit from every drede and tene,
As she that iuste cause hadde him to triste,
Made him swich feste, it Ioye was to sene,
Whan she his trouthe and clene entente wiste.
And as aboute a tree, with many a twiste, 1230
Bitrent and wryth the sote wode-binde,

Gan eche of hem in armes other winde.

And as the newe abaysshed nightingale,
That stinteth first whan she biginneth to singe,
Whan that she hereth any herde tale, 1235
Or in the hegges any wight steringe,
And after siker dooth hir voys out-ringe;
Right so Criseyde, whan hir drede stente,
Opned hir herte and tolde him hir entente.

And right as he that seeth his deeth y-shapen, 1240
And deye moot, in ought that he may gesse,
And sodeynly rescous doth him escapen,
And from his deeth is brought in sikernesse,
For al this world, in swich present gladnesse
Was Troilus, and hath his lady swete; 1245
With worse hap god lat us never mete!

Hir armes smale, hir streyghte bak and softe,
Hir sydes longe, fleshly, smothe, and whyte
He gan to stroke, and good thrift bad ful ofte
Hir snowish throte, hir brestes rounde and lyte; 1250
Thus in this hevene he gan him to delyte,
And ther-with-al a thousand tyme hir kiste;
That, what to done, for Ioye unnethe he wiste.

Than seyde he thus, `O, Love, O, Charitee,
Thy moder eek, Citherea the swete, 1255
After thy-self next heried be she,
Venus mene I, the wel-willy planete;
And next that, Imeneus, I thee grete;
For never man was to yow goddes holde
As I, which ye han brought fro cares colde. 1260

`Benigne Love, thou holy bond of thinges,
Who-so wol grace, and list thee nought honouren,
Lo, his desyr wol flee with-outen winges.
For, noldestow of bountee hem socouren
That serven best and most alwey labouren, 1265
Yet were al lost, that dar I wel seyn, certes,
But-if thy grace passed our desertes.

`And for thou me, that coude leest deserve
Of hem that nombred been un-to thy grace,
Hast holpen, ther I lykly was to sterve, 1270
And me bistowed in so heygh a place
That thilke boundes may no blisse pace,
I can no more, but laude and reverence
Be to thy bounte and thyn excellence!'

And therwith-al Criseyde anoon he kiste, 1275
Of which, certeyn, she felte no disese,
And thus seyde he, `Now wolde god I wiste,
Myn herte swete, how I yow mighte plese!
What man,' quod he, `was ever thus at ese
As I, on whiche the faireste and the beste 1280
That ever I say, deyneth hir herte reste.

`Here may men seen that mercy passeth right;
The experience of that is felt in me,
That am unworthy to so swete a wight.
But herte myn, of your benignitee, 1285
So thenketh, though that I unworthy be,
Yet mot I nede amenden in som wyse,
Right thourgh the vertu of your heyghe servyse.

`And for the love of god, my lady dere,
Sin god hath wrought me for I shal yow serve, 1290
As thus I mene, that ye wol be my stere,
To do me live, if that yow liste, or sterve,
So techeth me how that I may deserve
Your thank, so that I, thurgh myn ignoraunce,
Ne do no-thing that yow be displesaunce. 1295

`For certes, fresshe wommanliche wyf,
This dar I seye, that trouthe and diligence,
That shal ye finden in me al my lyf,
Ne wol not, certeyn, breken your defence;
And if I do, present or in absence, 1300
For love of god, lat slee me with the dede,
If that it lyke un-to your womanhede.'

`Y-wis,' quod she, `myn owne hertes list,
My ground of ese, and al myn herte dere,
Graunt mercy, for on that is al my trist; 1305
But late us falle awey fro this matere;
For it suffyseth, this that seyd is here.
And at o word, with-outen repentaunce,
Wel-come, my knight, my pees, my suffisaunce!'

Of hir delyt, or Ioyes oon the leste 1310
Were impossible to my wit to seye;
But iuggeth, ye that han ben at the feste,
Of swich gladnesse, if that hem liste pleye!
I can no more, but thus thise ilke tweye
That night, be-twixen dreed and sikernesse, 1315
Felten in love the grete worthinesse.

O blisful night, of hem so longe y-sought,

How blithe un-to hem bothe two thou were!
Why ne hadde I swich on with my soule y-bought,
Ye, or the leeste Ioye that was there? 1320
A-wey, thou foule daunger and thou fere,
And lat hem in this hevene blisse dwelle,
That is so heygh, that al ne can I telle!

But sooth is, though I can not tellen al,
As can myn auctor, of his excellence, 1325
Yet have I seyd, and, god to-forn, I shal
In every thing al hoolly his sentence.
And if that I, at loves reverence,
Have any word in eched for the beste,
Doth therwith-al right as your-selven leste. 1330

For myne wordes, here and every part,
I speke hem alle under correccioun
Of yow, that feling han in loves art,
And putte it al in your discrecioun
To encrese or maken diminucioun 1335
Of my langage, and that I yow bi-seche;
But now to purpos of my rather speche.

Thise ilke two, that ben in armes laft,
So looth to hem a-sonder goon it were,
That ech from other wende been biraft, 1340
Or elles, lo, this was hir moste fere,
That al this thing but nyce dremes were;
For which ful ofte ech of hem seyde, `O swete,
Clippe ich yow thus, or elles I it mete?'

And, lord! So he gan goodly on hir see, 1345
That never his look ne bleynte from hir face,

And seyde, `O dere herte, may it be
That it be sooth, that ye ben in this place?'
`Ye, herte myn, god thank I of his grace!'
Quod tho Criseyde, and therwith-al him kiste, 1350
That where his spirit was, for Ioye he niste.

This Troilus ful ofte hir eyen two
Gan for to kisse, and seyde, `O eyen clere,
It were ye that wroughte me swich wo,
Ye humble nettes of my lady dere! 1355
Though ther be mercy writen in your chere,
God wot, the text ful hard is, sooth, to finde,
How coude ye with-outen bond me binde?'

Therwith he gan hir faste in armes take,
And wel an hundred tymes gan he syke, 1360
Nought swiche sorwfull sykes as men make
For wo, or elles whan that folk ben syke,
But esy sykes, swiche as been to lyke,
That shewed his affeccioun with-inne;
Of swiche sykes coude he nought bilinne. 1365

Sone after this they speke of sondry thinges,
As fil to purpos of this aventure,
And pleyinge entrechaungeden hir ringes,
Of which I can nought tellen no scripture;
But wel I woot, a broche, gold and asure, 1370
In whiche a ruby set was lyk an herte,
Criseyde him yaf, and stak it on his sherte.

Lord! trowe ye, a coveitous, a wreccbe,
That blameth love and holt of it despyt,
That, of tho pens that he can mokre and kecche, 1375

Was ever yet y-yeve him swich delyt,
As is in love, in oo poynt, in som plyt?
Nay, doutelees, for also god me save,
So parfit Ioye may no nigard have!

They wol sey `Yis,' but lord! So that they lye, 1380
Tho bisy wrecches, ful of wo and drede!
They callen love a woodnesse or folye,
But it shal falle hem as I shal yow rede;
They shul forgo the whyte and eke the rede,
And live in wo, ther god yeve hem mischaunce, 1385
And every lover in his trouthe avaunce!

As wolde god, tho wrecches, that dispyse
Servyse of love, hadde eres al-so longe
As hadde Myda, ful of coveityse,
And ther-to dronken hadde as hoot and stronge 1390
As Crassus dide for his affectis wronge,
To techen hem that they ben in the vyce,
And loveres nought, al-though they holde hem nyce!

Thise ilke two, of whom that I yow seye,
Whan that hir hertes wel assured were, 1395
Tho gonne they to speken and to pleye,
And eek rehercen how, and whanne, and where,
They knewe hem first, and every wo and fere
That passed was; but al swich hevinesse,
I thanke it god, was tourned to gladnesse. 1400

And ever-mo, whan that hem fel to speke
Of any thing of swich a tyme agoon,
With kissing al that tale sholde breke,
And fallen in a newe Ioye anoon,

And diden al hir might, sin they were oon, 1405
For to recoveren blisse and been at ese,
And passed wo with Ioye countrepeyse.

Reson wil not that I speke of sleep,
For it accordeth nought to my matere;
God woot, they toke of that ful litel keep, 1410
But lest this night, that was to hem so dere,
Ne sholde in veyn escape in no manere,
It was biset in Ioye and bisinesse
Of al that souneth in-to gentilnesse.

But whan the cok, comune astrologer, 1415
Gan on his brest to bete, and after crowe,
And Lucifer, the dayes messager,
Gan for to ryse, and out hir bemes throwe;
And estward roos, to him that coude it knowe,
Fortuna maior, than anoon Criseyde, 1420
With herte sore, to Troilus thus seyde: --

`Myn hertes lyf, my trist and my plesaunce,
That I was born, allas! What me is wo,
That day of us mot make desseveraunce!
For tyme it is to ryse, and hennes go, 1425
Or elles I am lost for evermo!
O night, allas! Why niltow over us hove,
As longe as whanne Almena lay by Iove?

`O blake night, as folk in bokes rede,
That shapen art by god this world to hyde 1430
At certeyn tymes with thy derke wede,
That under that men mighte in reste abyde,
Wel oughte bestes pleyne, and folk thee chyde,

That there-as day with labour wolde us breste,
That thou thus fleest, and deynest us nought reste! 1435

`Thou dost, allas! To shortly thyn offyce,
Thou rakel night, ther god, makere of kinde,
Thee, for thyn hast and thyn unkinde vyce,
So faste ay to our hemi-spere binde.
That never-more under the ground thou winde! 1440
For now, for thou so hyest out of Troye,
Have I forgon thus hastily my Ioye!'

This Troilus, that with tho wordes felte,
As thoughte him tho, for pietous distresse,
The blody teres from his herte melte, 1445
As he that never yet swich hevinesse
Assayed hadde, out of so greet gladnesse,
Gan therwith-al Criseyde his lady dere
In armes streyne, and seyde in this manere: --

`O cruel day, accusour of the Ioye 1450
That night and love han stole and faste y-wryen,
A-cursed be thy coming in-to Troye,
For every bore hath oon of thy bright yen!
Envyous day, what list thee so to spyen?
What hastow lost, why sekestow this place, 1455
Ther god thy lyght so quenche, for his grace?

`Allas! What han thise loveres thee agilt,
Dispitous day? Thyn be the pyne of helle!
For many a lovere hastow shent, and wilt;
Thy pouring in wol no-wher lete hem dwelle. 1460
What proferestow thy light here for to selle?
Go selle it hem that smale seles graven,

We wol thee nought, us nedeth no day haven.'

And eek the sonne Tytan gan he chyde,
And seyde, `O fool, wel may men thee dispyse, 1465
That hast the Dawing al night by thy syde,
And suffrest hir so sone up fro thee ryse,
For to disesen loveres in this wyse.
What! Holde your bed ther, thou, and eek thy Morwe!
I bidde god, so yeve yow bothe sorwe!' 1470

Therwith ful sore he sighte, and thus he seyde,
`My lady right, and of my wele or wo
The welle and rote, O goodly myn, Criseyde,
And shal I ryse, allas! And shal I go?
Now fele I that myn herte moot a-two! 1475
For how sholde I my lyf an houre save,
Sin that with yow is al the lyf I have?

`What shal I doon, for certes, I not how,
Ne whanne, allas! I shal the tyme see,
That in this plyt I may be eft with yow; 1480
And of my lyf, god woot, how that shal be,
Sin that desyr right now so byteth me,
That I am deed anoon, but I retourne.
How sholde I longe, allas! Fro yow soiourne?

`But nathelees, myn owene lady bright, 1485
Yit were it so that I wiste outrely,
That I, your humble servaunt and your knight,
Were in your herte set so fermely
As ye in myn, the which thing, trewely,
Me lever were than thise worldes tweyne, 1490
Yet sholde I bet enduren al my peyne.'

To that Cryseyde answerde right anoon,
And with a syk she seyde, `O herte dere,
The game, y-wis, so ferforth now is goon,
That first shal Phebus falle fro his spere, 1495
And every egle been the dowves fere,
And every roche out of his place sterte,
Er Troilus out of Criseydes herte!

`Ye he so depe in-with myn herte grave,
That, though I wolde it turne out of my thought, 1500
As wisly verray god my soule save,
To dyen in the peyne, I coude nought!
And, for the love of god that us bath wrought,
Lat in your brayn non other fantasye
So crepe, that it cause me to dye! 1505

`And that ye me wolde han as faste in minde
As I have yow, that wolde I yow bi-seche;
And, if I wiste soothly that to finde,
God mighte not a poynt my Ioyes eche!
But, herte myn, with-oute more speche, 1510
Beth to me trewe, or elles were it routhe;
For I am thyn, by god and by my trouthe!

`Beth glad for-thy, and live in sikernesse;
Thus seyde I never er this, ne shal to mo;
And if to yow it were a gret gladnesse 1515
To turne ayein, soone after that ye go,
As fayn wolde I as ye, it were so,
As wisly god myn herte bringe at reste!'
And him in armes took, and ofte keste.

Agayns his wil, sin it mot nedes be, 1520
This Troilus up roos, and faste him cledde,
And in his armes took his lady free
An hundred tyme, and on his wey him spedde,
And with swich wordes as his herte bledde,
He seyde, `Farewel, mr dere herte swete, 1525
Ther god us graunte sounde and sone to mete!'

To which no word for sorwe she answerde,
So sore gan his parting hir destreyne;
And Troilus un-to his palays ferde,
As woo bigon as she was, sooth to seyne; 1530
So hard him wrong of sharp desyr the peyne
For to ben eft there he was in plesaunce,
That it may never out of his remembraunce.

Retorned to his real palais, sone
He softe in-to his bed gan for to slinke, 1535
To slepe longe, as he was wont to done,
But al for nought; he may wel ligge and winke,
But sleep ne may ther in his herte sinke;
Thenkinge how she, for whom desyr him brende,
A thousand-fold was worth more than he wende. 1540

And in his thought gan up and doun to winde
Hir wordes alle, and every countenaunce,
And fermely impressen in his minde
The leste poynt that to him was plesaunce;
And verrayliche, of thilke remembraunce, 1545
Desyr al newe him brende, and lust to brede
Gan more than erst, and yet took he non hede.

Criseyde also, right in the same wyse,

Of Troilus gan in hir herte shette
His worthinesse, his lust, his dedes wyse, 1550
His gentilesse, and how she with him mette,
Thonkinge love he so wel hir bisette;
Desyring eft to have hir herte dere
In swich a plyt, she dorste make him chere.

Pandare, a-morwe which that comen was 1555
Un-to his nece, and gan hir fayre grete,
Seyde, `Al this night so reyned it, allas!
That al my drede is that ye, nece swete,
Han litel layser had to slepe and mete;
Al night,' quod he, `hath reyn so do me wake, 1560
That som of us, I trowe, hir hedes ake.'

And ner he com, and seyde, `How stont it now
This mery morwe, nece, how can ye fare?'
Criseyde answerde, `Never the bet for yow,
Fox that ye been, god yeve youre herte care! 1565
God help me so, ye caused al this fare,
Trow I,' quod she, `for alle your wordes whyte;
O! Who-so seeth yow knoweth yow ful lyte!'

With that she gan hir face for to wrye
With the shete, and wex for shame al reed; 1570
And Pandarus gan under for to prye,
And seyde, `Nece, if that I shal be deed,
Have here a swerd, and smyteth of myn heed.'
With that his arm al sodeynly he thriste
Under hir nekke, and at the laste hir kiste. 1575

I passe al that which chargeth nought to seye,
What! God foryaf his deeth, and she al-so

Foryaf, and with hir uncle gan to pleye,
For other cause was ther noon than so.
But of this thing right to the effect to go, 1580
Whan tyme was, hom til hir hous she wente,
And Pandarus hath fully his entente.

Now torne we ayein to Troilus,
That resteles ful longe a-bedde lay,
And prevely sente after Pandarus, 1585
To him to come in al the haste he may.
He com anoon, nought ones seyde he `nay,'
And Troilus ful sobrely he grette,
And doun upon his beddes syde him sette.

This Troilus, with al the affeccioun 1590
Of frendes love that herte may devyse,
To Pandarus on knees fil adoun,
And er that he wolde of the place aryse,
He gan him thonken in his beste wyse;
An hondred sythe he gan the tyme blesse, 1595
That he was born, to bringe him fro distresse.

He seyde, `O frend of frendes the alderbeste
That ever was, the sothe for to telle,
Thou hast in hevene y-brought my soule at reste
Fro Flegitoun, the fery flood of helle; 1600
That, though I mighte a thousand tymes selle,
Upon a day, my lyf in thy servyse,
It mighte nought a mote in that suffyse.

`The sonne, which that al the world may see,
Saw never yet, my lyf, that dar I leye, 1605
So inly fayr and goodly as is she,

Whos I am al, and shal, til that I deye;
And, that I thus am hires, dar I seye,
That thanked be the heighe worthinesse
Of love, and eek thy kinde bisinesse. 1610

`Thus hastow me no litel thing y-yive,
Fo which to thee obliged be for ay
My lyf, and why? For thorugh thyn help I live;
For elles deed hadde I be many a day.'
And with that word doun in his bed he lay, 1615
And Pandarus ful sobrely him herde
Til al was seyd, and than he thus answerde:

`My dere frend, if I have doon for thee
In any cas, god wot, it is me leef;
And am as glad as man may of it be, 1620
God help me so; but tak now a-greef
That I shal seyn, be war of this myscheef,
That, there-as thou now brought art in-to blisse,
That thou thy-self ne cause it nought to misse.

`For of fortunes sharpe adversitee 1625
The worst kinde of infortune is this,
A man to have ben in prosperitee,
And it remembren, whan it passed is.
Thou art wys y-nough, for-thy do nought amis;
Be not to rakel, though thou sitte warme,
For if thou be, certeyn, it wol thee harme. 1631

`Thou art at ese, and holde the wel ther-inne.
For also seur as reed is every fyr,
As greet a craft is kepe wel as winne;
Brydle alwey wel thy speche and thy desyr, 1635

For worldly Ioye halt not but by a wyr;
That preveth wel, it brest alday so ofte;
For-thy nede is to werke with it softe.'

Quod Troilus, `I hope, and god to-forn,
My dere frend, that I shal so me bere, 1640
That in my gilt ther shal no thing be lorn,
Ne I nil not rakle as for to greven here;
It nedeth not this matere ofte tere;
For wistestow myn herte wel, Pandare,
God woot, of this thou woldest litel care.' 1645

Tho gan he telle him of his glade night,
And wher-of first his herte dredde, and how,
And seyde, `Freend, as I am trewe knight,
And by that feyth I shal to god and yow,
I hadde it never half so hote as now; 1650
And ay the more that desyr me byteth
To love hir best, the more it me delyteth.

`I noot my-self not wisly what it is;
But now I fele a newe qualitee,
Ye, al another than I dide er this.' 1655
Pandare answerde, and seyde thus, that he
That ones may in hevene blisse be,
He feleth other weyes, dar I leye,
Than thilke tyme he first herde of it seye.

This is o word for al: this Troilus 1660
Was never ful to speke of this matere,
And for to preysen un-to Pandarus
The bountee of his righte lady dere,
And Pandarus to thanke and maken chere.

This tale ay was span-newe to biginne, 1665
Til that the night departed hem a-twinne.

Sone after this, for that fortune it wolde,
I-comen was the blisful tyme swete,
That Troilus was warned that he sholde,
Ther he was erst, Criseyde his lady mete; 1670
For which he felte his herte in Ioye flete;
And feythfully gan alle the goddes herie;
And lat see now if that he can be merie.

And holden was the forme and al the wyse,
Of hir cominge, and eek of his also, 1675
As it was erst, which nedeth nought devyse.
But playnly to the effect right for to go,
In Ioye and suerte Pandarus hem two
A-bedde broughte, whan that hem bothe leste,
And thus they ben in quiete and in reste. 1680

Nought nedeth it to yow, sin they ben met,
To aske at me if that they blythe were;
For if it erst was wel, tho was it bet
A thousand-fold, this nedeth not enquere.
A-gon was every sorwe and every fere; 1685
And bothe, y-wis, they hadde, and so they wende,
As muche Ioye as herte may comprende.

This is no litel thing of for to seye,
This passeth every wit for to devyse;
For eche of hem gan otheres lust obeye; 1690
Felicitee, which that thise clerkes wyse
Commenden so, ne may not here suffyse.
This Ioye may not writen been with inke,

This passeth al that herte may bithinke.

But cruel day, so wel-awey the stounde! 1695
Gan for to aproche, as they by signes knewe,
For whiche hem thoughte felen dethes wounde;
So wo was hem, that changen gan hir hewe,
And day they goonnen to dispyse al newe,
Calling it traytour, envyous, and worse, 1700
And bitterly the dayes light they curse.

Quod Troilus, `Allas! Now am I war
That Pirous and tho swifte stedes three,
Whiche that drawen forth the sonnes char,
Han goon som by-path in despyt of me; 1705
That maketh it so sone day to be;
And, for the sonne him hasteth thus to ryse,
Ne shal I never doon him sacrifyse!'

But nedes day departe moste hem sone,
And whanne hir speche doon was and hir chere, 1710
They twinne anoon as they were wont to done,
And setten tyme of meting eft y-fere;
And many a night they wroughte in this manere.
And thus Fortune a tyme ladde in Ioye
Criseyde, and eek this kinges sone of Troye. 1715

In suffisaunce, in blisse, and in singinges,
This Troilus gan al his lyf to lede;
He spendeth, Iusteth, maketh festeynges;
He yeveth frely ofte, and chaungeth wede,
And held aboute him alwey, out of drede, 1720
A world of folk, as cam him wel of kinde,
The fressheste and the beste he coude fynde;

That swich a voys was of hym and a stevene
Thorugh-out the world, of honour and largesse,
That it up rong un-to the yate of hevene. 1725
And, as in love, he was in swich gladnesse,
That in his herte he demede, as I gesse,
That there nis lovere in this world at ese
So wel as he, and thus gan love him plese.

The godlihede or beautee which that kinde 1730
In any other lady hadde y-set
Can not the mountaunce of a knot unbinde,
A-boute his herte, of al Criseydes net.
He was so narwe y-masked and y-knet,
That it undon on any manere syde, 1735
That nil not been, for ought that may betyde.

And by the hond ful ofte he wolde take
This Pandarus, and in-to gardin lede,
And swich a feste and swich a proces make
Him of Criseyde, and of hir womanhede, 1740
And of hir beautee, that, with-outen drede,
It was an hevene his wordes for to here;
And thanne he wolde singe in this manere.

`Love, that of erthe and see hath governaunce,
Love, that his hestes hath in hevene hye, 1745
Love, that with an holsom alliaunce
Halt peples ioyned, as him list hem gye,
Love, that knetteth lawe of companye,
And couples doth in vertu for to dwelle,
Bind this acord, that I have told and telle; 1750

'That that the world with feyth, which that is stable,
Dyverseth so his stoundes concordinge,
That elements that been so discordable
Holden a bond perpetuely duringe,
That Phebus mote his rosy day forth bringe, 1755
And that the mone hath lordship over the nightes,
Al this doth Love; ay heried be his mightes!

'That, that the see, that gredy is to flowen,
Constreyneth to a certeyn ende so
His flodes, that so fersly they ne growen 1760
To drenchen erthe and al for ever-mo;
And if that Love ought lete his brydel go,
Al that now loveth a-sonder sholde lepe,
And lost were al, that Love halt now to-hepe.

'So wolde god, that auctor is of kinde, 1765
That, with his bond, Love of his vertu liste
To cerclen hertes alle, and faste binde,
That from his bond no wight the wey out wiste.
And hertes colde, hem wolde I that he twiste
To make hem love, and that hem leste ay rewe 1770
On hertes sore, and kepe hem that ben trewe.'

In alle nedes, for the tounes werre,
He was, and ay the firste in armes dight;
And certeynly, but-if that bokes erre,
Save Ector, most y-drad of any wight; 1775
And this encrees of hardinesse and might
Cam him of love, his ladies thank to winne,
That altered his spirit so with-inne.

In tyme of trewe, on haukinge wolde he ryde,

Or elles hunten boor, bere, or lyoun; 1780
The smale bestes leet he gon bi-syde.
And whan that he com rydinge in-to toun,
Ful ofte his lady, from hir window doun,
As fresh as faucon comen out of muwe,
Ful redy was, him goodly to saluwe. 1785

And most of love and vertu was his speche,
And in despyt hadde alle wrecchednesse;
And doutelees, no nede was him biseche
To honouren hem that hadde worthinesse,
And esen hem that weren in distresse. 1790
And glad was he if any wight wel ferde,
That lover was, whan he it wiste or herde.

For sooth to seyn, he lost held every wight
But-if he were in loves heigh servyse,
I mene folk that oughte it been of right. 1795
And over al this, so wel coude he devyse
Of sentement, and in so unkouth wyse
Al his array, that every lover thoughte,
That al was wel, what-so he seyde or wroughte.

And though that he be come of blood royal, 1800
Him liste of pryde at no wight for to chase;
Benigne he was to ech in general,
For which he gat him thank in every place.
Thus wolde love, y-heried be his grace,
That Pryde, Envye, Ire, and Avaryce 1805
He gan to flee, and every other vyce.

Thou lady bright, the doughter to Dione,
Thy blinde and winged sone eek, daun Cupyde;

Ye sustren nyne eek, that by Elicone
In hil Parnaso listen for to abyde, 1810
That ye thus fer han deyned me to gyde,
I can no more, but sin that ye wol wende,
Ye heried been for ay, with-outen ende!

Thourgh yow have I seyd fully in my song
Theffect and Ioye of Troilus servyse, 1815
Al be that ther was som disese among,
As to myn auctor listeth to devyse.
My thridde book now ende ich in this wyse;
And Troilus in luste and in quiete
Is with Criseyde, his owne herte swete. 1820

Explicit Liber Tercius.

BOOK IV. Incipit Prohemium Liber Quartus.

But al to litel, weylaway the whyle,
Lasteth swich Ioye, y-thonked be Fortune!
That semeth trewest, whan she wol bygyle,
And can to foles so hir song entune,
That she hem hent and blent, traytour comune; 5
And whan a wight is from hir wheel y-throwe,
Than laugheth she, and maketh him the mowe.

From Troilus she gan hir brighte face
Awey to wrythe, and took of him non hede,
But caste him clene out of his lady grace, 10
And on hir wheel she sette up Diomede;
For which right now myn herte ginneth blede,
And now my penne, allas! With which I wryte,
Quaketh for drede of that I moot endyte.

For how Criseyde Troilus forsook, 15
Or at the leste, how that she was unkinde,
Mot hennes-forth ben matere of my book,
As wryten folk through which it is in minde.
Allas! That they sholde ever cause finde
To speke hir harm; and if they on hir lye, 20
Y-wis, hem-self sholde han the vilanye.

O ye Herines, Nightes doughtren three,
That endelees compleynen ever in pyne,
Megera, Alete, and eek Thesiphone;
Thou cruel Mars eek, fader to Quiryne, 25
This ilke ferthe book me helpeth fyne,
So that the los of lyf and love y-fere
Of Troilus be fully shewed here.

Explicit prohemium.

Incipit Quartus Liber.

Ligginge in ost, as I have seyd er this,
The Grekes stronge, aboute Troye toun, 30
Bifel that, whan that Phebus shyning is
Up-on the brest of Hercules Lyoun,
That Ector, with ful many a bold baroun,
Caste on a day with Grekes for to fighte,
As he was wont to greve hem what he mighte. 35

Not I how longe or short it was bitwene
This purpos and that day they fighte mente;
But on a day wel armed, bright and shene,
Ector, and many a worthy wight out wente,
With spere in hond and bigge bowes bente; 40
And in the herd, with-oute lenger lette,
Hir fomen in the feld anoon hem mette.

The longe day, with speres sharpe y-grounde,
With arwes, dartes, swerdes, maces felle,
They fighte and bringen hors and man to grounde, 45
And with hir axes out the braynes quelle.
But in the laste shour, sooth for to telle,

The folk of Troye hem-selven so misledden,
That with the worse at night homward they fledden.

At whiche day was taken Antenor, 50
Maugre Polydamas or Monesteo,
Santippe, Sarpedon, Polynestor,
Polyte, or eek the Troian daun Ripheo,
And othere lasse folk, as Phebuseo.
So that, for harm, that day the folk of Troye 55
Dredden to lese a greet part of hir Ioye.

Of Pryamus was yeve, at Greek requeste,
A tyme of trewe, and tho they gonnen trete,
Hir prisoneres to chaungen, moste and leste,
And for the surplus yeven sommes grete. 60
This thing anoon was couth in every strete,
Bothe in thassege, in toune, and every-where,
And with the firste it cam to Calkas ere.

Whan Calkas knew this tretis sholde holde,
In consistorie, among the Grekes, sone 65
He gan in thringe forth, with lordes olde,
And sette him there-as he was wont to done;
And with a chaunged face hem bad a bone,
For love of god, to don that reverence,
To stinte noyse, and yeve him audience. 70

Thanne seyde he thus, `Lo! Lordes myne, I was
Troian, as it is knowen out of drede;
And, if that yow remembre, I am Calkas,
That alderfirst yaf comfort to your nede,
And tolde wel how that ye sholden spede. 75
For dredelees, thorugh yow, shal, in a stounde,

Ben Troye y-brend, and beten doun to grounde.

`And in what forme, or in what maner wyse
This town to shende, and al your lust to acheve,
Ye han er this wel herd it me devyse;   80
This knowe ye, my lordes, as I leve.
And for the Grekes weren me so leve,
I com my-self in my propre persone,
To teche in this how yow was best to done;

`Havinge un-to my tresour ne my rente 85
Right no resport, to respect of your ese.
Thus al my good I loste and to yow wente,
Wening in this you, lordes, for to plese.
But al that los ne doth me no disese.
I vouche-sauf, as wisly have I Ioye, 90
For you to lese al that I have in Troye,

`Save of a doughter, that I lafte, allas!
Slepinge at hoom, whanne out of Troye I sterte.
O sterne, O cruel fader that I was!
How mighte I have in that so hard an herte? 95
Allas! I ne hadde y-brought hir in hir sherte!
For sorwe of which I wol not live to morwe,
But-if ye lordes rewe up-on my sorwe.

`For, by that cause I say no tyme er now
Hir to delivere, I holden have my pees; 100
But now or never, if that it lyke yow,
I may hir have right sone, doutelees.
O help and grace! Amonges al this prees,
Rewe on this olde caitif in destresse,
Sin I through yow have al this hevinesse! 105

`Ye have now caught and fetered in prisoun
Troians y-nowe; and if your willes be,
My child with oon may have redempcioun.
Now for the love of god and of bountee,
Oon of so fele, allas! So yeve him me. 110
What nede were it this preyere for to werne,
Sin ye shul bothe han folk and toun as yerne?

`On peril of my lyf, I shal nat lye,
Appollo hath me told it feithfully;
I have eek founde it be astronomye, 115
By sort, and by augurie eek trewely,
And dar wel seye, the tyme is faste by,
That fyr and flaumbe on al the toun shal sprede;
And thus shal Troye turne to asshen dede.

`For certeyn, Phebus and Neptunus bothe, 120
That makeden the walles of the toun,
Ben with the folk of Troye alwey so wrothe,
That thei wol bringe it to confusioun,
Right in despyt of king Lameadoun.
By-cause he nolde payen hem hir hyre, 125
The toun of Troye shal ben set on-fyre.'

Telling his tale alwey, this olde greye,
Humble in speche, and in his lokinge eke,
The salte teres from his eyen tweye
Ful faste ronnen doun by eyther cheke. 130
So longe he gan of socour hem by-seke
That, for to hele him of his sorwes sore,
They yave him Antenor, with-oute more.

But who was glad y-nough but Calkas tho?
And of this thing ful sone his nedes leyde 135
On hem that sholden for the tretis go,
And hem for Antenor ful ofte preyde
To bringen hoom king Toas and Criseyde;
And whan Pryam his save-garde sente,
Thembassadours to Troye streyght they wente. 140

The cause y-told of hir cominge, the olde
Pryam the king ful sone in general
Let here-upon his parlement to holde,
Of which the effect rehersen yow I shal.
Thembassadours ben answered for fynal, 145
Theschaunge of prisoners and al this nede
Hem lyketh wel, and forth in they procede.

This Troilus was present in the place,
Whan axed was for Antenor Criseyde,
For which ful sone chaungen gan his face, 150
As he that with tho wordes wel neigh deyde.
But nathelees, he no word to it seyde,
Lest men sholde his affeccioun espye;
With mannes herte he gan his sorwes drye.

And ful of anguissh and of grisly drede 155
Abood what lordes wolde un-to it seye;
And if they wolde graunte, as god forbede,
Theschaunge of hir, than thoughte he thinges tweye,
First, how to save hir honour, and what weye
He mighte best theschaunge of hir withstonde; 160
Ful faste he caste how al this mighte stonde.

Love him made al prest to doon hir byde,

And rather dye than she sholde go;
But resoun seyde him, on that other syde,
`With-oute assent of hir ne do not so, 165
Lest for thy werk she wolde be thy fo,
And seyn, that thorugh thy medling is y-blowe
Your bother love, there it was erst unknowe.'

For which he gan deliberen, for the beste,
That though the lordes wolde that she wente, 170
He wolde lat hem graunte what hem leste,
And telle his lady first what that they mente.
And whan that she had seyd him hir entente,
Ther-after wolde he werken also blyve,
Though al the world ayein it wolde stryve. 175

Ector, which that wel the Grekes herde,
For Antenor how they wolde han Criseyde,
Gan it withstonde, and sobrely answerde: --
`Sires, she nis no prisoner,' he seyde;
`I noot on yow who that this charge leyde, 180
But, on my part, ye may eft-sone hem telle,
We usen here no wommen for to selle.'

The noyse of peple up-stirte thanne at ones,
As breme as blase of straw y-set on fyre;
For infortune it wolde, for the nones, 185
They sholden hir confusioun desyre.
`Ector,' quod they, `what goost may yow enspyre
This womman thus to shilde and doon us lese
Daun Antenor? -- a wrong wey now ye chese --

`That is so wys, and eek so bold baroun, 190
And we han nede to folk, as men may see;

He is eek oon, the grettest of this toun;
O Ector, lat tho fantasyes be!
O king Priam,' quod they, `thus seggen we,
That al our voys is to for-gon Criseyde;' 195
And to deliveren Antenor they preyde.

O Iuvenal, lord! Trewe is thy sentence,
That litel witen folk what is to yerne
That they ne finde in hir desyr offence;
For cloud of errour let hem not descerne 200
What best is; and lo, here ensample as yerne.
This folk desiren now deliveraunce
Of Antenor, that broughte hem to mischaunce!

For he was after traytour to the toun
Of Troye; allas! They quitte him out to rathe; 205
O nyce world, lo, thy discrecioun!
Criseyde, which that never dide hem skathe,
Shal now no lenger in hir blisse bathe;
But Antenor, he shal com hoom to toune,
And she shal out; thus seyden here and howne. 210

For which delibered was by parlement
For Antenor to yelden out Criseyde,
And it pronounced by the president,
Al-theigh that Ector `nay' ful ofte preyde.
And fynaly, what wight that it with-seyde, 215
It was for nought, it moste been, and sholde;
For substaunce of the parlement it wolde.

Departed out of parlement echone,
This Troilus, with-oute wordes mo,
Un-to his chaumbre spedde him faste allone, 220

But-if it were a man of his or two,
The whiche he bad out faste for to go,
By-cause he wolde slepen, as he seyde,
And hastely up-on his bed him leyde.

And as in winter leves been biraft, 225
Eche after other, til the tree be bare,
So that ther nis but bark and braunche y-laft,
Lyth Troilus, biraft of ech wel-fare,
Y-bounden in the blake bark of care,
Disposed wood out of his wit to breyde, 230
So sore him sat the chaunginge of Criseyde.

He rist him up, and every dore he shette
And windowe eek, and tho this sorweful man
Up-on his beddes syde a-doun him sette,
Ful lyk a deed image pale and wan; 235
And in his brest the heped wo bigan
Out-breste, and he to werken in this wyse
In his woodnesse, as I shal yow devyse.

Right as the wilde bole biginneth springe
Now here, now there, y-darted to the herte, 240
And of his deeth roreth in compleyninge,
Right so gan he aboute the chaumbre sterte,
Smyting his brest ay with his festes smerte;
His heed to the wal, his body to the grounde
Ful ofte he swapte, him-selven to confounde. 245

His eyen two, for pitee of his herte,
Out stremeden as swifte welles tweye;
The heighe sobbes of his sorwes smerte
His speche him refte, unnethes mighte he seye,

`O deeth, allas! Why niltow do me deye? 250
A-cursed be the day which that nature
Shoop me to ben a lyves creature!'

But after, whan the furie and the rage
Which that his herte twiste and faste threste,
By lengthe of tyme somwhat gan asswage, 255
Up-on his bed he leyde him doun to reste;
But tho bigonne his teres more out-breste,
That wonder is, the body may suffyse
To half this wo, which that I yow devyse.

Than seyde he thus, `Fortune! Allas the whyle! 260
What have I doon, what have I thus a-gilt?
How mightestow for reuthe me bigyle?
Is ther no grace, and shal I thus be spilt?
Shal thus Criseyde awey, for that thou wilt?
Allas! How maystow in thyn herte finde 265
To been to me thus cruel and unkinde?

`Have I thee nought honoured al my lyve,
As thou wel wost, above the goddes alle?
Why wiltow me fro Ioye thus depryve?
O Troilus, what may men now thee calle 270
But wrecche of wrecches, out of honour falle
In-to miserie, in which I wol biwayle
Criseyde, allas! Til that the breeth me fayle?

`Allas, Fortune! If that my lyf in Ioye
Displesed hadde un-to thy foule envye, 275
Why ne haddestow my fader, king of Troye,
By-raft the lyf, or doon my bretheren dye,
Or slayn my-self, that thus compleyne and crye,

I, combre-world, that may of no-thing serve,
But ever dye, and never fully sterve? 280

`If that Criseyde allone were me laft,
Nought roughte I whider thou woldest me stere;
And hir, allas! Than hastow me biraft.
But ever-more, lo! This is thy manere,
To reve a wight that most is to him dere, 285
To preve in that thy gerful violence.
Thus am I lost, ther helpeth no defence!

`O verray lord of love, O god, allas!
That knowest best myn herte and al my thought,
What shal my sorwful lyf don in this cas 290
If I for-go that I so dere have bought?
Sin ye Cryseyde and me han fully brought
In-to your grace, and bothe our hertes seled,
How may ye suffre, allas! It be repeled?

`What I may doon, I shal, whyl I may dure 295
On lyve in torment and in cruel peyne,
This infortune or this disaventure,
Allone as I was born, y-wis, compleyne;
Ne never wil I seen it shyne or reyne;
But ende I wil, as Edippe, in derknesse 300
My sorwful lyf, and dyen in distresse.

`O wery goost, that errest to and fro,
Why niltow fleen out of the wofulleste
Body, that ever mighte on grounde go?
O soule, lurkinge in this wo, unneste, 305
Flee forth out of myn herte, and lat it breste,
And folwe alwey Criseyde, thy lady dere;

Thy righte place is now no lenger here!

`O wofulle eyen two, sin your disport
Was al to seen Criseydes eyen brighte, 310
What shal ye doon but, for my discomfort,
Stonden for nought, and wepen out your sighte?
Sin she is queynt, that wont was yow to lighte,
In veyn fro-this-forth have I eyen tweye
Y-formed, sin your vertue is a-weye. 315

`O my Criseyde, O lady sovereyne
Of thilke woful soule that thus cryeth,
Who shal now yeven comfort to the peyne?
Allas, no wight; but when myn herte dyeth,
My spirit, which that so un-to yow hyeth, 320
Receyve in gree, for that shal ay yow serve;
For-thy no fors is, though the body sterve.

`O ye loveres, that heighe upon the wheel
Ben set of Fortune, in good aventure,
God leve that ye finde ay love of steel, 325
And longe mot your lyf in Ioye endure!
But whan ye comen by my sepulture,
Remembreth that your felawe resteth there;
For I lovede eek, though I unworthy were.

`O olde, unholsom, and mislyved man, 330
Calkas I mene, allas! What eyleth thee
To been a Greek, sin thou art born Troian?
O Calkas, which that wilt my bane be,
In cursed tyme was thou born for me!
As wolde blisful Iove, for his Ioye, 335
That I thee hadde, where I wolde, in Troye!'

A thousand sykes, hottere than the glede,
Out of his brest ech after other wente,
Medled with pleyntes newe, his wo to fede,
For which his woful teres never stente; 340
And shortly, so his peynes him to-rente,
And wex so mat, that Ioye nor penaunce
He feleth noon, but lyth forth in a traunce.

Pandare, which that in the parlement
Hadde herd what every lord and burgeys seyde, 345
And how ful graunted was, by oon assent,
For Antenor to yelden so Criseyde,
Gan wel neigh wood out of his wit to breyde,
So that, for wo, he niste what he mente;
But in a rees to Troilus he wente. 350

A certeyn knight, that for the tyme kepte
The chaumbre-dore, un-dide it him anoon;
And Pandare, that ful tendreliche wepte,
In-to the derke chaumbre, as stille as stoon,
Toward the bed gan softely to goon, 355
So confus, that he niste what to seye;
For verray wo his wit was neigh aweye.

And with his chere and loking al to-torn,
For sorwe of this, and with his armes folden,
He stood this woful Troilus biforn, 360
And on his pitous face he gan biholden;
But lord, so often gan his herte colden,
Seing his freend in wo, whos hevinesse
His herte slow, as thoughte him, for distresse.

This woful wight, this Troilus, that felte 365
His freend Pandare y-comen him to see,
Gan as the snow ayein the sonne melte,
For which this sorwful Pandare, of pitee,
Gan for to wepe as tendreliche as he;
And specheles thus been thise ilke tweye, 370
That neyther mighte o word for sorwe seye.

But at the laste this woful Troilus,
Ney deed for smert, gan bresten out to rore,
And with a sorwful noyse he seyde thus,
Among his sobbes and his sykes sore, 375
`Lo! Pandare, I am deed, with-outen more.
Hastow nought herd at parlement,' he seyde,
`For Antenor how lost is my Criseyde?'

This Pandarus, ful deed and pale of hewe,
Ful pitously answerde and seyde, `Yis! 380
As wisly were it fals as it is trewe,
That I have herd, and wot al how it is.
O mercy, god, who wolde have trowed this?
Who wolde have wend that, in so litel a throwe,
Fortune our Ioye wolde han over-throwe? 385

`For in this world ther is no creature,
As to my doom, that ever saw ruyne
Straungere than this, thorugh cas or aventure.
But who may al eschewe, or al devyne?
Swich is this world; for-thy I thus defyne, 390
Ne trust no wight to finden in Fortune
Ay propretee; hir yeftes been comune.

`But tel me this, why thou art now so mad

To sorwen thus? Why lystow in this wyse,
Sin thy desyr al holly hastow had, 395
So that, by right, it oughte y-now suffyse?
But I, that never felte in my servyse
A frendly chere or loking of an ye,
Lat me thus wepe and wayle, til I dye.

`And over al this, as thou wel wost thy-selve, 400
This town is ful of ladies al aboute;
And, to my doom, fairer than swiche twelve
As ever she was, shal I finde, in som route,
Ye, oon or two, with-outen any doute.
For-thy be glad, myn owene dere brother, 405
If she be lost, we shal recovere another.

`What, god for-bede alwey that ech plesaunce
In o thing were, and in non other wight!
If oon can singe, another can wel daunce;
If this be goodly, she is glad and light; 410
And this is fayr, and that can good a-right.
Ech for his vertu holden is for dere,
Bothe heroner and faucon for rivere.

`And eek, as writ Zanzis, that was ful wys,
"The newe love out chaceth ofte the olde;" 415
And up-on newe cas lyth newe avys.
Thenk eek, thy-self to saven artow holde;
Swich fyr, by proces, shal of kinde colde.
For sin it is but casuel plesaunce,
Som cas shal putte it out of remembraunce. 420

`For al-so seur as day cometh after night,
The newe love, labour or other wo,

Or elles selde seinge of a wight,
Don olde affecciouns alle over-go.
And, for thy part, thou shalt have oon of tho 425
To abrigge with thy bittre peynes smerte;
Absence of hir shal dryve hir out of herte.'

Thise wordes seyde he for the nones alle,
To helpe his freend, lest he for sorwe deyde.
For douteles, to doon his wo to falle, 430
He roughte not what unthrift that he seyde.
But Troilus, that neigh for sorwe deyde,
Tok litel hede of al that ever he mente;
Oon ere it herde, at the other out it wente:

But at the laste answerde and seyde, `Freend, 435
This lechecraft, or heled thus to be,
Were wel sitting, if that I were a feend,
To traysen hir that trewe is unto me!
I pray god, lat this consayl never y-thee;
But do me rather sterve anon-right here 440
Er I thus do as thou me woldest lere.

`She that I serve, y-wis, what so thou seye,
To whom myn herte enhabit is by right,
Shal han me holly hires til that I deye.
For, Pandarus, sin I have trouthe hir hight, 445
I wol not been untrewe for no wight;
But as hir man I wol ay live and sterve,
And never other creature serve.

`And ther thou seyst, thou shalt as faire finde
As she, lat be, make no comparisoun 450
To creature y-formed here by kinde.

O leve Pandare, in conclusioun,
I wol not be of thyn opinioun,
Touching al this; for whiche I thee biseche,
So hold thy pees; thou sleest me with thy speche. 455

`Thow biddest me I sholde love an-other
Al freshly newe, and lat Criseyde go!
It lyth not in my power, leve brother.
And though I mighte, I wolde not do so.
But canstow pleyen raket, to and fro, 460
Netle in, dokke out, now this, now that, Pandare?
Now foule falle hir, for thy wo that care!

`Thow farest eek by me, thou Pandarus,
As he, that whan a wight is wo bi-goon,
He cometh to him a pas, and seyth right thus, 465
"Thenk not on smert, and thou shalt fele noon."
Thou most me first transmuwen in a stoon,
And reve me my passiounes alle,
Er thou so lightly do my wo to falle.

`The deeth may wel out of my brest departe 470
The lyf, so longe may this sorwe myne;
But fro my soule shal Criseydes darte
Out never-mo; but doun with Proserpyne,
Whan I am deed, I wol go wone in pyne;
And ther I wol eternaly compleyne 475
My wo, and how that twinned be we tweyne.

`Thow hast here maad an argument, for fyn,
How that it sholde a lasse peyne be
Criseyde to for-goon, for she was myn,
And live in ese and in felicitee. 480

Why gabbestow, that seydest thus to me
That "him is wors that is fro wele y-throwe,
Than he hadde erst non of that wele y-knowe?"

`But tel me now, sin that thee thinketh so light
To chaungen so in love, ay to and fro, 485
Why hastow not don bisily thy might
To chaungen hir that doth thee al thy wo?
Why niltow lete hir fro thyn herte go?
Why niltow love an-other lady swete,
That may thyn herte setten in quiete? 490

`If thou hast had in love ay yet mischaunce,
And canst it not out of thyn herte dryve,
I, that livede in lust and in plesaunce
With hir as muche as creature on-lyve,
How sholde I that foryete, and that so blyve? 495
O where hastow ben hid so longe in muwe,
That canst so wel and formely arguwe?

`Nay, nay, god wot, nought worth is al thy reed,
For which, for what that ever may bifalle,
With-outen wordes mo, I wol be deed. 500
O deeth, that endere art of sorwes alle,
Com now, sin I so ofte after thee calle,
For sely is that deeth, soth for to seyne,
That, ofte y-cleped, cometh and endeth peyne.

`Wel wot I, whyl my lyf was in quiete, 505
Er thou me slowe, I wolde have yeven hyre;
But now thy cominge is to me so swete,
That in this world I no-thing so desyre.
O deeth, sin with this sorwe I am a-fyre,

Thou outher do me anoon yn teres drenche, 510
Or with thy colde strook myn hete quenche!

`Sin that thou sleest so fele in sondry wyse
Ayens hir wil, unpreyed, day and night,
Do me, at my requeste, this servyse,
Delivere now the world, so dostow right, 515
Of me, that am the wofulleste wight
That ever was; for tyme is that I sterve,
Sin in this world of right nought may I serve.'

This Troilus in teres gan distille,
As licour out of alambyk ful faste; 520
And Pandarus gan holde his tunge stille,
And to the ground his eyen doun he caste.
But nathelees, thus thoughte he at the laste,
`What, parde, rather than my felawe deye,
Yet shal I som-what more un-to him seye:' 525

And seyde, `Freend, sin thou hast swich distresse,
And sin thee list myn arguments to blame,
Why nilt thy-selven helpen doon redresse,
And with thy manhod letten al this grame?
Go ravisshe hir ne canstow not for shame! 530
And outher lat hir out of toune fare,
Or hold hir stille, and leve thy nyce fare.

`Artow in Troye, and hast non hardiment
To take a womman which that loveth thee,
And wolde hir-selven been of thyn assent? 535
Now is not this a nyce vanitee?
Rys up anoon, and lat this weping be,
And kyth thou art a man, for in this houre

I wil be deed, or she shal bleven oure.'

To this answerde him Troilus ful softe, 540
And seyde, `Parde, leve brother dere,
Al this have I my-self yet thought ful ofte,
And more thing than thou devysest here.
But why this thing is laft, thou shalt wel here;
And whan thou me hast yeve an audience, 545
Ther-after mayst thou telle al thy sentence.

`First, sin thou wost this toun hath al this werre
For ravisshing of wommen so by might,
It sholde not be suffred me to erre,
As it stant now, ne doon so gret unright. 550
I sholde han also blame of every wight,
My fadres graunt if that I so withstode,
Sin she is chaunged for the tounes goode.

`I have eek thought, so it were hir assent,
To aske hir at my fader, of his grace; 555
Than thenke I, this were hir accusement,
Sin wel I woot I may hir not purchace.
For sin my fader, in so heigh a place
As parlement, hath hir eschaunge enseled,
He nil for me his lettre be repeled. 560

`Yet drede I most hir herte to pertourbe
With violence, if I do swich a game;
For if I wolde it openly distourbe,
It moste been disclaundre to hir name.
And me were lever deed than hir defame, 565
As nolde god but-if I sholde have
Hir honour lever than my lyf to save!

`Thus am I lost, for ought that I can see;
For certeyn is, sin that I am hir knight,
I moste hir honour levere han than me 570
In every cas, as lovere oughte of right.
Thus am I with desyr and reson twight;
Desyr for to destourben hir me redeth,
And reson nil not, so myn herte dredeth.'

Thus wepinge that he coude never cesse, 575
He seyde, `Allas! How shal I, wrecche, fare?
For wel fele I alwey my love encresse,
And hope is lasse and lasse alwey, Pandare!
Encressen eek the causes of my care;
So wel-a-wey, why nil myn herte breste? 580
For, as in love, ther is but litel reste.'

Pandare answerde, `Freend, thou mayst, for me,
Don as thee list; but hadde ich it so hote,
And thyn estat, she sholde go with me;
Though al this toun cryede on this thing by note, 585
I nolde sette at al that noyse a grote.
For when men han wel cryed, than wol they roune;
A wonder last but nyne night never in toune.

`Devyne not in reson ay so depe
Ne curteysly, but help thy-self anoon; 590
Bet is that othere than thy-selven wepe,
And namely, sin ye two been al oon.
Rys up, for by myn heed, she shal not goon;
And rather be in blame a lyte y-founde
Than sterve here as a gnat, with-oute wounde. 595

`It is no shame un-to yow, ne no vyce
Hir to with-holden, that ye loveth most.
Paraunter, she mighte holden thee for nyce
To lete hir go thus to the Grekes ost.
Thenk eek Fortune, as wel thy-selven wost, 600
Helpeth hardy man to his enpryse,
And weyveth wrecches, for hir cowardyse.

`And though thy lady wolde a litel hir greve,
Thou shalt thy pees ful wel here-after make,
But as for me, certayn, I can not leve 605
That she wolde it as now for yvel take.
Why sholde than for ferd thyn herte quake?
Thenk eek how Paris hath, that is thy brother,
A love; and why shaltow not have another?

`And Troilus, o thing I dar thee swere, 610
That if Criseyde, whiche that is thy leef,
Now loveth thee as wel as thou dost here,
God helpe me so, she nil nat take a-greef,
Though thou do bote a-noon in this mischeef.
And if she wilneth fro thee for to passe, 615
Thanne is she fals; so love hir wel the lasse.

`For-thy tak herte, and thenk, right as a knight,
Thourgh love is broken alday every lawe.
Kyth now sumwhat thy corage and thy might,
Have mercy on thy-self, for any awe. 620
Lat not this wrecched wo thin herte gnawe,
But manly set the world on sixe and sevene;
And, if thou deye a martir, go to hevene.

`I wol my-self be with thee at this dede,

Though ich and al my kin, up-on a stounde, 625
Shulle in a strete as dogges liggen dede,
Thourgh-girt with many a wyd and blody wounde.
In every cas I wol a freend be founde.
And if thee list here sterven as a wrecche,
A-dieu, the devel spede him that it recche!' 630

This Troilus gan with tho wordes quiken,
And seyde, `Freend, graunt mercy, ich assente;
But certaynly thou mayst not me so priken,
Ne peyne noon ne may me so tormente,
That, for no cas, it is not myn entente, 635
At shorte wordes, though I dyen sholde,
To ravisshe hir, but-if hir-self it wolde.'

`Why, so mene I,' quod Pandarus, `al this day.
But tel me than, hastow hir wil assayed,
That sorwest thus?' And he answerde, `Nay.'
`Wher-of artow,' quod Pandare, `than a-mayed, 640
That nost not that she wol ben y-vel apayed
To ravisshe hir, sin thou hast not ben there,
But-if that Iove tolde it in thyn ere?

`For-thy rys up, as nought ne were, anoon, 645
And wash thy face, and to the king thou wende,
Or he may wondren whider thou art goon.
Thou most with wisdom him and othere blende;
Or, up-on cas, he may after thee sende
Er thou be war; and shortly, brother dere, 650
Be glad, and lat me werke in this matere.

`For I shal shape it so, that sikerly
Thou shalt this night som tyme, in som manere,

Com speke with thy lady prevely,
And by hir wordes eek, and by hir chere, 655
Thou shalt ful sone aperceyve and wel here
Al hir entente, and in this cas the beste;
And fare now wel, for in this point I reste.'

The swifte Fame, whiche that false thinges
Egal reporteth lyk the thinges trewe, 660
Was thorugh-out Troye y-fled with preste winges
Fro man to man, and made this tale al newe,
How Calkas doughter, with hir brighte hewe,
At parlement, with-oute wordes more,
I-graunted was in chaunge of Antenore. 665

The whiche tale anoon-right as Criseyde
Had herd, she, which that of hir fader roughte,
As in this cas, right nought, ne whanne he deyde,
Ful bisily to Iuppiter bisoughte
Yeve hem mischaunce that this tretis broughte. 670
But shortly, lest thise tales sothe were,
She dorste at no wight asken it, for fere.

As she that hadde hir herte and al hir minde
On Troilus y-set so wonder faste,
That al this world ne mighte hir love unbinde, 675
Ne Troilus out of hir herte caste;
She wol ben his, whyl that hir lyf may laste.
And thus she brenneth bothe in love and drede,
So that she niste what was best to rede.

But as men seen in toune, and al aboute, 680
That wommen usen frendes to visyte,
So to Criseyde of wommen com a route

For pitous Ioye, and wenden hir delyte;
And with hir tales, dere y-nough a myte,
These wommen, whiche that in the cite dwelle, 685
They sette hem doun, and seyde as I shal telle.

Quod first that oon, `I am glad, trewely,
By-cause of yow, that shal your fader see.'
A-nother seyde, `Y-wis, so nam not I,
For al to litel hath she with us be.' 690
Quod tho the thridde, `I hope, y-wis, that she
Shal bringen us the pees on every syde,
That, whan she gooth, almighty god hir gyde!'

Tho wordes and tho wommanisshe thinges,
She herde hem right as though she thennes were; 695
For, god it wot, hir herte on other thing is,
Although the body sat among hem there.
Hir advertence is alwey elles-where;
For Troilus ful faste hir soule soughte;
With-outen word, alwey on him she thoughte. 700

Thise wommen, that thus wenden hir to plese,
Aboute nought gonne alle hir tales spende;
Swich vanitee ne can don hir non ese,
As she that, al this mene whyle. brende
Of other passioun than that they wende, 705
So that she felte almost hir herte deye
For wo, and wery of that companye.

For which no lenger mighte she restreyne
Hir teres, so they gonnen up to welle,
That yaven signes of the bitter peyne 710
In whiche hir spirit was, and moste dwelle;

Remembring hir, fro heven unto which helle
She fallen was, sith she forgoth the sighte
Of Troilus, and sorowfully she sighte.

And thilke foles sittinge hir aboute 715
Wenden, that she wepte and syked sore
By-cause that she sholde out of that route
Departe, and never pleye with hem more.
And they that hadde y-knowen hir of yore
Seye hir so wepe, and thoughte it kindenesse, 720
And eche of hem wepte eek for hir destresse;

And bisily they gonnen hir conforten
Of thing, god wot, on which she litel thoughte;
And with hir tales wenden hir disporten,
And to be glad they often hir bisoughte. 725
But swich an ese ther-with they hir wroughte
Right as a man is esed for to fele,
For ache of heed, to clawen him on his hele!

But after al this nyce vanitee
They took hir leve, and hoom they wenten alle. 730
Criseyde, ful of sorweful pitee,
In-to hir chaumbre up wente out of the halle,
And on hir bed she gan for deed to falle,
In purpos never thennes for to ryse;
And thus she wroughte, as I shal yow devyse. 735

Hir ounded heer, that sonnish was of hewe,
She rente, and eek hir fingres longe and smale
She wrong ful ofte, and bad god on hir rewe,
And with the deeth to doon bote on hir bale.
Hir hewe, whylom bright, that tho was pale, 740

Bar witnes of hir wo and hir constreynte;
And thus she spak, sobbinge, in hir compleynte:

`Alas!' quod she, `out of this regioun
I, woful wrecche and infortuned wight,
And born in corsed constellacioun, 745
Mot goon, and thus departen fro my knight;
Wo worth, allas! That ilke dayes light
On which I saw him first with eyen tweyne,
That causeth me, and I him, al this peyne!'

Therwith the teres from hir eyen two 750
Doun fille, as shour in Aperill ful swythe;
Hir whyte brest she bet, and for the wo
After the deeth she cryed a thousand sythe,
Sin he that wont hir wo was for to lythe,
She mot for-goon; for which disaventure 755
She held hir-self a forlost creature.

She seyde, `How shal he doon, and I also?
How sholde I live, if that I from him twinne?
O dere herte eek, that I love so,
Who shal that sorwe sleen that ye ben inne? 760
O Calkas, fader, thyn be al this sinne!
O moder myn, that cleped were Argyve,
Wo worth that day that thou me bere on lyve!

`To what fyn sholde I live and sorwen thus?
How sholde a fish with-oute water dure? 765
What is Criseyde worth, from Troilus?
How sholde a plaunte or lyves creature
Live, with-oute his kinde noriture?
For which ful oft a by-word here I seye,

That "rotelees, mot grene sone deye." 770

`I shal don thus, sin neither swerd ne darte
Dar I non handle, for the crueltee,
That ilke day that I from yow departe,
If sorwe of that nil not my bane be,
Than shal no mete or drinke come in me 775
Til I my soule out of my breste unshethe;
And thus my-selven wol I do to dethe.

`And, Troilus, my clothes everichoon
Shul blake been, in tokeninge, herte swete,
That I am as out of this world agoon, 780
That wont was yow to setten in quiete;
And of myn ordre, ay til deeth me mete,
The observaunce ever, in your absence,
Shal sorwe been, compleynte, and abstinence.

`Myn herte and eek the woful goost ther-inne 785
Biquethe I, with your spirit to compleyne
Eternally, for they shal never twinne.
For though in erthe y-twinned be we tweyne,
Yet in the feld of pitee, out of peyne,
That hight Elysos, shul we been y-fere, 790
As Orpheus and Erudice, his fere.

`Thus, herte myn, for Antenor, allas!
I sone shal be chaunged, as I wene.
But how shul ye don in this sorwful cas,
How shal youre tendre herte this sustene? 795
But herte myn, for-yet this sorwe and tene,
And me also; for, soothly for to seye,
So ye wel fare, I recche not to deye.'

How mighte it ever y-red ben or y-songe,
The pleynte that she made in hir distresse? 800
I noot; but, as for me, my litel tonge,
If I discreven wolde hir hevinesse,
It sholde make hir sorwe seme lesse
Than that it was, and childishly deface
Hir heigh compleynte, and therfore I it pace. 805

Pandare, which that sent from Troilus
Was to Criseyde, as ye han herd devyse,
That for the beste it was accorded thus,
And he ful glad to doon him that servyse,
Un-to Criseyde, in a ful secree wyse, 810
Ther-as she lay in torment and in rage,
Com hir to telle al hoolly his message,

And fond that she hir-selven gan to trete
Ful pitously; for with hir salte teres
Hir brest, hir face, y-bathed was ful wete; 815
The mighty tresses of hir sonnish heres,
Unbroyden, hangen al aboute hir eres;
Which yaf him verray signal of martyre
Of deeth, which that hir herte gan desyre.

Whan she him saw, she gan for sorwe anoon 820
Hir tery face a-twixe hir armes hide,
For which this Pandare is so wo bi-goon,
That in the hous he mighte unnethe abyde,
As he that pitee felte on every syde.
For if Criseyde hadde erst compleyned sore, 825
Tho gan she pleyne a thousand tymes more.

And in hir aspre pleynte than she seyde,
`Pandare first of Ioyes mo than two
Was cause causinge un-to me, Criseyde,
That now transmuwed been in cruel wo. 830
Wher shal I seye to yow "wel come" or no,
That alderfirst me broughte in-to servyse
Of love, allas! That endeth in swich wyse?

`Endeth than love in wo? Ye, or men lyeth!
And alle worldly blisse, as thinketh me. 835
The ende of blisse ay sorwe it occupyeth;
And who-so troweth not that it so be,
Lat him upon me, woful wrecche, y-see,
That my-self hate, and ay my birthe acorse,
Felinge alwey, fro wikke I go to worse. 840

`Who-so me seeth, he seeth sorwe al at ones,
Peyne, torment, pleynte, wo, distresse.
Out of my woful body harm ther noon is,
As anguish, langour, cruel bitternesse,
A-noy, smert, drede, fury, and eek siknesse. 845
I trowe, y-wis, from hevene teres reyne,
For pitee of myn aspre and cruel peyne!   `

`And thou, my suster, ful of discomfort,'
Quod Pandarus, `what thenkestow to do?
Why ne hastow to thy-selven som resport, 850
Why woltow thus thy-selve, allas, for-do?
Leef al this werk and tak now hede to
That I shal seyn, and herkne, of good entente,
This, which by me thy Troilus thee sente.'

Torned hir tho Criseyde, a wo makinge 855

So greet that it a deeth was for to see: --
`Allas!' quod she, `what wordes may ye bringe?
What wol my dere herte seyn to me,
Which that I drede never-mo to see?
Wol he have pleynte or teres, er I wende? 860
I have y-nowe, if he ther-after sende!'

She was right swich to seen in hir visage
As is that wight that men on bere binde;
Hir face, lyk of Paradys the image,
Was al y-chaunged in another kinde. 865
The pleye, the laughtre men was wont to finde
On hir, and eek hir Ioyes everychone,
Ben fled, and thus lyth now Criseyde allone.

Aboute hir eyen two a purpre ring
Bi-trent, in sothfast tokninge of hir peyne, 870
That to biholde it was a dedly thing,
For which Pandare mighte not restreyne
The teres from his eyen for to reyne.
But nathelees, as he best mighte, he seyde
From Troilus thise wordes to Criseyde. 875

`Lo, nece, I trowe ye han herd al how
The king, with othere lordes, for the beste,
Hath mad eschaunge of Antenor and yow,
That cause is of this sorwe and this unreste.
But how this cas doth Troilus moleste, 880
That may non erthely mannes tonge seye;
For verray wo his wit is al aweye.

`For which we han so sorwed, he and I,
That in-to litel bothe it hadde us slawe;

But thurgh my conseil this day, fynally, 885
He somwhat is fro weping now with-drawe.
And semeth me that he desyreth fawe
With yow to been al night, for to devyse
Remede in this, if ther were any wyse.

`This, short and pleyne, theffect of my message, 890
As ferforth as my wit can comprehende.
For ye, that been of torment in swich rage,
May to no long prologe as now entende;
And her-upon ye may answere him sende.
And, for the love of god, my nece dere, 895
So leef this wo er Troilus be here.'

`Gret is my wo,' quod she, and sighte sore,
As she that feleth dedly sharp distresse;
`But yet to me his sorwe is muchel more,
That love him bet than he him-self, I gesse. 900
Allas! For me hath he swich hevinesse?
Can he for me so pitously compleyne?
Y-wis, his sorwe doubleth al my peyne.

`Grevous to me, god wot, is for to twinne,'
Quod she, `but yet it hardere is to me 905
To seen that sorwe which that he is inne;
For wel wot I, it wol my bane be;
And deye I wol in certayn,' tho quod she;
`But bidde him come, er deeth, that thus me threteth,
Dryve out that goost which in myn herte beteth.' 910

Thise wordes seyd, she on hir armes two
Fil gruf, and gan to wepe pitously.
Quod Pandarus, `Allas! Why do ye so,

Syn wel ye woot the tyme is faste by,
That he shal come? Arys up hastely, 915
That he yow nat biwopen thus ne finde,
But ye wol have him wood out of his minde!

`For wiste he that ye ferde in this manere,
He wolde him-selve slee; and if I wende
To han this fare, he sholde not come here 920
For al the good that Pryam may despende.
For to what fyn he wolde anoon pretende,
That knowe I wel; and for-thy yet I seye,
So leef this sorwe, or platly he wol deye.

`And shapeth yow his sorwe for to abregge, 925
And nought encresse, leve nece swete;
Beth rather to him cause of flat than egge,
And with som wysdom ye his sorwes bete.
What helpeth it to wepen ful a strete,
Or though ye bothe in salte teres dreynte? 930
Bet is a tyme of cure ay than of pleynte.

`I mene thus; whan I him hider bringe,
Sin ye ben wyse, and bothe of oon assent,
So shapeth how distourbe your goinge,
Or come ayen, sone after ye be went. 935
Wommen ben wyse in short avysement;
And lat sen how your wit shal now avayle;
And what that I may helpe, it shal not fayle.'

`Go,' quod Criseyde, `and uncle, trewely,
I shal don al my might, me to restreyne 940
From weping in his sighte, and bisily,
Him for to glade, I shal don al my peyne,

And in myn herte seken every veyne;
If to this soor ther may be founden salve,
It shal not lakken, certain, on myn halve.' 945

Goth Pandarus, and Troilus he soughte,
Til in a temple he fond him allone,
As he that of his lyf no lenger roughte;
But to the pitouse goddes everichone
Ful tendrely he preyde, and made his mone, 950
To doon him sone out of this world to pace;
For wel he thoughte ther was non other grace.

And shortly, al the sothe for to seye,
He was so fallen in despeyr that day,
That outrely he shoop him for to deye. 955
For right thus was his argument alwey:
He seyde, he nas but loren, waylawey!
`For al that comth, comth by necessitee;
Thus to be lorn, it is my destinee.

`For certaynly, this wot I wel,' he seyde, 960
`That for-sight of divyne purveyaunce
Hath seyn alwey me to for-gon Criseyde,
Sin god seeth every thing, out of doutaunce,
And hem disponeth, thourgh his ordenaunce,
In hir merytes sothly for to be, 965
As they shul comen by predestinee.

`But nathelees, allas! Whom shal I leve?
For ther ben grete clerkes many oon,
That destinee thorugh argumentes preve;
And som men seyn that nedely ther is noon; 970
But that free chois is yeven us everichoon.

O, welaway! So sleye arn clerkes olde,
That I not whos opinion I may holde.

`For som men seyn, if god seth al biforn,
Ne god may not deceyved ben, pardee, 975
Than moot it fallen, though men hadde it sworn,
That purveyaunce hath seyn bifore to be.
Wherfor I seye, that from eterne if he
Hath wist biforn our thought eek as our dede,
We have no free chois, as these clerkes rede. 980

`For other thought nor other dede also
Might never be, but swich as purveyaunce,
Which may not ben deceyved never-mo,
Hath feled biforn, with-outen ignoraunce.
For if ther mighte been a variaunce 985
To wrythen out fro goddes purveyinge,
Ther nere no prescience of thing cominge;

`But it were rather an opinioun
Uncerteyn, and no stedfast forseinge;
And certes, that were an abusioun, 990
That god shuld han no parfit cleer witinge
More than we men that han doutous weninge.
But swich an errour up-on god to gesse
Were fals and foul, and wikked corsednesse.

`Eek this is an opinioun of somme 995
That han hir top ful heighe and smothe y-shore;
They seyn right thus, that thing is not to come
For that the prescience hath seyn bifore
That it shal come; but they seyn that therfore
That it shal come, therfore the purveyaunce 1000

Wot it biforn with-outen ignoraunce;

`And in this manere this necessitee
Retorneth in his part contrarie agayn.
For needfully bihoveth it not to be
That thilke thinges fallen in certayn 1005
That ben purveyed; but nedely, as they seyn,
Bihoveth it that thinges, whiche that falle,
That they in certayn ben purveyed alle.

`I mene as though I laboured me in this,
To enqueren which thing cause of which thing be; 1010
As whether that the prescience of god is
The certayn cause of the necessitee
Of thinges that to comen been, pardee;
Or if necessitee of thing cominge
Be cause certeyn of the purveyinge. 1015

`But now ne enforce I me nat in shewinge
How the ordre of causes stant; but wel wot I,
That it bihoveth that the bifallinge
Of thinges wist biforen certeynly
Be necessarie, al seme it not ther-by 1020
That prescience put falling necessaire
To thing to come, al falle it foule or faire.

`For if ther sit a man yond on a see,
Than by necessitee bihoveth it
That, certes, thyn opinioun soth be, 1025
That wenest or coniectest that he sit;
And ferther-over now ayenward yit,
Lo, right so it is of the part contrarie,
As thus; (now herkne, for I wol not tarie):

`I seye, that if the opinioun of thee 1030
Be sooth, for that he sit, than seye I this,
That he mot sitten by necessitee;
And thus necessitee in either is.
For in him nede of sittinge is, y-wis,
And in thee nede of sooth; and thus, forsothe, 1035
Ther moot necessitee ben in yow bothe.

`But thou mayst seyn, the man sit not therfore,
That thyn opinioun of sitting soth is;
But rather, for the man sit ther bifore,
Therfore is thyn opinioun sooth, y-wis. 1040
And I seye, though the cause of sooth of this
Comth of his sitting, yet necessitee
Is entrechaunged, bothe in him and thee.

`Thus on this same wyse, out of doutaunce,
I may wel maken, as it semeth me, 1045
My resoninge of goddes purveyaunce,
And of the thinges that to comen be;
By whiche reson men may wel y-see,
That thilke thinges that in erthe falle,
That by necessitee they comen alle. 1050

`For al-though that, for thing shal come, y-wis,
Therfore is it purveyed, certaynly,
Nat that it comth for it purveyed is:
Yet nathelees, bihoveth it nedfully,
That thing to come be purveyed, trewely; 1055
Or elles, thinges that purveyed be,
That they bityden by necessitee.

`And this suffyseth right y-now, certeyn,
For to destroye our free chois every del. --
But now is this abusion, to seyn, 1060
That fallinge of the thinges temporel
Is cause of goddes prescience eternel.
Now trewely, that is a fals sentence,
That thing to come sholde cause his prescience.

`What mighte I wene, and I hadde swich a thought, 1065
But that god purveyth thing that is to come
For that it is to come, and elles nought?
So mighte I wene that thinges alle and some,
That whylom been bifalle and over-come,
Ben cause of thilke sovereyn purveyaunce, 1070
That for-wot al with-outen ignoraunce.

`And over al this, yet seye I more herto,
That right as whan I woot ther is a thing,
Y-wis, that thing mot nedefully be so;
Eek right so, whan I woot a thing coming, 1075
So mot it come; and thus the bifalling
Of thinges that ben wist bifore the tyde,
They mowe not been eschewed on no syde.'

Than seyde he thus, `Almighty Iove in trone,
That wost of al this thing the soothfastnesse, 1080
Rewe on my sorwe, or do me deye sone,
Or bring Criseyde and me fro this distresse.'
And whyl he was in al this hevinesse,
Disputinge with him-self in this matere,
Com Pandare in, and seyde as ye may here. 1085

`O mighty god,' quod Pandarus, `in trone,

Ey! Who seigh ever a wys man faren so?
Why, Troilus, what thenkestow to done?
Hastow swich lust to been thyn owene fo?
What, parde, yet is not Criseyde a-go! 1090
Why list thee so thy-self for-doon for drede,
That in thyn heed thyn eyen semen dede?

`Hastow not lived many a yeer biforn
With-outen hir, and ferd ful wel at ese?
Artow for hir and for non other born? 1095
Hath kinde thee wroughte al-only hir to plese?
Lat be, and thenk right thus in thy disese.
That, in the dees right as ther fallen chaunces,
Right so in love, ther come and goon plesaunces.

`And yet this is a wonder most of alle, 1100
Why thou thus sorwest, sin thou nost not yit,
Touching hir goinge, how that it shal falle,
Ne if she can hir-self distorben it.
Thou hast not yet assayed al hir wit.
A man may al by tyme his nekke bede 1105
Whan it shal of, and sorwen at the nede.

`For-thy take hede of that that I shal seye;
I have with hir y-spoke and longe y-be,
So as accorded was bitwixe us tweye.
And ever-mor me thinketh thus, that she 1110
Hath som-what in hir hertes prevetee,
Wher-with she can, if I shal right arede,
Distorbe al this, of which thou art in drede.

`For which my counseil is, whan it is night,
Thou to hir go, and make of this an ende; 1115

And blisful Iuno, thourgh hir grete mighte,
Shal, as I hope, hir grace un-to us sende.
Myn herte seyth, "Certeyn, she shal not wende;"
And for-thy put thyn herte a whyle in reste;
And hold this purpos, for it is the beste.' 1120

This Troilus answerde, and sighte sore,
`Thou seyst right wel, and I wil do right so;'
And what him liste, he seyde un-to it more.
And whan that it was tyme for to go,
Ful prevely him-self, with-outen mo, 1125
Un-to hir com, as he was wont to done;
And how they wroughte, I shal yow telle sone.

Soth is, that whan they gonne first to mete,
So gan the peyne hir hertes for to twiste,
That neither of hem other mighte grete, 1130
But hem in armes toke and after kiste.
The lasse wofulle of hem bothe niste
Wher that he was, ne mighte o word out-bringe,
As I seyde erst, for wo and for sobbinge.

Tho woful teres that they leten falle 1135
As bittre weren, out of teres kinde,
For peyne, as is ligne aloes or galle.
So bittre teres weep nought, as I finde,
The woful Myrra through the bark and rinde.
That in this world ther nis so hard an herte, 1140
That nolde han rewed on hir peynes smerte.

But whan hir woful wery gostes tweyne
Retorned been ther-as hem oughte dwelle,
And that som-what to wayken gan the peyne

By lengthe of pleynte, and ebben gan the welle 1145
Of hire teres, and the herte unswelle,
With broken voys, al hoors for-shright, Criseyde
To Troilus thise ilke wordes seyde:

`O Iove, I deye, and mercy I beseche!
Help, Troilus!' And ther-with-al hir face 1150
Upon his brest she leyde, and loste speche;
Hir woful spirit from his propre place,
Right with the word, alwey up poynt to pace.
And thus she lyth with hewes pale and grene,
That whylom fresh and fairest was to sene. 1155

This Troilus, that on hir gan biholde,
Clepinge hir name, (and she lay as for deed,
With-oute answere, and felte hir limes colde,
Hir eyen throwen upward to hir heed),
This sorwful man can now noon other reed, 1160
But ofte tyme hir colde mouth he kiste;
Wher him was wo, god and him-self it wiste!

He rist him up, and long streight he hir leyde;
For signe of lyf, for ought he can or may,
Can he noon finde in no-thing on Criseyde, 1165
For which his song ful ofte is `weylaway!'
But whan he saugh that specheles she lay,
With sorwful voys and herte of blisse al bare,
He seyde how she was fro this world y-fare!

So after that he longe hadde hir compleyned, 1170
His hondes wrong, and seyde that was to seye,
And with his teres salte hir brest bireyned,
He gan tho teris wypen of ful dreye,

And pitously gan for the soule preye,
And seyde, `O lord, that set art in thy trone, 1175
Rewe eek on me, for I shal folwe hir sone!'

She cold was and with-outen sentement,
For aught he woot, for breeth ne felte he noon;
And this was him a preignant argument
That she was forth out of this world agoon; 1180
And whan he seigh ther was non other woon,
He gan hir limes dresse in swich manere
As men don hem that shul be leyd on bere.

And after this, with sterne and cruel herte,
His swerd a-noon out of his shethe he twighte, 1185
Him-self to sleen, how sore that him smerte,
So that his sowle hir sowle folwen mighte,
Ther-as the doom of Mynos wolde it dighte;
Sin love and cruel Fortune it ne wolde,
That in this world he lenger liven sholde. 1190

Thanne seyde he thus, fulfild of heigh desdayn,
`O cruel Iove, and thou, Fortune adverse,
This al and som, that falsly have ye slayn
Criseyde, and sin ye may do me no werse,
Fy on your might and werkes so diverse! 1195
Thus cowardly ye shul me never winne;
Ther shal no deeth me fro my lady twinne.

`For I this world, sin ye han slayn hir thus,
Wol lete, and folowe hir spirit lowe or hye;
Shal never lover seyn that Troilus 1200
Dar not, for fere, with his lady dye;
For certeyn, I wol bere hir companye.

But sin ye wol not suffre us liven here,
Yet suffreth that our soules ben y-fere.

`And thou, citee, whiche that I leve in wo, 1205
And thou, Pryam, and bretheren al y-fere,
And thou, my moder, farwel! For I go;
And Attropos, make redy thou my bere!
And thou, Criseyde, o swete herte dere,
Receyve now my spirit!' wolde he seye, 1210
With swerd at herte, al redy for to deye

But as god wolde, of swough ther-with she abreyde,
And gan to syke, and `Troilus' she cryde;
And he answerde, `Lady myn Criseyde,
Live ye yet?' and leet his swerd doun glyde. 1215
`Ye, herte myn, that thanked be Cupyde!'
Quod she, and ther-with-al she sore sighte;
And he bigan to glade hir as he mighte;

Took hir in armes two, and kiste hir ofte,
And hir to glade he dide al his entente; 1220
For which hir goost, that flikered ay on-lofte,
In-to hir woful herte ayein it wente.
But at the laste, as that hir eyen glente
A-syde, anoon she gan his swerd aspye,
As it lay bare, and gan for fere crye, 1225

And asked him, why he it hadde out-drawe?
And Troilus anoon the cause hir tolde,
And how himself ther-with he wolde have slawe.
For which Criseyde up-on him gan biholde,
And gan him in hir armes faste folde, 1230
And seyde, `O mercy, god, lo, which a dede!

Allas! How neigh we were bothe dede!

`Thanne if I ne hadde spoken, as grace was,
Ye wolde han slayn your-self anoon?' quod she.
`Ye, douteless;' and she answerde, `Allas! 1235
For, by that ilke lord that made me,
I nolde a forlong wey on-lyve han be,
After your deeth, to han been crouned quene
Of al the lond the sonne on shyneth shene.

`But with this selve swerd, which that here is, 1240
My-selve I wolde han slayn!' -- quod she tho;
`But ho, for we han right y-now of this,
And late us ryse and streight to bedde go
And there lat ys speken of oure wo.
For, by the morter which that I see brenne, 1245
Knowe I ful wel that day is not fer henne.'

Whan they were in hir bedde, in armes folde,
Nought was it lyk tho nightes here-biforn;
For pitously ech other gan biholde,
As they that hadden al hir blisse y-lorn, 1250
Biwaylinge ay the day that they were born.
Til at the last this sorwful wight Criseyde
To Troilus these ilke wordes seyde: --

`Lo, herte myn, wel wot ye this,' quod she,
`That if a wight alwey his wo compleyne, 1255
And seketh nought how holpen for to be,
It nis but folye and encrees of peyne;
And sin that here assembled be we tweyne
To finde bote of wo that we ben inne,
It were al tyme sone to biginne. 1260

`I am a womman, as ful wel ye woot,
And as I am avysed sodeynly,
So wol I telle yow, whyl it is hoot.
Me thinketh thus, that nouther ye nor I
Oughte half this wo to make skilfully. 1265
For there is art y-now for to redresse
That yet is mis, and sleen this hevinesse.

`Sooth is, the wo, the whiche that we ben inne,
For ought I woot, for no-thing elles is
But for the cause that we sholden twinne. 1270
Considered al, ther nis no-more amis.
But what is thanne a remede un-to this,
But that we shape us sone for to mete?
This al and som, my dere herte swete.

`Now that I shal wel bringen it aboute 1275
To come ayein, sone after that I go,
Ther-of am I no maner thing in doute.
For dredeles, with-inne a wouke or two,
I shal ben here; and, that it may be so
By alle right, and in a wordes fewe, 1280
I shal yow wel an heep of weyes shewe.

`For which I wol not make long sermoun,
For tyme y-lost may not recovered be;
But I wol gon to my conclusioun,
And to the beste, in ought that I can see. 1285
And, for the love of god, for-yeve it me
If I speke ought ayein your hertes reste;
For trewely, I speke it for the beste;

`Makinge alwey a protestacioun,
That now these wordes, whiche that I shal seye, 1290
Nis but to shewe yow my mocioun,
To finde un-to our helpe the beste weye;
And taketh it non other wyse, I preye.
For in effect what-so ye me comaunde,
That wol I doon, for that is no demaunde. 1295

`Now herkneth this, ye han wel understonde,
My goinge graunted is by parlement
So ferforth, that it may not be with-stonde
For al this world, as by my Iugement.
And sin ther helpeth noon avysement 1300
To letten it, lat it passe out of minde;
And lat us shape a bettre wey to finde.

`The sothe is, that the twinninge of us tweyne
Wol us disese and cruelliche anoye.
But him bihoveth som-tyme han a peyne, 1305
That serveth love, if that he wol have Ioye.
And sin I shal no ferthere out of Troye
Than I may ryde ayein on half a morwe,
It oughte lesse causen us to sorwe.

`So as I shal not so ben hid in muwe, 1310
That day by day, myn owene herte dere,
Sin wel ye woot that it is now a trewe,
Ye shal ful wel al myn estat y-here.
And er that truwe is doon, I shal ben here,
And thanne have ye bothe Antenor y-wonne 1315
And me also; beth glad now, if ye conne;

`And thenk right thus, "Criseyde is now agoon,

But what! She shal come hastely ayeyn;"
And whanne, allas? By god, lo, right anoon,
Er dayes ten, this dar I saufly seyn. 1320
And thanne at erste shul we been so fayn,
So as we shulle to-gederes ever dwelle,
That al this world ne mighte our blisse telle.

`I see that ofte, ther-as we ben now,
That for the beste, our counseil for to hyde, 1325
Ye speke not with me, nor I with yow
In fourtenight; ne see yow go ne ryde.
May ye not ten dayes thanne abyde,
For myn honour, in swich an aventure?
Y-wis, ye mowen elles lite endure! 1330

`Ye knowe eek how that al my kin is here,
But-if that onliche it my fader be;
And eek myn othere thinges alle y-fere,
And nameliche, my dere herte, ye,
Whom that I nolde leven for to see 1335
For al this world, as wyd as it hath space;
Or elles, see ich never Ioves face!

`Why trowe ye my fader in this wyse
Coveiteth so to see me, but for drede
Lest in this toun that folkes me dispyse 1340
By-cause of him, for his unhappy dede?
What woot my fader what lyf that I lede?
For if he wiste in Troye how wel I fare,
Us neded for my wending nought to care.

`Ye seen that every day eek, more and more, 1345
Men trete of pees; and it supposed is,

That men the quene Eleyne shal restore,
And Grekes us restore that is mis.
So though ther nere comfort noon but this,
That men purposen pees on every syde, 1350
Ye may the bettre at ese of herte abyde.

`For if that it be pees, myn herte dere,
The nature of the pees mot nedes dryve
That men moste entrecomunen y-fere,
And to and fro eek ryde and gon as blyve 1355
Alday as thikke as been flen from an hyve;
And every wight han libertee to bleve
Where-as him list the bet, with-outen leve.

`And though so be that pees ther may be noon,
Yet hider, though ther never pees ne were, 1360
I moste come; for whider sholde I goon,
Or how mischaunce sholde I dwelle there
Among tho men of armes ever in fere?
For which, as wisly god my soule rede,
I can not seen wher-of ye sholden drede. 1365

`Have here another wey, if it so be
That al this thing ne may yow not suffyse.
My fader, as ye knowen wel, pardee,
Is old, and elde is ful of coveityse,
And I right now have founden al the gyse, 1370
With-oute net, wher-with I shal him hente;
And herkeneth how, if that ye wole assente.

`Lo, Troilus, men seyn that hard it is
The wolf ful, and the wether hool to have;
This is to seyn, that men ful ofte, y-wis, 1375

Mot spenden part, the remenant for to save.
For ay with gold men may the herte grave
Of him that set is up-on coveityse;
And how I mene, I shal it yow devyse.

`The moeble which that I have in this toun 1380
Un-to my fader shal I take, and seye,
That right for trust and for savacioun
It sent is from a freend of his or tweye,
The whiche freendes ferventliche him preye
To senden after more, and that in hye, 1385
Whyl that this toun stant thus in Iupartye.

`And that shal been an huge quantitee,
Thus shal I seyn, but, lest it folk aspyde,
This may be sent by no wight but by me;
I shal eek shewen him, if pees bityde, 1390
What frendes that ich have on every syde
Toward the court, to doon the wrathe pace
Of Priamus, and doon him stonde in grace.

`So what for o thing and for other, swete,
I shal him so enchaunten with my sawes, 1395
That right in hevene his sowle is, shal he mete!
For al Appollo, or his clerkes lawes,
Or calculinge avayleth nought three hawes;
Desyr of gold shal so his sowle blende,
That, as me lyst, I shal wel make an ende. 1400

`And if he wolde ought by his sort it preve
If that I lye, in certayn I shal fonde
Distorben him, and plukke him by the sleve,
Makinge his sort, and beren him on honde,

He hath not wel the goddes understonde. 1405
For goddes speken in amphibologyes,
And, for o sooth they tellen twenty lyes.

`Eek drede fond first goddes, I suppose,
Thus shal I seyn, and that his cowarde herte
Made him amis the goddes text to glose, 1410
Whan he for ferde out of his Delphos sterte.
And but I make him sone to converte,
And doon my reed with-inne a day or tweye,
I wol to yow oblige me to deye.'

And treweliche, as writen wel I finde, 1415
That al this thing was seyd of good entente;
And that hir herte trewe was and kinde
Towardes him, and spak right as she mente,
And that she starf for wo neigh, whan she wente,
And was in purpos ever to be trewe; 1420
Thus writen they that of hir werkes knewe.

This Troilus, with herte and eres spradde,
Herde al this thing devysen to and fro;
And verraylich him semed that he hadde
The selve wit; but yet to lete hir go 1425
His herte misforyaf him ever-mo.
But fynally, he gan his herte wreste
To trusten hir, and took it for the beste.

For which the grete furie of his penaunce
Was queynt with hope, and ther-with hem bitwene 1430
Bigan for Ioye the amorouse daunce.
And as the briddes, whan the sonne is shene,
Delyten in hir song in leves grene,

Right so the wordes that they spake y-fere
Delyted hem, and made hir hertes clere. 1435

But natheles, the wending of Criseyde,
For al this world, may nought out of his minde;
For which ful ofte he pitously hir preyde,
That of hir heste he might hir trewe finde,
And seyde hire, `Certes, if ye be unkinde, 1440
And but ye come at day set in-to Troye,
Ne shal I never have hele, honour, ne Ioye.

`For al-so sooth as sonne up-rist on morwe,
And, god! So wisly thou me, woful wrecche,
To reste bringe out of this cruel sorwe, 1445
I wol my-selven slee if that ye drecche.
But of my deeth though litel be to recche,
Yet, er that ye me cause so to smerte,
Dwel rather here, myn owene swete herte!

`For trewely, myn owene lady dere, 1450
Tho sleightes yet that I have herd yow stere
Ful shaply been to failen alle y-fere.
For thus men seyn, "That oon thenketh the bere,
But al another thenketh his ledere."
Your sire is wys, and seyd is, out of drede, 1455
"Men may the wyse at-renne, and not at-rede."

`It is ful hard to halten unespyed
Bifore a crepul, for he can the craft;
Your fader is in sleighte as Argus yed;
For al be that his moeble is him biraft, 1460
His olde sleighte is yet so with him laft,
Ye shal not blende him for your womanhede,

Ne feyne a-right, and that is al my drede.

`I noot if pees shal ever-mo bityde;
But, pees or no, for ernest ne for game, 1465
I woot, sin Calkas on the Grekis syde
Hath ones been, and lost so foule his name,
He dar no more come here ayein for shame;
For which that weye, for ought I can espye,
To trusten on, nis but a fantasye. 1470

`Ye shal eek seen, your fader shal yow glose
To been a wyf, and as he can wel preche,
He shal som Grek so preyse and wel alose,
That ravisshen he shal yow with his speche,
Or do yow doon by force as he shal teche. 1475
And Troilus, of whom ye nil han routhe,
Shal causeles so sterven in his trouthe!

`And over al this, your fader shal despyse
Us alle, and seyn this citee nis but lorn;
And that thassege never shal aryse, 1480
For-why the Grekes han it alle sworn
Til we be slayn, and doun our walles torn.
And thus he shal yow with his wordes fere,
That ay drede I, that ye wol bleve there.

`Ye shul eek seen so many a lusty knight 1485
A-mong the Grekes, ful of worthinesse,
And eche of hem with herte, wit, and might
To plesen yow don al his besinesse,
That ye shul dullen of the rudenesse
Of us sely Troianes, but-if routhe 1490
Remorde yow, or vertue of your trouthe.

`And this to me so grevous is to thinke,
That fro my brest it wol my soule rende;
Ne dredeles, in me ther may not sinke
A good opinioun, if that ye wende; 1495
For-why your faderes sleighte wol us shende.
And if ye goon, as I have told yow yore,
So thenk I nam but deed, with-oute more.

`For which, with humble, trewe, and pitous herte,
A thousand tymes mercy I yow preye; 1500
So reweth on myn aspre peynes smerte,
And doth somwhat, as that I shal yow seye,
And lat us stele away bitwixe us tweye;
And thenk that folye is, whan man may chese,
For accident his substaunce ay to lese. 1505

`I mene this, that sin we mowe er day
Wel stele away, and been to-gider so,
What wit were it to putten in assay,
In cas ye sholden to your fader go,
If that ye mighte come ayein or no? 1510
Thus mene I, that it were a gret folye
To putte that sikernesse in Iupertye.

`And vulgarly to speken of substaunce
Of tresour, may we bothe with us lede
Y-nough to live in honour and plesaunce, 1515
Til in-to tyme that we shal ben dede;
And thus we may eschewen al this drede.
For everich other wey ye can recorde,
Myn herte, y-wis, may not ther-with acorde.

`And hardily, ne dredeth no poverte, 1520
For I have kin and freendes elles-where
That, though we comen in oure bare sherte,
Us sholde neither lakke gold ne gere,
But been honured whyl we dwelten there.
And go we anoon, for, as in myn entente, 1525
This is the beste, if that ye wole assente.'

Criseyde, with a syk, right in this wyse
Answerde, `Y-wis, my dere herte trewe,
We may wel stele away, as ye devyse,
And finde swich unthrifty weyes newe; 1530
But afterward, ful sore it wol us rewe.
And help me god so at my moste nede
As causeles ye suffren al this drede!

`For thilke day that I for cherisshinge
Or drede of fader, or of other wight, 1535
Or for estat, delyt, or for weddinge,
Be fals to yow, my Troilus, my knight,
Saturnes doughter, Iuno, thorugh hir might,
As wood as Athamante do me dwelle
Eternaly in Stix, the put of helle! 1540

`And this on every god celestial
I swere it yow; and eek on eche goddesse,
On every Nymphe and deite infernal,
On Satiry and Fauny more and lesse,
That halve goddes been of wildernesse; 1545
And Attropos my threed of lyf to-breste
If I be fals; now trowe me if thow leste!

`And thou, Simoys, that as an arwe clere

Thorugh Troye rennest ay downward to the see,
Ber witnesse of this word that seyd is here, 1550
That thilke day that ich untrewe be
To Troilus, myn owene herte free,
That thou retorne bakwarde to thy welle,
And I with body and soule sinke in helle!

`But that ye speke, awey thus for to go 1555
And leten alle your freendes, god for-bede,
For any womman, that ye sholden so,
And namely, sin Troye hath now swich nede
Of help; and eek of o thing taketh hede,
If this were wist, my lif laye in balaunce, 1560
And your honour; god shilde us fro mischaunce!

`And if so be that pees her-after take,
As alday happeth, after anger, game,
Why, lord! The sorwe and wo ye wolden make,
That ye ne dorste come ayein for shame! 1565
And er that ye Iuparten so your name,
Beth nought to hasty in this hote fare;
For hasty man ne wanteth never care.

`What trowe ye the peple eek al aboute
Wolde of it seye? It is ful light to arede. 1570
They wolden seye, and swere it, out of doute,
That love ne droof yow nought to doon this dede,
But lust voluptuous and coward drede.
Thus were al lost, y-wis, myn herte dere,
Your honour, which that now shyneth so clere. 1575

`And also thenketh on myn honestee,
That floureth yet, how foule I sholde it shende,

And with what filthe it spotted sholde be,
If in this forme I sholde with yow wende.
Ne though I livede un-to the worldes ende, 1580
My name sholde I never ayeinward winne;
Thus were I lost, and that were routhe and sinne.

`And for-thy slee with reson al this hete;
Men seyn, "The suffraunt overcometh," pardee;
Eek "Who-so wol han leef, he lief mot lete;" 1585
Thus maketh vertue of necessitee
By pacience, and thenk that lord is he
Of fortune ay, that nought wol of hir recche;
And she ne daunteth no wight but a wrecche.

`And trusteth this, that certes, herte swete, 1590
Er Phebus suster, Lucina the shene,
The Leoun passe out of this Ariete,
I wol ben here, with-outen any wene.
I mene, as helpe me Iuno, hevenes quene,
The tenthe day, but-if that deeth me assayle, 1595
I wol yow seen with-outen any fayle.'

`And now, so this be sooth,' quod Troilus,
`I shal wel suffre un-to the tenthe day,
Sin that I see that nede it moot be thus.
But, for the love of god, if it be may, 1600
So lat us stele prively away;
For ever in oon, as for to live in reste,
Myn herte seyth that it wol been the beste.'

`O mercy, god, what lyf is this?' quod she;
`Allas, ye slee me thus for verray tene! 1605
I see wel now that ye mistrusten me;

For by your wordes it is wel y-sene.
Now, for the love of Cynthia the shene,
Mistrust me not thus causeles, for routhe;
Sin to be trewe I have yow plight my trouthe. 1610

`And thenketh wel, that som tyme it is wit
To spende a tyme, a tyme for to winne;
Ne, pardee, lorn am I nought fro yow yit,
Though that we been a day or two a-twinne.
Dryf out the fantasyes yow with-inne; 1615
And trusteth me, and leveth eek your sorwe,
Or here my trouthe, I wol not live til morwe.

`For if ye wiste how sore it doth me smerte,
Ye wolde cesse of this; for god, thou wost,
The pure spirit wepeth in myn herte, 1620
To see yow wepen that I love most,
And that I moot gon to the Grekes ost.
Ye, nere it that I wiste remedye
To come ayein, right here I wolde dye!

`But certes, I am not so nyce a wight 1625
That I ne can imaginen a wey
To come ayein that day that I have hight.
For who may holde thing that wol a-way?
My fader nought, for al his queynte pley.
And by my thrift, my wending out of Troye 1630
Another day shal torne us alle to Ioye.

`For-thy, with al myn herte I yow beseke,
If that yow list don ought for my preyere,
And for the love which that I love yow eke,
That er that I departe fro yow here, 1635

That of so good a comfort and a chere
I may you seen, that ye may bringe at reste
Myn herte, which that is at point to breste.

`And over al this I pray yow,' quod she tho,
`Myn owene hertes soothfast suffisaunce, 1640
Sin I am thyn al hool, with-outen mo,
That whyl that I am absent, no plesaunce
Of othere do me fro your remembraunce.
For I am ever a-gast, for-why men rede,
That "love is thing ay ful of bisy drede." 1645

`For in this world ther liveth lady noon,
If that ye were untrewe, as god defende!
That so bitraysed were or wo bigoon
As I, that alle trouthe in yow entende.
And douteles, if that ich other wende, 1650
I nere but deed; and er ye cause finde,
For goddes love, so beth me not unkinde.'

To this answerde Troilus and seyde,
`Now god, to whom ther nis no cause y-wrye,
Me glade, as wis I never un-to Criseyde, 1655
Sin thilke day I saw hir first with ye,
Was fals, ne never shal til that I dye.
At shorte wordes, wel ye may me leve;
I can no more, it shal be founde at preve.'

`Graunt mercy, goode myn, y-wis,' quod she, 1660
`And blisful Venus lat me never sterve
Er I may stonde of plesaunce in degree
To quyte him wel, that so wel can deserve;
And whyl that god my wit wol me conserve,

I shal so doon, so trewe I have yow founde, 1665
That ay honour to me-ward shal rebounde.

`For trusteth wel, that your estat royal
Ne veyn delyt, nor only worthinesse
Of yow in werre, or torney marcial,
Ne pompe, array, nobley, or eek richesse, 1670
Ne made me to rewe on your distresse;
But moral vertue, grounded upon trouthe,
That was the cause I first hadde on yow routhe!

`Eek gentil herte and manhod that ye hadde,
And that ye hadde, as me thoughte, in despyt 1675
Every thing that souned in-to badde,
As rudenesse and poeplish appetyt;
And that your reson brydled your delyt,
This made, aboven every creature,
That I was your, and shal, whyl I may dure. 1680

`And this may lengthe of yeres not for-do,
Ne remuable fortune deface;
But Iuppiter, that of his might may do
The sorwful to be glad, so yeve us grace,
Er nightes ten, to meten in this place, 1685
So that it may your herte and myn suffyse;
And fareth now wel, for tyme is that ye ryse.'

And after that they longe y-pleyned hadde,
And ofte y-kist, and streite in armes folde,
The day gan ryse, and Troilus him cladde, 1690
And rewfulliche his lady gan biholde,
As he that felte dethes cares colde,
And to hir grace he gan him recomaunde;

Wher him was wo, this holde I no demaunde.

For mannes heed imaginen ne can, 1695
Ne entendement considere, ne tonge telle
The cruel peynes of this sorwful man,
That passen every torment doun in helle.
For whan he saugh that she ne mighte dwelle,
Which that his soule out of his herte rente, 1700
With-outen more, out of the chaumbre he wente.

Explicit Liber Quartus.

BOOK V. Incipit Liber Quintus.

Aprochen gan the fatal destinee
That Ioves hath in disposicioun,
And to yow, angry Parcas, sustren three,
Committeth, to don execucioun;
For which Criseyde moste out of the toun, 5
And Troilus shal dwelle forth in pyne
Til Lachesis his threed no lenger twyne. --

The golden-tressed Phebus heighe on-lofte
Thryes hadde alle with his bemes shene
The snowes molte, and Zephirus as ofte 10
Y-brought ayein the tendre leves grene,
Sin that the sone of Ecuba the quene
Bigan to love hir first, for whom his sorwe
Was al, that she departe sholde a-morwe.

Ful redy was at pryme Dyomede, 15
Criseyde un-to the Grekes ost to lede,
For sorwe of which she felt hir herte blede,
As she that niste what was best to rede.
And trewely, as men in bokes rede,
Men wiste never womman han the care, 20
Ne was so looth out of a toun to fare.

This Troilus, with-outen reed or lore,
As man that hath his Ioyes eek forlore,
Was waytinge on his lady ever-more
As she that was the soothfast crop and more 25
Of al his lust, or Ioyes here-tofore.
But Troilus, now farewel al thy Ioye,
For shaltow never seen hir eft in Troye!

Soth is, that whyl he bood in this manere,
He gan his wo ful manly for to hyde. 30
That wel unnethe it seen was in his chere;
But at the yate ther she sholde oute ryde
With certeyn folk, he hoved hir tabyde,
So wo bigoon, al wolde he nought him pleyne,
That on his hors unnethe he sat for peyne. 35

For ire he quook, so gan his herte gnawe,
Whan Diomede on horse gan him dresse,
And seyde un-to him-self this ilke sawe,
`Allas,' quod he, `thus foul a wrecchednesse
Why suffre ich it, why nil ich it redresse? 40
Were it not bet at ones for to dye
Than ever-more in langour thus to drye?

`Why nil I make at ones riche and pore
To have y-nough to done, er that she go?
Why nil I bringe al Troye upon a rore? 45
Why nil I sleen this Diomede also?
Why nil I rather with a man or two
Stele hir a-way? Why wol I this endure?
Why nil I helpen to myn owene cure?'

But why he nolde doon so fel a dede, 50

That shal I seyn, and why him liste it spare;
He hadde in herte alweyes a maner drede,
Lest that Criseyde, in rumour of this fare,
Sholde han ben slayn; lo, this was al his care.
And ellis, certeyn, as I seyde yore, 55
He hadde it doon, with-outen wordes more.

Criseyde, whan she redy was to ryde,
Ful sorwfully she sighte, and seyde `Allas!'
But forth she moot, for ought that may bityde,
And forth she rit ful sorwfully a pas. 60
Ther nis non other remedie in this cas.
What wonder is though that hir sore smerte,
Whan she forgoth hir owene swete herte?

This Troilus, in wyse of curteisye,
With hauke on hond, and with an huge route 65
Of knightes, rood and dide hir companye,
Passinge al the valey fer with-oute,
And ferther wolde han riden, out of doute,
Ful fayn, and wo was him to goon so sone;
But torne he moste, and it was eek to done. 70

And right with that was Antenor y-come
Out of the Grekes ost, and every wight
Was of it glad, and seyde he was wel-come.
And Troilus, al nere his herte light,
He peyned him with al his fulle might 75
Him to with-holde of wepinge at the leste,
And Antenor he kiste, and made feste.

And ther-with-al he moste his leve take,
And caste his eye upon hir pitously,

And neer he rood, his cause for to make, 80
To take hir by the honde al sobrely.
And lord! So she gan wepen tendrely!
And he ful softe and sleighly gan hir seye,
`Now hold your day, and dooth me not to deye.'

With that his courser torned he a-boute 85
With face pale, and un-to Diomede
No word he spak, ne noon of al his route;
Of which the sone of Tydeus took hede,
As he that coude more than the crede
In swich a craft, and by the reyne hir hente; 90
And Troilus to Troye homwarde he wente.

This Diomede, that ladde hir by the brydel,
Whan that he saw the folk of Troye aweye,
Thoughte, `Al my labour shal not been on ydel,
If that I may, for somwhat shal I seye, 95
For at the worste it may yet shorte our weye.
I have herd seyd, eek tymes twyes twelve,
"He is a fool that wol for-yete him-selve."'

But natheles this thoughte he wel ynough,
`That certaynly I am aboute nought, 100
If that I speke of love, or make it tough;
For douteles, if she have in hir thought
Him that I gesse, he may not been y-brought
So sone awey; but I shal finde a mene,
That she not wite as yet shal what I mene.' 105

This Diomede, as he that coude his good,
Whan this was doon, gan fallen forth in speche
Of this and that, and asked why she stood

In swich disese, and gan hir eek biseche,
That if that he encrese mighte or eche 110
With any thing hir ese, that she sholde
Comaunde it him, and seyde he doon it wolde.

For trewely he swoor hir, as a knight,
That ther nas thing with whiche he mighte hir plese,
That he nolde doon his peyne and al his might 115
To doon it, for to doon hir herte an ese.
And preyede hir, she wolde hir sorwe apese,
And seyde, `Y-wis, we Grekes con have Ioye
To honouren yow, as wel as folk of Troye.'

He seyde eek thus, `I woot, yow thinketh straunge, 120
No wonder is, for it is to yow newe,
Thaqueintaunce of these Troianis to chaunge,
For folk of Grece, that ye never knewe.
But wolde never god but-if as trewe
A Greek ye shulde among us alle finde 125
As any Troian is, and eek as kinde.

`And by the cause I swoor yow right, lo, now,
To been your freend, and helply, to my might,
And for that more aqueintaunce eek of yow
Have ich had than another straunger wight, 130
So fro this forth, I pray yow, day and night,
Comaundeth me, how sore that me smerte,
To doon al that may lyke un-to your herte;

`And that ye me wolde as your brother trete,
And taketh not my frendship in despyt; 135
And though your sorwes be for thinges grete,
Noot I not why, but out of more respyt,

Myn herte hath for to amende it greet delyt.
And if I may your harmes not redresse,
I am right sory for your hevinesse, 140

`And though ye Troians with us Grekes wrothe
Han many a day be, alwey yet, pardee,
O god of love in sooth we serven bothe.
And, for the love of god, my lady free,
Whom so ye hate, as beth not wroth with me. 145
For trewely, ther can no wight yow serve,
That half so looth your wraththe wolde deserve.

`And nere it that we been so neigh the tente
Of Calkas, which that seen us bothe may,
I wolde of this yow telle al myn entente; 150
But this enseled til another day.
Yeve me your hond, I am, and shal ben ay,
God help me so, whyl that my lyf may dure,
Your owene aboven every creature.

`Thus seyde I never er now to womman born; 155
For god myn herte as wisly glade so,
I lovede never womman here-biforn
As paramours, ne never shal no mo.
And, for the love of god, beth not my fo;
Al can I not to yow, my lady dere, 160
Compleyne aright, for I am yet to lere.

`And wondreth not, myn owene lady bright,
Though that I speke of love to you thus blyve;
For I have herd or this of many a wight,
Hath loved thing he never saugh his lyve. 165
Eek I am not of power for to stryve

Ayens the god of love, but him obeye
I wol alwey, and mercy I yow preye.

`Ther been so worthy knightes in this place,
And ye so fair, that everich of hem alle 170
Wol peynen him to stonden in your grace.
But mighte me so fair a grace falle,
That ye me for your servaunt wolde calle,
So lowly ne so trewely you serve
Nil noon of hem, as I shal, til I sterve.' 175

Criseide un-to that purpos lyte answerde,
As she that was with sorwe oppressed so
That, in effect, she nought his tales herde,
But here and there, now here a word or two.
Hir thoughte hir sorwful herte brast a-two. 180
For whan she gan hir fader fer aspye,
Wel neigh doun of hir hors she gan to sye.

But natheles she thonked Diomede
Of al his travaile, and his goode chere,
And that him liste his friendship hir to bede; 185
And she accepteth it in good manere,
And wolde do fayn that is him leef and dere;
And trusten him she wolde, and wel she mighte,
As seyde she, and from hir hors she alighte.

Hir fader hath hir in his armes nome, 190
And tweynty tyme he kiste his doughter swete,
And seyde, `O dere doughter myn, wel-come!'
She seyde eek, she was fayn with him to mete,
And stood forth mewet, milde, and mansuete.
But here I leve hir with hir fader dwelle, 195

And forth I wol of Troilus yow telle.

To Troye is come this woful Troilus,
In sorwe aboven alle sorwes smerte,
With felon look, and face dispitous.
Tho sodeinly doun from his hors he sterte, 200
And thorugh his paleys, with a swollen herte,
To chambre he wente; of no-thing took he hede,
Ne noon to him dar speke a word for drede.

And there his sorwes that he spared hadde
He yaf an issue large, and `Deeth!' he cryde; 205
And in his throwes frenetyk and madde
He cursed Iove, Appollo, and eek Cupyde,
He cursed Ceres, Bacus, and Cipryde,
His burthe, him-self, his fate, and eek nature,
And, save his lady, every creature. 210

To bedde he goth, and weyleth there and torneth
In furie, as dooth he, Ixion in helle;
And in this wyse he neigh til day soiorneth.
But tho bigan his herte a lyte unswelle
Thorugh teres which that gonnen up to welle; 215
And pitously he cryde up-on Criseyde,
And to him-self right thus he spak, and seyde: --

`Wher is myn owene lady lief and dere,
Wher is hir whyte brest, wher is it, where?
Wher ben hir armes and hir eyen clere, 220
That yesternight this tyme with me were?
Now may I wepe allone many a tere,
And graspe aboute I may, but in this place,
Save a pilowe, I finde nought tenbrace.

`How shal I do? Whan shal she com ayeyn? 225
I noot, allas! Why leet ich hir to go?
As wolde god, ich hadde as tho be sleyn!
O herte myn, Criseyde, O swete fo!
O lady myn, that I love and no mo!
To whom for ever-mo myn herte I dowe; 230
See how I deye, ye nil me not rescowe!

`Who seeth yow now, my righte lode-sterre?
Who sit right now or stant in your presence?
Who can conforten now your hertes werre?
Now I am gon, whom yeve ye audience? 235
Who speketh for me right now in myn absence?
Allas, no wight; and that is al my care;
For wel wot I, as yvel as I ye fare.

`How sholde I thus ten dayes ful endure,
Whan I the firste night have al this tene? 240
How shal she doon eek, sorwful creature?
For tendernesse, how shal she this sustene,
Swich wo for me? O pitous, pale, and grene
Shal been your fresshe wommanliche face
For langour, er ye torne un-to this place.' 245

And whan he fil in any slomeringes,
Anoon biginne he sholde for to grone,
And dremen of the dredfulleste thinges
That mighte been; as, mete he were allone
In place horrible, makinge ay his mone, 250
Or meten that he was amonges alle
His enemys, and in hir hondes falle.

And ther-with-al his body sholde sterte,
And with the stert al sodeinliche awake,
And swich a tremour fele aboute his herte, 255
That of the feer his body sholde quake;
And there-with-al he sholde a noyse make,
And seme as though he sholde falle depe
From heighe a-lofte; and than he wolde wepe,

And rewen on him-self so pitously, 260
That wonder was to here his fantasye.
Another tyme he sholde mightily
Conforte him-self, and seyn it was folye,
So causeles swich drede for to drye,
And eft biginne his aspre sorwes newe, 265
That every man mighte on his sorwes rewe.

Who coude telle aright or ful discryve
His wo, his pleynt, his langour, and his pyne?
Nought al the men that han or been on-lyve.
Thou, redere, mayst thy-self ful wel devyne 270
That swich a wo my wit can not defyne.
On ydel for to wryte it sholde I swinke,
Whan that my wit is wery it to thinke.

On hevene yet the sterres were sene,
Al-though ful pale y-waxen was the mone; 275
And whyten gan the orisonte shene
Al estward, as it woned is for to done.
And Phebus with his rosy carte sone
Gan after that to dresse him up to fare,
Whan Troilus hath sent after Pandare. 280

This Pandare, that of al the day biforn

Ne mighte han comen Troilus to see,
Al-though he on his heed it hadde y-sworn,
For with the king Pryam alday was he,
So that it lay not in his libertee 285
No-wher to gon, but on the morwe he wente
To Troilus, whan that he for him sente.

For in his herte he coude wel devyne,
That Troilus al night for sorwe wook;
And that he wolde telle him of his pyne, 290
This knew he wel y-nough, with-oute book.
For which to chaumbre streight the wey he took,
And Troilus tho sobreliche he grette,
And on the bed ful sone he gan him sette.

`My Pandarus,' quod Troilus, `the sorwe 295
Which that I drye, I may not longe endure.
I trowe I shal not liven til to-morwe;
For whiche I wolde alwey, on aventure,
To thee devysen of my sepulture
The forme, and of my moeble thou dispone 300
Right as thee semeth best is for to done.

`But of the fyr and flaumbe funeral
In whiche my body brenne shal to glede,
And of the feste and pleyes palestral
At my vigile, I prey thee tak good hede 305
That be wel; and offre Mars my stede,
My swerd, myn helm, and, leve brother dere,
My sheld to Pallas yef, that shyneth clere.

`The poudre in which myn herte y-brend shal torne,
That preye I thee thou take and it conserve 310

In a vessel, that men clepeth an urne,
Of gold, and to my lady that I serve,
For love of whom thus pitously I sterve,
So yeve it hir, and do me this plesaunce,
To preye hir kepe it for a remembraunce. 315

`For wel I fele, by my maladye,
And by my dremes now and yore ago,
Al certeinly, that I mot nedes dye.
The owle eek, which that hight Ascaphilo,
Hath after me shright alle thise nightes two. 320
And, god Mercurie! Of me now, woful wrecche,
The soule gyde, and, whan thee list, it fecche!'

Pandare answerde, and seyde, `Troilus,
My dere freend, as I have told thee yore,
That it is folye for to sorwen thus, 325
And causeles, for whiche I can no-more.
But who-so wol not trowen reed ne lore,
I can not seen in him no remedye,
But lete him worthen with his fantasye.

`But Troilus, I pray thee tel me now, 330
If that thou trowe, er this, that any wight
Hath loved paramours as wel as thou?
Ye, god wot, and fro many a worthy knight
Hath his lady goon a fourtenight,
And he not yet made halvendel the fare. 335
What nede is thee to maken al this care?

`Sin day by day thou mayst thy-selven see
That from his love, or elles from his wyf,
A man mot twinnen of necessitee,

Ye, though he love hir as his owene lyf; 340
Yet nil he with him-self thus maken stryf.
For wel thow wost, my leve brother dere,
That alwey freendes may nought been y-fere.

`How doon this folk that seen hir loves wedded
By freendes might, as it bi-tit ful ofte, 345
And seen hem in hir spouses bed y-bedded?
God woot, they take it wysly, faire and softe.
For-why good hope halt up hir herte on-lofte,
And for they can a tyme of sorwe endure;
As tyme hem hurt, a tyme doth hem cure. 350

`So sholdestow endure, and late slyde
The tyme, and fonde to ben glad and light.
Ten dayes nis so longe not tabyde.
And sin she thee to comen hath bihight,
She nil hir hestes breken for no wight. 355
For dred thee not that she nil finden weye
To come ayein, my lyf that dorste I leye.

`Thy swevenes eek and al swich fantasye
Dryf out, and lat hem faren to mischaunce;
For they procede of thy malencolye, 360
That doth thee fele in sleep al this penaunce.
A straw for alle swevenes signifiaunce!
God helpe me so, I counte hem not a bene,
Ther woot no man aright what dremes mene.

`For prestes of the temple tellen this, 365
That dremes been the revelaciouns
Of goddes, and as wel they telle, y-wis,
That they ben infernals illusiouns;

And leches seyn, that of complexiouns
Proceden they, or fast, or glotonye. 370
Who woot in sooth thus what they signifye?

`Eek othere seyn that thorugh impressiouns,
As if a wight hath faste a thing in minde,
That ther-of cometh swiche avisiouns;
And othere seyn, as they in bokes finde, 375
That, after tymes of the yeer by kinde,
Men dreme, and that theffect goth by the mone;
But leve no dreem, for it is nought to done.

`Wel worth of dremes ay thise olde wyves,
And treweliche eek augurie of thise foules; 380
For fere of which men wenen lese her lyves,
As ravenes qualm, or shryking of thise oules.
To trowen on it bothe fals and foul is.
Allas, allas, so noble a creature
As is a man, shal drede swich ordure! 385

`For which with al myn herte I thee beseche,
Un-to thy-self that al this thou foryive;
And rys up now with-oute more speche,
And lat us caste how forth may best be drive
This tyme, and eek how freshly we may live 390
Whan that she cometh, the which shal be right sone;
God help me so, the beste is thus to done.

`Rys, lat us speke of lusty lyf in Troye
That we han lad, and forth the tyme dryve;
And eek of tyme cominge us reioye, 395
That bringen shal our blisse now so blyve;
And langour of these twyes dayes fyve

We shal ther-with so foryete or oppresse,
That wel unnethe it doon shal us duresse.

`This toun is ful of lordes al aboute, 400
And trewes lasten al this mene whyle.
Go we pleye us in som lusty route
To Sarpedon, not hennes but a myle.
And thus thou shalt the tyme wel bigyle,
And dryve it forth un-to that blisful morwe, 405
That thou hir see, that cause is of thy sorwe.

`Now rys, my dere brother Troilus;
For certes, it noon honour is to thee
To wepe, and in thy bedde to iouken thus.
For trewely, of o thing trust to me, 410
If thou thus ligge a day, or two, or three,
The folk wol wene that thou, for cowardyse,
Thee feynest syk, and that thou darst not ryse.'

This Troilus answerde, `O brother dere,
This knowen folk that han y-suffred peyne, 415
That though he wepe and make sorwful chere,
That feleth harm and smert in every veyne,
No wonder is; and though I ever pleyne,
Or alwey wepe, I am no-thing to blame,
Sin I have lost the cause of al my game. 420

`But sin of fyne force I moot aryse,
I shal aryse as sone as ever I may;
And god, to whom myn herte I sacrifyse,
So sende us hastely the tenthe day!
For was ther never fowl so fayn of May, 425
As I shal been, whan that she cometh in Troye,

That cause is of my torment and my Ioye.

`But whider is thy reed,' quod Troilus,
`That we may pleye us best in al this toun?'
`Bi god, my conseil is,' quod Pandarus, 430
`To ryde and pleye us with king Sarpedoun.'
So longe of this they speken up and doun,
Til Troilus gan at the laste assente
To ryse, and forth to Sarpedoun they wente.

This Sarpedoun, as he that honourable 435
Was ever his lyve, and ful of heigh prowesse,
With al that mighte y-served been on table,
That deyntee was, al coste it greet richesse,
He fedde hem day by day, that swich noblesse,
As seyden bothe the moste and eek the leste, 440
Was never er that day wist at any feste.

Nor in this world ther is non instrument
Delicious, through wind, or touche, of corde,
As fer as any wight hath ever y-went,
That tonge telle or herte may recorde, 445
That at that feste it nas wel herd acorde;
Ne of ladies eek so fayr a companye
On daunce, er tho, was never y-seyn with ye.

But what avayleth this to Troilus,
That for his sorwe no-thing of it roughte? 450
For ever in oon his herte pietous
Ful bisily Criseyde his lady soughte.
On hir was ever al that his herte thoughte,
Now this, now that, so faste imagininge,
That glade, y-wis, can him no festeyinge. 455

These ladies eek that at this feste been,
Sin that he saw his lady was a-weye,
It was his sorwe upon hem for to seen,
Or for to here on instrumentz so pleye.
For she, that of his herte berth the keye, 460
Was absent, lo, this was his fantasye,
That no wight sholde make melodye.

Nor ther nas houre in al the day or night,
Whan he was ther-as no wight mighte him here,
That he ne seyde, `O lufsom lady bright, 465
How have ye faren, sin that ye were here?
Wel-come, y-wis, myn owene lady dere.'
But welaway, al this nas but a mase;
Fortune his howve entended bet to glase.

The lettres eek, that she of olde tyme 470
Hadde him y-sent, he wolde allone rede,
An hundred sythe, a-twixen noon and pryme;
Refiguringe hir shap, hir womanhede,
With-inne his herte, and every word and dede
That passed was, and thus he droof to an ende 475
The ferthe day, and seyde, he wolde wende.

And seyde, `Leve brother Pandarus,
Intendestow that we shal here bleve
Til Sarpedoun wol forth congeyen us?
Yet were it fairer that we toke our leve. 480
For goddes love, lat us now sone at eve
Our leve take, and homward lat us torne;
For trewely, I nil not thus soiourne.'

Pandare answerde, `Be we comen hider
To fecchen fyr, and rennen hoom ayeyn? 485
God helpe me so, I can not tellen whider
We mighten goon, if I shal soothly seyn,
Ther any wight is of us more fayn
Than Sarpedoun; and if we hennes hye
Thus sodeinly, I holde it vilanye. 490

`Sin that we seyden that we wolde bleve
With him a wouke; and now, thus sodeinly,
The ferthe day to take of him oure leve,
He wolde wondren on it, trewely!
Lat us holde forth our purpos fermely; 495
And sin that ye bihighten him to byde,
Hold forward now, and after lat us ryde.'

Thus Pandarus, with alle peyne and wo,
Made him to dwelle; and at the woukes ende,
Of Sarpedoun they toke hir leve tho, 500
And on hir wey they spedden hem to wende.
Quod Troilus, `Now god me grace sende,
That I may finden, at myn hom-cominge,
Criseyde comen!' And ther-with gan he singe.

`Ye, hasel-wode!' thoughte this Pandare, 505
And to him-self ful softely he seyde,
`God woot, refreyden may this hote fare,
Er Calkas sende Troilus Criseyde!'
But natheles, he Iaped thus, and seyde,
And swor, y-wis, his herte him wel bihighte, 510
She wolde come as sone as ever she mighte.

Whan they un-to the paleys were y-comen

Of Troilus, they doun of hors alighte,
And to the chambre hir wey than han they nomen.
And in-to tyme that it gan to nighte, 515
They spaken of Crysede the brighte.
And after this, whan that hem bothe leste,
They spedde hem fro the soper un-to reste.

On morwe, as sone as day bigan to clere,
This Troilus gan of his sleep tabrayde, 520
And to Pandare, his owene brother dere,
`For love of god,' ful pitously he seyde,
`As go we seen the paleys of Criseyde;
For sin we yet may have namore feste,
So lat us seen hir paleys at the leste.' 525

And ther-with-al, his meyne for to blende,
A cause he fond in toune for to go,
And to Criseydes hous they gonnen wende.
But lord! This sely Troilus was wo!
Him thoughte his sorweful herte braste a-two. 530
For whan he saugh hir dores sperred alle,
Wel neigh for sorwe a-doun he gan to falle.

Therwith, whan he was war and gan biholde
How shet was every windowe of the place,
As frost, him thoughte, his herte gan to colde; 535
For which with chaunged deedlich pale face,
With-outen word, he forth bigan to pace;
And, as god wolde, he gan so faste ryde,
That no wight of his contenance aspyde.

Than seyde he thus; `O paleys desolat, 540
O hous, of houses whylom best y-hight,

O paleys empty and disconsolat,
O thou lanterne, of which queynt is the light,
O paleys, whylom day, that now art night,
Wel oughtestow to falle, and I to dye, 545
Sin she is went that wont was us to gye!

`O paleys, whylom croune of houses alle,
Enlumined with sonne of alle blisse!
O ring, fro which the ruby is out-falle,
O cause of wo, that cause hast been of lisse! 550
Yet, sin I may no bet, fayn wolde I kisse
Thy colde dores, dorste I for this route;
And fare-wel shryne, of which the seynt is oute!'

Ther-with he caste on Pandarus his ye
With chaunged face, and pitous to biholde; 555
And whan he mighte his tyme aright aspye,
Ay as he rood, to Pandarus he tolde
His newe sorwe, and eek his Ioyes olde,
So pitously and with so dede an hewe,
That every wight mighte on his sorwe rewe. 560

Fro thennesforth he rydeth up and doun,
And every thing com him to remembraunce
As he rood forbi places of the toun
In whiche he whylom hadde al his plesaunce.
`Lo, yond saugh I myn owene lady daunce; 565
And in that temple, with hir eyen clere,
Me coughte first my righte lady dere.

`And yonder have I herd ful lustily
My dere herte laugh, and yonder pleye
Saugh I hir ones eek ful blisfully. 570

And yonder ones to me gan she seye,
"Now goode swete, love me wel, I preye."
And yond so goodly gan she me biholde,
That to the deeth myn herte is to hir holde.

`And at that corner, in the yonder hous, 575
Herde I myn alderlevest lady dere
So wommanly, with voys melodious,
Singen so wel, so goodly, and so clere,
That in my soule yet me thinketh I here
The blisful soun; and, in that yonder place, 580
My lady first me took un-to hir grace.'

Thanne thoughte he thus, `O blisful lord Cupyde,
Whanne I the proces have in my memorie,
How thou me hast wereyed on every syde,
Men might a book make of it, lyk a storie. 585
What nede is thee to seke on me victorie,
Sin I am thyn, and hoolly at thy wille?
What Ioye hastow thyn owene folk to spille?

`Wel hastow, lord, y-wroke on me thyn ire,
Thou mighty god, and dredful for to greve! 590
Now mercy, lord, thou wost wel I desire
Thy grace most, of alle lustes leve,
And live and deye I wol in thy bileve,
For which I naxe in guerdon but a bone,
That thou Criseyde ayein me sende sone. 595

`Distreyne hir herte as faste to retorne
As thou dost myn to longen hir to see;
Than woot I wel, that she nil nought soiorne.
Now, blisful lord, so cruel thou ne be

Un-to the blood of Troye, I preye thee, 600
As Iuno was un-to the blood Thebane,
For which the folk of Thebes caughte hir bane.'

And after this he to the yates wente
Ther-as Criseyde out-rood a ful good paas,
And up and doun ther made he many a wente, 605
And to him-self ful ofte he seyde `Allas!
From hennes rood my blisse and my solas!
As wolde blisful god now, for his Ioye,
I mighte hir seen ayein come in-to Troye!

`And to the yonder hille I gan hir gyde, 610
Allas! And there I took of hir my leve!
And yond I saugh hir to hir fader ryde,
For sorwe of which myn herte shal to-cleve.
And hider hoom I com whan it was eve;
And here I dwelle out-cast from alle Ioye, 615
And shal, til I may seen hir eft in Troye.'

And of him-self imagened he ofte
To ben defet, and pale, and waxen lesse
Than he was wont, and that men seyden softe,
`What may it be? Who can the sothe gesse 620
Why Troilus hath al this hevinesse?'
And al this nas but his malencolye,
That he hadde of him-self swich fantasye.

Another tyme imaginen he wolde
That every wight that wente by the weye 625
Had of him routhe, and that they seyen sholde,
`I am right sory Troilus wole deye.'
And thus he droof a day yet forth or tweye.

As ye have herd, swich lyf right gan he lede,
As he that stood bitwixen hope and drede. 630

For which him lyked in his songes shewe
Thencheson of his wo, as he best mighte,
And made a song of wordes but a fewe,
Somwhat his woful herte for to lighte.
And whan he was from every mannes sighte, 635
With softe voys he, of his lady dere,
That was absent, gan singe as ye may here.

`O sterre, of which I lost have al the light,
With herte soor wel oughte I to bewayle,
That ever derk in torment, night by night, 640
Toward my deeth with wind in stere I sayle;
For which the tenthe night if that I fayle
The gyding of thy bemes brighte an houre,
My ship and me Caribdis wole devoure.'

This song whan he thus songen hadde, sone 645
He fil ayein in-to his sykes olde;
And every night, as was his wone to done,
He stood the brighte mone to beholde,
And al his sorwe he to the mone tolde;
And seyde, `Y-wis, whan thou art horned newe, 650
I shal be glad, if al the world be trewe!

`I saugh thyn hornes olde eek by the morwe,
Whan hennes rood my righte lady dere,
That cause is of my torment and my sorwe;
For whiche, O brighte Lucina the clere, 655
For love of god, ren faste aboute thy spere!
For whan thyn hornes newe ginne springe,

Than shal she come, that may my blisse bringe!'

The day is more, and lenger every night,
Than they be wont to be, him thoughte tho; 660
And that the sonne wente his course unright
By lenger wey than it was wont to go;
And seyde, `Y-wis, me dredeth ever-mo,
The sonnes sone, Pheton, be on-lyve,
And that his fadres cart amis he dryve.' 665

Upon the walles faste eek wolde he walke,
And on the Grekes ost he wolde see,
And to him-self right thus he wolde talke,
`Lo, yonder is myn owene lady free,
Or elles yonder, ther tho tentes be! 670
And thennes comth this eyr, that is so sote,
That in my soule I fele it doth me bote.

`And hardely this wind, that more and more
Thus stoundemele encreseth in my face,
Is of my ladyes depe sykes sore. 675
I preve it thus, for in non othere place
Of al this toun, save onliche in this space,
Fele I no wind that souneth so lyk peyne;
It seyth, "Allas! Why twinned be we tweyne?"'

This longe tyme he dryveth forth right thus, 680
Til fully passed was the nynthe night;
And ay bi-syde him was this Pandarus,
That bisily dide alle his fulle might
Him to comforte, and make his herte light;
Yevinge him hope alwey, the tenthe morwe 685
That she shal come, and stinten al his sorwe.

Up-on that other syde eek was Criseyde,
With wommen fewe, among the Grekes stronge;
For which ful ofte a day `Allas,' she seyde,
`That I was born! Wel may myn herte longe 690
After my deeth; for now live I to longe!
Allas! And I ne may it not amende;
For now is wors than ever yet I wende.

`My fader nil for no-thing do me grace
To goon ayein, for nought I can him queme; 695
And if so be that I my terme passe,
My Troilus shal in his herte deme
That I am fals, and so it may wel seme.
Thus shal I have unthank on every syde;
That I was born, so weylaway the tyde! 700

`And if that I me putte in Iupartye,
To stele awey by nighte, and it bifalle
That I be caught, I shal be holde a spye;
Or elles, lo, this drede I most of alle,
If in the hondes of som wrecche I falle, 705
I am but lost, al be myn herte trewe;
Now mighty god, thou on my sorwe rewe!'

Ful pale y-waxen was hir brighte face,
Hir limes lene, as she that al the day
Stood whan she dorste, and loked on the place 710
Ther she was born, and ther she dwelt hadde ay.
And al the night wepinge, allas! she lay.
And thus despeired, out of alle cure,
She ladde hir lyf, this woful creature.

Ful ofte a day she sighte eek for destresse, 715
And in hir-self she wente ay portrayinge
Of Troilus the grete worthinesse,
And alle his goodly wordes recordinge
Sin first that day hir love bigan to springe.
And thus she sette hir woful herte a-fyre 720
Through remembraunce of that she gan desyre.

In al this world ther nis so cruel herte
That hir hadde herd compleynen in hir sorwe,
That nolde han wopen for hir peynes smerte,
So tendrely she weep, bothe eve and morwe. 725
Hir nedede no teres for to borwe.
And this was yet the worste of al hir peyne,
Ther was no wight to whom she dorste hir pleyne.

Ful rewfully she loked up-on Troye,
Biheld the toures heighe and eek the halles; 730
`Allas!' quod she, `The plesaunce and the Ioye
The whiche that now al torned in-to galle is,
Have I had ofte with-inne yonder walles!
O Troilus, what dostow now,' she seyde;
`Lord! Whether yet thou thenke up-on Criseyde? 735

`Allas! I ne hadde trowed on your lore,
And went with yow, as ye me radde er this!
Thanne hadde I now not syked half so sore.
Who mighte han seyd, that I had doon a-mis
To stele awey with swich on as he is? 740
But al to late cometh the letuarie,
Whan men the cors un-to the grave carie.

`To late is now to speke of this matere;

Prudence, allas! Oon of thyn eyen three
Me lakked alwey, er that I come here; 745
On tyme y-passed, wel remembred me;
And present tyme eek coude I wel y-see.
But futur tyme, er I was in the snare,
Coude I not seen; that causeth now my care.

`But natheles, bityde what bityde, 750
I shal to-morwe at night, by est or weste,
Out of this ost stele on som maner syde,
And go with Troilus wher-as him leste.
This purpos wol I holde, and this is beste.
No fors of wikked tonges Ianglerye, 755
For ever on love han wrecches had envye.

`For who-so wole of every word take hede,
Or rewlen him by every wightes wit,
Ne shal he never thryven, out of drede.
For that that som men blamen ever yit, 760
Lo, other maner folk commenden it.
And as for me, for al swich variaunce,
Felicitee clepe I my suffisaunce.

`For which, with-outen any wordes mo,
To Troye I wol, as for conclusioun.' 765
But god it wot, er fully monthes two,
She was ful fer fro that entencioun.
For bothe Troilus and Troye toun
Shal knotteles through-out hir herte slyde;
For she wol take a purpos for tabyde. 770

This Diomede, of whom yow telle I gan,
Goth now, with-inne him-self ay arguinge

With al the sleighte and al that ever he can,
How he may best, with shortest taryinge,
In-to his net Criseydes herte bringe. 775
To this entente he coude never fyne;
To fisshen hir, he leyde out hook and lyne.

But natheles, wel in his herte he thoughte,
That she nas nat with-oute a love in Troye,
For never, sithen he hir thennes broughte, 780
Ne coude he seen her laughe or make Ioye.
He nist how best hir herte for tacoye.
`But for to assaye,' he seyde, `it nought ne greveth;
For he that nought nassayeth, nought nacheveth.'

Yet seide he to him-self upon a night, 785
`Now am I not a fool, that woot wel how
Hir wo for love is of another wight,
And here-up-on to goon assaye hir now?
I may wel wite, it nil not been my prow.
For wyse folk in bokes it expresse, 790
"Men shal not wowe a wight in hevinesse."

`But who-so mighte winnen swich a flour
From him, for whom she morneth night and day,
He mighte seyn, he were a conquerour.'
And right anoon, as he that bold was ay, 795
Thoughte in his herte, `Happe how happe may,
Al sholde I deye, I wole hir herte seche;
I shal no more lesen but my speche.'

This Diomede, as bokes us declare,
Was in his nedes prest and corageous; 800
With sterne voys and mighty limes square,

Hardy, testif, strong, and chevalrous
Of dedes, lyk his fader Tideus.
And som men seyn, he was of tunge large;
And heir he was of Calidoine and Arge. 805

Criseyde mene was of hir stature,
Ther-to of shap, of face, and eek of chere,
Ther mighte been no fairer creature.
And ofte tyme this was hir manere,
To gon y-tressed with hir heres clere 810
Doun by hir coler at hir bak bihinde,
Which with a threde of gold she wolde binde.

And, save hir browes ioyneden y-fere,
Ther nas no lak, in ought I can espyen;
But for to speken of hir eyen clere, 815
Lo, trewely, they writen that hir syen,
That Paradys stood formed in hir yen.
And with hir riche beautee ever-more
Strof love in hir, ay which of hem was more.

She sobre was, eek simple, and wys with-al, 820
The beste y-norisshed eek that mighte be,
And goodly of hir speche in general,
Charitable, estatliche, lusty, and free;
Ne never-mo ne lakkede hir pitee;
Tendre-herted, slydinge of corage; 825
But trewely, I can not telle hir age.

And Troilus wel waxen was in highte,
And complet formed by proporcioun
So wel, that kinde it not amenden mighte;
Yong, fresshe, strong, and hardy as lyoun; 830

Trewe as steel in ech condicioun;
On of the beste enteched creature,
That is, or shal, whyl that the world may dure.

And certainly in storie it is y-founde,
That Troilus was never un-to no wight, 835
As in his tyme, in no degree secounde
In durring don that longeth to a knight.
Al mighte a geaunt passen him of might,
His herte ay with the firste and with the beste
Stood paregal, to durre don that him leste. 840

But for to tellen forth of Diomede: --
It fil that after, on the tenthe day,
Sin that Criseyde out of the citee yede,
This Diomede, as fresshe as braunche in May,
Com to the tente ther-as Calkas lay, 845
And feyned him with Calkas han to done;
But what he mente, I shal yow telle sone.

Criseyde, at shorte wordes for to telle,
Welcomed him, and doun by hir him sette;
And he was ethe y-nough to maken dwelle. 850
And after this, with-outen longe lette,
The spyces and the wyn men forth hem fette;
And forth they speke of this and that y-fere,
As freendes doon, of which som shal ye here.

He gan first fallen of the werre in speche 855
Bitwixe hem and the folk of Troye toun;
And of thassege he gan hir eek byseche,
To telle him what was hir opinioun.
Fro that demaunde he so descendeth doun

To asken hir, if that hir straunge thoughte 860
The Grekes gyse, and werkes that they wroughte?

And why hir fader tarieth so longe
To wedden hir un-to som worthy wight?
Criseyde, that was in hir peynes stronge
For love of Troilus, hir owene knight, 865
As fer-forth as she conning hadde or might,
Answerde him tho; but, as of his entente,
It semed not she wiste what he mente.

But natheles, this ilke Diomede
Gan in him-self assure, and thus he seyde, 870
`If ich aright have taken of yow hede,
Me thinketh thus, O lady myn, Criseyde,
That sin I first hond on your brydel leyde,
Whan ye out come of Troye by the morwe,
Ne coude I never seen yow but in sorwe. 875

`Can I not seyn what may the cause be
But-if for love of som Troyan it were,
The which right sore wolde athinken me
That ye, for any wight that dwelleth there,
Sholden spille a quarter of a tere, 880
Or pitously your-selven so bigyle;
For dredelees, it is nought worth the whyle.

`The folk of Troye, as who seyth, alle and some
In preson been, as ye your-selven see;
Nor thennes shal not oon on-lyve come 885
For al the gold bitwixen sonne and see.
Trusteth wel, and understondeth me.
Ther shal not oon to mercy goon on-lyve,

Al were he lord of worldes twyes fyve!

`Swich wreche on hem, for fecching of Eleyne, 890
Ther shal be take, er that we hennes wende,
That Manes, which that goddes ben of peyne,
Shal been agast that Grekes wol hem shende.
And men shul drede, un-to the worldes ende,
From hennes-forth to ravisshe any quene, 895
So cruel shal our wreche on hem be sene.

`And but-if Calkas lede us with ambages,
That is to seyn, with double wordes slye,
Swich as men clepe a "word with two visages,"
Ye shal wel knowen that I nought ne lye, 900
And al this thing right seen it with your ye,
And that anoon; ye nil not trowe how sone;
Now taketh heed, for it is for to done.

`What wene ye your wyse fader wolde
Han yeven Antenor for yow anoon, 905
If he ne wiste that the citee sholde
Destroyed been? Why, nay, so mote I goon!
He knew ful wel ther shal not scapen oon
That Troyan is; and for the grete fere,
He dorste not, ye dwelte lenger there. 910

`What wole ye more, lufsom lady dere?
Lat Troye and Troyan fro your herte pace!
Dryf out that bittre hope, and make good chere,
And clepe ayein the beautee of your face,
That ye with salte teres so deface. 915
For Troye is brought in swich a Iupartye,
That, it to save, is now no remedye.

`And thenketh wel, ye shal in Grekes finde,
A more parfit love, er it be night,
Than any Troian is, and more kinde, 920
And bet to serven yow wol doon his might.
And if ye vouche sauf, my lady bright,
I wol ben he to serven yow my-selve,
Yee, lever than he lord of Greces twelve!'

And with that word he gan to waxen reed, 925
And in his speche a litel wight he quook,
And caste a-syde a litel wight his heed,
And stinte a whyle; and afterward awook,
And sobreliche on hir he threw his look,
And seyde, `I am, al be it yow no Ioye, 930
As gentil man as any wight in Troye.

`For if my fader Tydeus,' he seyde,
`Y-lived hadde, I hadde been, er this,
Of Calidoine and Arge a king, Criseyde!
And so hope I that I shal yet, y-wis. 935
But he was slayn, allas! The more harm is,
Unhappily at Thebes al to rathe,
Polymites and many a man to scathe.

`But herte myn, sin that I am your man,
And been the ferste of whom I seche grace, 940
To serven you as hertely as I can,
And ever shal, whyl I to live have space,
So, er that I departe out of this place,
Ye wol me graunte, that I may to-morwe,
At bettre leyser, telle yow my sorwe.' 945

What shold I telle his wordes that he seyde?
He spak y-now, for o day at the meste;
It preveth wel, he spak so that Criseyde
Graunted, on the morwe, at his requeste,
For to speken with him at the leste, 950
So that he nolde speke of swich matere;
And thus to him she seyde, as ye may here:

As she that hadde hir herte on Troilus
So faste, that ther may it noon arace;
And straungely she spak, and seyde thus; 955
`O Diomede, I love that ilke place
Ther I was born; and Ioves, for his grace,
Delivere it sone of al that doth it care!
God, for thy might, so leve it wel to fare!

`That Grekes wolde hir wraththe on Troye wreke, 960
If that they mighte, I knowe it wel, y-wis.
But it shal not bifallen as ye speke;
And god to-forn, and ferther over this,
I wot my fader wys and redy is;
And that he me hath bought, as ye me tolde, 965
So dere, I am the more un-to him holde.

`That Grekes been of heigh condicioun,
I woot eek wel; but certein, men shal finde
As worthy folk with-inne Troye toun,
As conning, and as parfit and as kinde, 970
As been bitwixen Orcades and Inde.
And that ye coude wel your lady serve,
I trowe eek wel, hir thank for to deserve.

`But as to speke of love, y-wis,' she seyde,

`I hadde a lord, to whom I wedded was, 975
The whos myn herte al was, til that he deyde;
And other love, as helpe me now Pallas,
Ther in myn herte nis, ne nevere was.
And that ye been of noble and heigh kinrede,
I have wel herd it tellen, out of drede. 980

`And that doth me to han so gret a wonder,
That ye wol scornen any womman so.
Eek, god wot, love and I be fer a-sonder!
I am disposed bet, so mote I go,
Un-to my deeth, to pleyne and maken wo. 985
What I shal after doon, I can not seye;
But trewely, as yet me list not pleye.

`Myn herte is now in tribulacioun,
And ye in armes bisy, day by day.
Here-after, whan ye wonnen han the toun, 990
Paraunter, thanne so it happen may,
That whan I see that I never er say,
Than wole I werke that I never wroughte!
This word to yow y-nough suffysen oughte.

`To-morwe eek wol I speken with yow fayn, 995
So that ye touchen nought of this matere.
And whan yow list, ye may come here ayeyn;
And, er ye gon, thus muche I seye yow here;
As help me Pallas with hir heres clere,
If that I sholde of any Greek han routhe, 1000
It sholde be your-selven, by my trouthe!

`I sey not therfore that I wol yow love,
Ne I sey not nay, but in conclusioun,

I mene wel, by god that sit above:' --
And ther-with-al she caste hir eyen doun, 1005
And gan to syke, and seyde, `O Troye toun,
Yet bidde I god, in quiete and in reste
I may yow seen, or do myn herte breste.'

But in effect, and shortly for to seye,
This Diomede al freshly newe ayeyn 1010
Gan pressen on, and faste hir mercy preye;
And after this, the sothe for to seyn,
Hir glove he took, of which he was ful fayn.
And fynally, whan it was waxen eve,
And al was wel, he roos and took his leve. 1015

The brighte Venus folwede and ay taughte
The wey, ther brode Phebus doun alighte;
And Cynthea hir char-hors over-raughte
To whirle out of the Lyon, if she mighte;
And Signifer his candelse shewed brighte, 1020
Whan that Criseyde un-to hir bedde wente
In-with hir fadres faire brighte tente.

Retorning in hir soule ay up and doun
The wordes of this sodein Diomede,
His greet estat, and peril of the toun, 1025
And that she was allone and hadde nede
Of freendes help; and thus bigan to brede
The cause why, the sothe for to telle,
That she tok fully purpos for to dwelle.

The morwe com, and goostly for to speke, 1030
This Diomede is come un-to Criseyde,
And shortly, lest that ye my tale breke,

So wel he for him-selve spak and seyde,
That alle hir sykes sore adoun he leyde.
And fynally, the sothe for to seyne,   1035
He refte hir of the grete of al hir peyne.

And after this the story telleth us,
That she him yaf the faire baye stede,
The which he ones wan of Troilus;
And eek a broche (and that was litel nede)   1040
That Troilus was, she yaf this Diomede.
And eek, the bet from sorwe him to releve,
She made him were a pencel of hir sleve.

I finde eek in stories elles-where,
Whan through the body hurt was Diomede   1045
Of Troilus, tho weep she many a tere,
Whan that she saugh his wyde woundes blede;
And that she took to kepen him good hede,
And for to hele him of his sorwes smerte.
Men seyn, I not, that she yaf him hir herte.   1050

But trewely, the story telleth us,
Ther made never womman more wo
Than she, whan that she falsed Troilus.
She seyde, `Allas! For now is clene a-go
My name of trouthe in love, for ever-mo!   1055
For I have falsed oon, the gentileste
That ever was, and oon the worthieste!

`Allas, of me, un-to the worldes ende,
Shal neither been y-writen nor y-songe
No good word, for thise bokes wol me shende.   1060
O, rolled shal I been on many a tonge;

Through-out the world my belle shal be ronge;
And wommen most wol hate me of alle.
Allas, that swich a cas me sholde falle!

`They wol seyn, in as muche as in me is,   1065
I have hem don dishonour, weylawey!
Al be I not the first that dide amis,
What helpeth that to do my blame awey?
But sin I see there is no bettre way,
And that to late is now for me to rewe,   1070
To Diomede algate I wol be trewe.

`But Troilus, sin I no better may,
And sin that thus departen ye and I,
Yet preye I god, so yeve yow right good day
As for the gentileste, trewely,   1075
That ever I say, to serven feithfully,
And best can ay his lady honour kepe:' --
And with that word she brast anon to wepe.

`And certes yow ne haten shal I never,
And freendes love, that shal ye han of me,   1080
And my good word, al mighte I liven ever.
And, trewely, I wolde sory be
For to seen yow in adversitee.
And giltelees, I woot wel, I yow leve;
But al shal passe; and thus take I my leve.'   1085

But trewely, how longe it was bitwene,
That she for-sook him for this Diomede,
Ther is non auctor telleth it, I wene.
Take every man now to his bokes hede;
He shal no terme finden, out of drede.   1090

For though that he bigan to wowe hir sone,
Er he hir wan, yet was ther more to done.

Ne me ne list this sely womman chyde
Ferther than the story wol devyse.
Hir name, allas! Is publisshed so wyde, 1095
That for hir gilt it oughte y-noe suffyse.
And if I mighte excuse hir any wyse,
For she so sory was for hir untrouthe,
Y-wis, I wolde excuse hir yet for routhe.

This Troilus, as I biforn have told, 1100
Thus dryveth forth, as wel as he hath might.
But often was his herte hoot and cold,
And namely, that ilke nynthe night,
Which on the morwe she hadde him byhight
To come ayein: god wot, ful litel reste 1105
Hadde he that night; no-thing to slepe him leste.

The laurer-crouned Phebus, with his hete,
Gan, in his course ay upward as he wente,
To warmen of the est see the wawes wete,
And Nisus doughter song with fresh entente, 1110
Whan Troilus his Pandare after sente;
And on the walles of the toun they pleyde,
To loke if they can seen ought of Criseyde.

Til it was noon, they stoden for to see
Who that ther come; and every maner wight, 1115
That cam fro fer, they seyden it was she,
Til that they coude knowen him a-right.
Now was his herte dul, now was it light;
And thus by-iaped stonden for to stare

Aboute nought, this Troilus and Pandare. 1120

To Pandarus this Troilus tho seyde,
`For ought I wot, bi-for noon, sikerly,
In-to this toun ne comth nought here Criseyde.
She hath y-now to done, hardily,
To winnen from hir fader, so trowe I; 1125
Hir olde fader wol yet make hir dyne
Er that she go; god yeve his herte pyne!'

Pandare answerde, `It may wel be, certeyn;
And for-thy lat us dyne, I thee biseche;
And after noon than maystw thou come ayeyn.' 1130
And hoom they go, with-oute more speche;
And comen ayein, but longe may they seche
Er that they finde that they after cape;
Fortune hem bothe thenketh for to Iape.

Quod Troilus, `I see wel now, that she 1135
Is taried with hir olde fader so,
That er she come, it wole neigh even be.
Com forth, I wol un-to the yate go.
Thise portours been unkonninge ever-mo;
And I wol doon hem holden up the yate 1140
As nought ne were, al-though she come late.'

The day goth faste, and after that comth eve,
And yet com nought to Troilus Criseyde.
He loketh forth by hegge, by tree, by greve,
And fer his heed over the wal he leyde. 1145
And at the laste he torned him, and seyde.
`By god, I woot hir mening now, Pandare!
Al-most, y-wis, al newe was my care.

'Now douteles, this lady can hir good;
I woot, she meneth ryden prively. 1150
I comende hir wysdom, by myn hood!
She wol not maken peple nycely
Gaure on hir, whan she comth; but softely
By nighte in-to the toun she thenketh ryde.
And, dere brother, thenk not longe to abyde. 1155

'We han nought elles for to don, y-wis.
And Pandarus, now woltow trowen me?
Have here my trouthe, I see hir! Yond she is.
Heve up thyn eyen, man! Maystow not see?'
Pandare answerde, 'Nay, so mote I thee! 1160
Al wrong, by god; what seystow, man, wher art?
That I see yond nis but a fare-cart.'

'Allas, thou seist right sooth,' quod Troilus;
'But, hardely, it is not al for nought
That in myn herte I now reioyse thus. 1165
It is ayein som good I have a thought.
Noot I not how, but sin that I was wrought,
Ne felte I swich a confort, dar I seye;
She comth to-night, my lyf, that dorste I leye!'

Pandare answerde, 'It may be wel, y-nough'; 1170
And held with him of al that ever he seyde;
But in his herte he thoughte, and softe lough,
And to him-self ful sobrely he seyde:
'From hasel-wode, ther Ioly Robin pleyde,
Shal come al that thou abydest here; 1175
Ye, fare-wel al the snow of ferne yere!'

The wardein of the yates gan to calle
The folk which that with-oute the yates were,
And bad hem dryven in hir bestes alle,
Or al the night they moste bleven there. 1180
And fer with-in the night, with many a tere,
This Troilus gan hoomward for to ryde;
For wel he seeth it helpeth nought tabyde.

But natheles, he gladded him in this;
He thoughte he misacounted hadde his day, 1185
And seyde, `I understonde have al a-mis.
For thilke night I last Criseyde say,
She seyde, "I shal ben here, if that I may,
Er that the mone, O dere herte swete!
The Lyon passe, out of this Ariete." 1190

`For which she may yet holde al hir biheste.'
And on the morwe un-to the yate he wente,
And up and down, by west and eek by este,
Up-on the walles made he many a wente.
But al for nought; his hope alwey him blente; 1195
For which at night, in sorwe and sykes sore,
He wente him hoom, with-outen any more.

This hope al clene out of his herte fledde,
He nath wher-on now lenger for to honge;
But for the peyne him thoughte his herte bledde, 1200
So were his throwes sharpe and wonder stronge.
For when he saugh that she abood so longe,
He niste what he iuggen of it mighte,
Sin she hath broken that she him bihighte.

The thridde, ferthe, fifte, sixte day 1205

After tho dayes ten, of which I tolde,
Bitwixen hope and drede his herte lay,
Yet som-what trustinge on hir hestes olde.
But whan he saugh she nolde hir terme holde,
He can now seen non other remedye, 1210
But for to shape him sone for to dye.

Ther-with the wikked spirit, god us blesse,
Which that men clepeth wode Ialousye,
Gan in him crepe, in al this hevinesse;
For which, by-cause he wolde sone dye, 1215
He ne eet ne dronk, for his malencolye,
And eek from every companye he fledde;
This was the lyf that al the tyme he ledde.

He so defet was, that no maner man
Unneth mighte him knowe ther he wente; 1220
So was he lene, and ther-to pale and wan,
And feble, that he walketh by potente;
And with his ire he thus himselven shente.
But who-so axed him wher-of him smerte,
He seyde, his harm was al aboute his herte. 1225

Pryam ful ofte, and eek his moder dere,
His bretheren and his sustren gonne him freyne
Why he so sorwful was in al his chere,
And what thing was the cause of al his peyne?
But al for nought; he nolde his cause pleyne, 1230
But seyde, he felte a grevous maladye
A-boute his herte, and fayn he wolde dye.

So on a day he leyde him doun to slepe,
And so bifel that in his sleep him thoughte,

That in a forest faste he welk to wepe 1235
For love of hir that him these peynes wroughte;
And up and doun as he the forest soughte,
He mette he saugh a boor with tuskes grete,
That sleep ayein the brighte sonnes hete.

And by this boor, faste in his armes folde, 1240
Lay kissing ay his lady bright Criseyde:
For sorwe of which, whan he it gan biholde,
And for despyt, out of his slepe he breyde,
And loude he cryde on Pandarus, and seyde,
`O Pandarus, now knowe I crop and rote! 1245
I nam but deed; ther nis non other bote!

`My lady bright Criseyde hath me bitrayed,
In whom I trusted most of any wight,
She elles-where hath now hir herte apayed;
The blisful goddes, through hir grete might, 1250
Han in my dreem y-shewed it ful right.
Thus in my dreem Criseyde I have biholde' --
And al this thing to Pandarus he tolde.

`O my Criseyde, allas! What subtiltee.
What newe lust, what beautee, what science, 1255
What wratthe of iuste cause have ye to me?
What gilt of me, what fel experience
Hath fro me raft, allas! Thyn advertence?
O trust, O feyth, O depe aseuraunce,
Who hath me reft Criseyde, al my plesaunce? 1260

`Allas! Why leet I you from hennes go,
For which wel neigh out of my wit I breyde?
Who shal now trowe on any othes mo?

God wot I wende, O lady bright, Criseyde,
That every word was gospel that ye seyde! 1265
But who may bet bigylen, yf him liste,
Than he on whom men weneth best to triste?

`What shal I doon, my Pandarus, allas!
I fele now so sharpe a newe peyne,
Sin that ther is no remedie in this cas, 1270
That bet were it I with myn hondes tweyne
My-selven slow, than alwey thus to pleyne.
For through my deeth my wo sholde han an ende,
Ther every day with lyf my-self I shende.'

Pandare answerde and seyde, `Allas the whyle 1275
That I was born; have I not seyd er this,
That dremes many a maner man bigyle?
And why? For folk expounden hem a-mis.
How darstow seyn that fals thy lady is,
For any dreem, right for thyn owene drede? 1280
Lat be this thought, thou canst no dremes rede.

`Paraunter, ther thou dremest of this boor,
It may so be that it may signifye
Hir fader, which that old is and eek hoor,
Ayein the sonne lyth, on poynt to dye, 1285
And she for sorwe ginneth wepe and crye,
And kisseth him, ther he lyth on the grounde;
Thus shuldestow thy dreem a-right expounde.'

`How mighte I thanne do?' quod Troilus,
`To knowe of this, ye, were it never so lyte?' 1290
`Now seystow wysly,' quod this Pandarus,
`My reed is this, sin thou canst wel endyte,

That hastely a lettre thou hir wryte,
Thorugh which thou shalt wel bringen it aboute,
To knowe a sooth of that thou art in doute. 1295

`And see now why; for this I dar wel seyn,
That if so is that she untrewe be,
I can not trowe that she wol wryte ayeyn.
And if she wryte, thou shalt ful sone see,
As whether she hath any libertee 1300
To come ayein, or ellis in som clause,
If she be let, she wol assigne a cause.

`Thou hast not writen hir sin that she wente,
Nor she to thee, and this I dorste leye,
Ther may swich cause been in hir entente, 1305
That hardely thou wolt thy-selven seye,
That hir a-bood the beste is for yow tweye.
Now wryte hir thanne, and thou shalt fele sone
A sothe of al; ther is no more to done.'

Acorded been to this conclusioun, 1310
And that anoon, these ilke lordes two;
And hastely sit Troilus adoun,
And rolleth in his herte to and fro,
How he may best discryven hir his wo.
And to Criseyde, his owene lady dere, 1315
He wroot right thus, and seyde as ye may here.

`Right fresshe flour, whos I have been and shal,
With-outen part of elles-where servyse,
With herte, body, lyf, lust, thought, and al;
I, woful wight, in every humble wyse 1320
That tonge telle or herte may devyse,

As ofte as matere occupyeth place,
Me recomaunde un-to your noble grace.

`Lyketh it yow to witen, swete herte,
As ye wel knowe how longe tyme agoon 1325
That ye me lefte in aspre peynes smerte,
Whan that ye wente, of which yet bote noon
Have I non had, but ever wers bigoon
Fro day to day am I, and so mot dwelle,
While it yow list, of wele and wo my welle. 1330

`For which to yow, with dredful herte trewe,
I wryte, as he that sorwe dryfth to wryte,
My wo, that every houre encreseth newe,
Compleyninge as I dar or can endyte.
And that defaced is, that may ye wyte 1335
The teres, which that fro myn eyen reyne,
That wolde speke, if that they coude, and pleyne.

`Yow first biseche I, that your eyen clere
To look on this defouled ye not holde;
And over al this, that ye, my lady dere, 1340
Wol vouche-sauf this lettre to biholde.
And by the cause eek of my cares colde,
That sleeth my wit, if ought amis me asterte,
For-yeve it me, myn owene swete herte.

`If any servant dorste or oughte of right 1345
Up-on his lady pitously compleyne,
Than wene I, that ich oughte be that wight,
Considered this, that ye these monthes tweyne
Han taried, ther ye seyden, sooth to seyne,
But dayes ten ye nolde in ost soiourne, 1350

But in two monthes yet ye not retourne.

`But for-as-muche as me mot nedes lyke
Al that yow list, I dar not pleyne more,
But humbely with sorwful sykes syke;
Yow wryte ich myn unresty sorwes sore, 1355
Fro day to day desyring ever-more
To knowen fully, if your wil it were,
How ye han ferd and doon, whyl ye be there.

`The whos wel-fare and hele eek god encresse
In honour swich, that upward in degree 1360
It growe alwey, so that it never cesse;
Right as your herte ay can, my lady free,
Devyse, I prey to god so mote it be.
And graunte it that ye sone up-on me rewe
As wisly as in al I am yow trewe. 1365

`And if yow lyketh knowen of the fare
Of me, whos wo ther may no wight discryve,
I can no more but, cheste of every care,
At wrytinge of this lettre I was on-lyve,
Al redy out my woful gost to dryve; 1370
Which I delaye, and holde him yet in honde,
Upon the sight of matere of your sonde.

`Myn eyen two, in veyn with which I see,
Of sorweful teres salte arn waxen welles;
My song, in pleynte of myn adversitee; 1375
My good, in harm; myn ese eek waxen helle is.
My Ioye, in wo; I can sey yow nought elles,
But turned is, for which my lyf I warie,
Everich Ioye or ese in his contrarie.

`Which with your cominge hoom ayein to Troye 1380
Ye may redresse, and, more a thousand sythe
Than ever ich hadde, encressen in me Ioye.
For was ther never herte yet so blythe
To han his lyf, as I shal been as swythe
As I yow see; and, though no maner routhe 1385
Commeve yow, yet thinketh on your trouthe.

`And if so be my gilt hath deeth deserved,
Or if yow list no more up-on me see,
In guerdon yet of that I have you served,
Biseche I yow, myn hertes lady free, 1390
That here-upon ye wolden wryte me,
For love of god, my righte lode-sterre,
Ther deeth may make an ende of al my werre.

`If other cause aught doth yow for to dwelle,
That with your lettre ye me recomforte; 1395
For though to me your absence is an helle,
With pacience I wol my wo comporte,
And with your lettre of hope I wol desporte.
Now wryteth, swete, and lat me thus not pleyne;
With hope, or deeth, delivereth me fro peyne. 1400

`Y-wis, myn owene dere herte trewe,
I woot that, whan ye next up-on me see,
So lost have I myn hele and eek myn hewe,
Criseyde shal nought conne knowe me!
Y-wis, myn hertes day, my lady free, 1405
So thursteth ay myn herte to biholde
Your beautee, that my lyf unnethe I holde.

`I sey no more, al have I for to seye
To you wel more than I telle may;
But whether that ye do me live or deye, 1410
Yet pray I god, so yeve yow right good day.
And fareth wel, goodly fayre fresshe may,
As ye that lyf or deeth me may comaunde;
And to your trouthe ay I me recomaunde

`With hele swich that, but ye yeven me 1415
The same hele, I shal noon hele have.
In you lyth, whan yow liste that it so be,
The day in which me clothen shal my grave.
In yow my lyf, in yow might for to save
Me from disese of alle peynes smerte; 1420
And fare now wel, myn owene swete herte!
                    Le vostre T.'

This lettre forth was sent un-to Criseyde,
Of which hir answere in effect was this;
Ful pitously she wroot ayein, and seyde,
That also sone as that she might, y-wis, 1425
She wolde come, and mende al that was mis.
And fynally she wroot and seyde him thanne,
She wolde come, ye, but she niste whenne.

But in hir lettre made she swich festes,
That wonder was, and swereth she loveth him best, 1430
Of which he fond but botmelees bihestes.
But Troilus, thou mayst now, est or west,
Pype in an ivy leef, if that thee lest;
Thus gooth the world; god shilde us fro mischaunce,
And every wight that meneth trouthe avaunce! 1435

Encresen gan the wo fro day to night
Of Troilus, for taryinge of Criseyde;
And lessen gan his hope and eek his might,
For which al doun he in his bed him leyde;
He ne eet, ne dronk, ne sleep, ne word he seyde, 1440
Imagininge ay that she was unkinde;
For which wel neigh he wex out of his minde.

This dreem, of which I told have eek biforn,
May never come out of his remembraunce;
He thoughte ay wel he hadde his lady lorn, 1445
And that Ioves, of his purveyaunce,
Him shewed hadde in sleep the signifiaunce
Of hir untrouthe and his disaventure,
And that the boor was shewed him in figure.

For which he for Sibille his suster sente, 1450
That called was Cassandre eek al aboute;
And al his dreem he tolde hir er he stente,
And hir bisoughte assoilen him the doute
Of the stronge boor, with tuskes stoute;
And fynally, with-inne a litel stounde, 1455
Cassandre him gan right thus his dreem expounde.

She gan first smyle, and seyde, `O brother dere,
If thou a sooth of this desyrest knowe,
Thou most a fewe of olde stories here,
To purpos, how that fortune over-throwe 1460
Hath lordes olde; through which, with-inne a throwe,
Thou wel this boor shalt knowe, and of what kinde
He comen is, as men in bokes finde.

`Diane, which that wrooth was and in ire

For Grekes nolde doon hir sacrifyse, 1465
Ne encens up-on hir auter sette a-fyre,
She, for that Grekes gonne hir so dispyse,
Wrak hir in a wonder cruel wyse.
For with a boor as greet as oxe in stalle
She made up frete hir corn and vynes alle. 1470

`To slee this boor was al the contree reysed,
A-monges which ther com, this boor to see,
A mayde, oon of this world the best y-preysed;
And Meleagre, lord of that contree,
He lovede so this fresshe mayden free 1475
That with his manhod, er he wolde stente,
This boor he slow, and hir the heed he sente;

`Of which, as olde bokes tellen us,
Ther roos a contek and a greet envye;
And of this lord descended Tydeus 1480
By ligne, or elles olde bokes lye;
But how this Meleagre gan to dye
Thorugh his moder, wol I yow not telle,
For al to long it were for to dwelle.'

[Argument of the 12 Books of Statius' "Thebais"]

Associat profugum Tideo primus Polimitem;
Tidea legatum docet insidiasque secundus;
Tercius Hemoniden canit et vates latitantes;
Quartus habet reges ineuntes prelia septem;
Mox furie Lenne quinto narratur et anguis;
Archimori bustum sexto ludique leguntur;
Dat Graios Thebes et vatem septimus vmbria;
Octauo cecidit Tideus, spes, vita Pelasgia;

Ypomedon nono moritur cum Parthonopeo;
Fulmine percussus, decimo Capaneus superatur;
Vndecimo sese perimunt per vulnera fratres;
Argiuam flentem narrat duodenus et igneum.

She tolde eek how Tydeus, er she stente, 1485
Un-to the stronge citee of Thebes,
To cleyme kingdom of the citee, wente,
For his felawe, daun Polymites,
Of which the brother, daun Ethyocles,
Ful wrongfully of Thebes held the strengthe; 1490
This tolde she by proces, al by lengthe.

She tolde eek how Hemonides asterte,
Whan Tydeus slough fifty knightes stoute.
She tolde eek al the prophesyes by herte,
And how that sevene kinges, with hir route, 1495
Bisegeden the citee al aboute;
And of the holy serpent, and the welle,
And of the furies, al she gan him telle.

Of Archimoris buryinge and the pleyes,
And how Amphiorax fil through the grounde, 1500
How Tydeus was slayn, lord of Argeyes,
And how Ypomedoun in litel stounde
Was dreynt, and deed Parthonope of wounde;
And also how Cappaneus the proude
With thonder-dint was slayn, that cryde loude. 1505

She gan eek telle him how that either brother,
Ethyocles and Polimyte also,
At a scarmyche, eche of hem slough other,
And of Argyves wepinge and hir wo;

And how the town was brent she tolde eek tho. 1510
And so descendeth doun from gestes olde
To Diomede, and thus she spak and tolde.

`This ilke boor bitokneth Diomede,
Tydeus sone, that doun descended is
Fro Meleagre, that made the boor to blede. 1515
And thy lady, wher-so she be, y-wis,
This Diomede hir herte hath, and she his.
Weep if thou wolt, or leef; for, out of doute,
This Diomede is inne, and thou art oute.'

`Thou seyst nat sooth,' quod he, `thou sorceresse, 1520
With al thy false goost of prophesye!
Thou wenest been a greet devyneresse;
Now seestow not this fool of fantasye
Peyneth hir on ladyes for to lye?
Awey!' quod he. `Ther Ioves yeve thee sorwe! 1525
Thou shalt be fals, paraunter, yet to-morwe!

`As wel thou mightest lyen on Alceste,
That was of creatures, but men lye,
That ever weren, kindest and the beste.
For whanne hir housbonde was in Iupartye 1530
To dye him-self, but-if she wolde dye,
She chees for him to dye and go to helle,
And starf anoon, as us the bokes telle.'

Cassandre goth, and he with cruel herte
For-yat his wo, for angre of hir speche; 1535
And from his bed al sodeinly he sterte,
As though al hool him hadde y-mad a leche.
And day by day he gan enquere and seche

A sooth of this, with al his fulle cure;
And thus he dryeth forth his aventure. 1540

Fortune, whiche that permutacioun
Of thinges hath, as it is hir committed
Through purveyaunce and disposicioun
Of heighe Iove, as regnes shal ben flitted
Fro folk in folk, or whan they shal ben smitted, 1545
Gan pulle awey the fetheres brighte of Troye
Fro day to day, til they ben bare of Ioye.

Among al this, the fyn of the parodie
Of Ector gan approchen wonder blyve;
The fate wolde his soule sholde unbodie, 1550
And shapen hadde a mene it out to dryve;
Ayeins which fate him helpeth not to stryve;
But on a day to fighten gan he wende,
At which, allas! He coughte his lyves ende.

For which me thinketh every maner wight 1555
That haunteth armes oughte to biwayle
The deeth of him that was so noble a knight;
For as he drough a king by thaventayle,
Unwar of this, Achilles through the mayle
And through the body gan him for to ryve; 1560
And thus this worthy knight was brought of lyve.

For whom, as olde bokes tellen us,
Was mad swich wo, that tonge it may not telle;
And namely, the sorwe of Troilus,
That next him was of worthinesse welle. 1565
And in this wo gan Troilus to dwelle,
That, what for sorwe, and love, and for unreste,

Ful ofte a day he bad his herte breste.

But natheles, though he gan him dispeyre,
And dradde ay that his lady was untrewe, 1570
Yet ay on hir his herte gan repeyre.
And as these loveres doon, he soughte ay newe
To gete ayein Criseyde, bright of hewe.
And in his herte he wente hir excusinge,
That Calkas causede al hir taryinge. 1575

And ofte tyme he was in purpos grete
Him-selven lyk a pilgrim to disgyse,
To seen hir; but he may not contrefete
To been unknowen of folk that weren wyse,
Ne finde excuse aright that may suffyse, 1580
If he among the Grekes knowen were;
For which he weep ful ofte many a tere.

To hir he wroot yet ofte tyme al newe
Ful pitously, he lefte it nought for slouthe,
Biseching hir that, sin that he was trewe, 1585
She wolde come ayein and holde hir trouthe.
For which Criseyde up-on a day, for routhe,
I take it so, touchinge al this matere,
Wrot him ayein, and seyde as ye may here.

`Cupydes sone, ensample of goodlihede, 1590
O swerd of knighthod, sours of gentilesse!
How might a wight in torment and in drede
And helelees, yow sende as yet gladnesse?
I hertelees, I syke, I in distresse;
Sin ye with me, nor I with yow may dele, 1595
Yow neither sende ich herte may nor hele.

`Your lettres ful, the papir al y-pleynted,
Conceyved hath myn hertes pietee;
I have eek seyn with teres al depeynted
Your lettre, and how that ye requeren me 1600
To come ayein, which yet ne may not be.
But why, lest that this lettre founden were,
No mencioun ne make I now, for fere.

`Grevous to me, god woot, is your unreste,
Your haste, and that, the goddes ordenaunce, 1605
It semeth not ye take it for the beste.
Nor other thing nis in your remembraunce,
As thinketh me, but only your plesaunce.
But beth not wrooth, and that I yow biseche;
For that I tarie, is al for wikked speche. 1610

`For I have herd wel more than I wende,
Touchinge us two, how thinges han y-stonde;
Which I shal with dissimulinge amende.
And beth nought wrooth, I have eek understonde,
How ye ne doon but holden me in honde. 1615
But now no fors, I can not in yow gesse
But alle trouthe and alle gentilesse.

`Comen I wol, but yet in swich disioynte
I stonde as now, that what yeer or what day
That this shal be, that can I not apoynte. 1620
But in effect, I prey yow, as I may,
Of your good word and of your frendship ay.
For trewely, whyl that my lyf may dure,
As for a freend, ye may in me assure.

`Yet preye I yow on yvel ye ne take, 1625
That it is short which that I to yow wryte;
I dar not, ther I am, wel lettres make,
Ne never yet ne coude I wel endyte.
Eek greet effect men wryte in place lite.
Thentente is al, and nought the lettres space; 1630
And fareth now wel, god have you in his grace!
    La vostre C.'

This Troilus this lettre thoughte al straunge,
Whan he it saugh, and sorwefully he sighte;
Him thoughte it lyk a kalendes of chaunge;
But fynally, he ful ne trowen mighte 1635
That she ne wolde him holden that she highte;
For with ful yvel wil list him to leve
That loveth wel, in swich cas, though him greve.

But natheles, men seyn that, at the laste,
For any thing, men shal the sothe see; 1640
And swich a cas bitidde, and that as faste,
That Troilus wel understood that she
Nas not so kinde as that hir oughte be.
And fynally, he woot now, out of doute,
That al is lost that he hath been aboute. 1645

Stood on a day in his malencolye
This Troilus, and in suspecioun
Of hir for whom he wende for to dye.
And so bifel, that through-out Troye toun,
As was the gyse, y-bore was up and doun 1650
A maner cote-armure, as seyth the storie,
Biforn Deiphebe, in signe of his victorie,

The whiche cote, as telleth Lollius,
Deiphebe it hadde y-rent from Diomede
The same day; and whan this Troilus 1655
It saugh, he gan to taken of it hede,
Avysing of the lengthe and of the brede,
And al the werk; but as he gan biholde,
Ful sodeinly his herte gan to colde,

As he that on the coler fond with-inne 1660
A broche, that he Criseyde yaf that morwe
That she from Troye moste nedes twinne,
In remembraunce of him and of his sorwe;
And she him leyde ayein hir feyth to borwe
To kepe it ay; but now, ful wel he wiste, 1665
His lady nas no lenger on to triste.

He gooth him hoom, and gan ful sone sende
For Pandarus; and al this newe chaunce,
And of this broche, he tolde him word and ende,
Compleyninge of hir hertes variaunce, 1670
His longe love, his trouthe, and his penaunce;
And after deeth, with-outen wordes more,
Ful faste he cryde, his reste him to restore.

Than spak he thus, `O lady myn Criseyde,
Wher is your feyth, and wher is your biheste? 1675
Wher is your love, wher is your trouthe,' he seyde;
`Of Diomede have ye now al this feste!
Allas, I wolde have trowed at the leste.
That, sin ye nolde in trouthe to me stonde,
That ye thus nolde han holden me in honde! 1680

`Who shal now trowe on any othes mo?

Allas, I never wolde han wend, er this,
That ye, Criseyde, coude han chaunged so;
Ne, but I hadde a-gilt and doon amis,
So cruel wende I not your herte, y-wis, 1685
To slee me thus; allas, your name of trouthe
Is now for-doon, and that is al my routhe.

`Was ther non other broche yow liste lete
To feffe with your newe love,' quod he,
`But thilke broche that I, with teres wete, 1690
Yow yaf, as for a remembraunce of me?
Non other cause, allas, ne hadde ye
But for despyt, and eek for that ye mente
Al-outrely to shewen your entente!

`Through which I see that clene out of your minde 1695
Ye han me cast, and I ne can nor may,
For al this world, with-in myn herte finde
To unloven yow a quarter of a day!
In cursed tyme I born was, weylaway!
That ye, that doon me al this wo endure, 1700
Yet love I best of any creature.

`Now god,' quod he, `me sende yet the grace
That I may meten with this Diomede!
And trewely, if I have might and space,
Yet shal I make, I hope, his sydes blede. 1705
O god,' quod he, `that oughtest taken hede
To fortheren trouthe, and wronges to punyce,
Why niltow doon a vengeaunce of this vyce?

`O Pandare, that in dremes for to triste
Me blamed hast, and wont art oft up-breyde, 1710

Now maystow see thy-selve, if that thee liste,
How trewe is now thy nece, bright Criseyde!
In sondry formes, god it woot,' he seyde,
`The goddes shewen bothe Ioye and tene
In slepe, and by my dreme it is now sene. 1715

`And certaynly, with-oute more speche,
From hennes-forth, as ferforth as I may,
Myn owene deeth in armes wol I seche;
I recche not how sone be the day!
But trewely, Criseyde, swete may, 1720
Whom I have ay with al my might y-served,
That ye thus doon, I have it nought deserved.'

This Pandarus, that alle these thinges herde,
And wiste wel he seyde a sooth of this,
He nought a word ayein to him answerde; 1725
For sory of his frendes sorwe he is,
And shamed, for his nece hath doon a-mis;
And stant, astoned of these causes tweye,
As stille as stoon; a word ne coude he seye.

But at the laste thus he spak, and seyde, 1730
`My brother dere, I may thee do no-more.
What shulde I seyn? I hate, y-wis, Criseyde!
And, god wot, I wol hate hir evermore!
And that thou me bisoughtest doon of yore,
Havinge un-to myn honour ne my reste 1735
Right no reward, I dide al that thee leste.

`If I dide ought that mighte lyken thee,
It is me leef; and of this treson now,
God woot, that it a sorwe is un-to me!

And dredelees, for hertes ese of yow, 1740
Right fayn wolde I amende it, wiste I how.
And fro this world, almighty god I preye,
Delivere hir sone; I can no-more seye.'

Gret was the sorwe and pleynt of Troilus;
But forth hir cours fortune ay gan to holde. 1745
Criseyde loveth the sone of Tydeus,
And Troilus mot wepe in cares colde.
Swich is this world; who-so it can biholde,
In eche estat is litel hertes reste;
God leve us for to take it for the beste! 1750

In many cruel batayle, out of drede,
Of Troilus, this ilke noble knight,
As men may in these olde bokes rede,
Was sene his knighthod and his grete might.
And dredelees, his ire, day and night, 1755
Ful cruelly the Grekes ay aboughte;
And alwey most this Diomede he soughte.

And ofte tyme, I finde that they mette
With blody strokes and with wordes grete,
Assayinge how hir speres weren whette; 1760
And god it woot, with many a cruel hete
Gan Troilus upon his helm to bete.
But natheles, fortune it nought ne wolde,
Of others hond that either deyen sholde. --

And if I hadde y-taken for to wryte 1765
The armes of this ilke worthy man,
Than wolde I of his batailles endyte.
But for that I to wryte first bigan

Of his love, I have seyd as that I can.
His worthy dedes, who-so list hem here, 1770
Reed Dares, he can telle hem alle y-fere.

Bisechinge every lady bright of hewe,
And every gentil womman, what she be,
That al be that Criseyde was untrewe,
That for that gilt she be not wrooth with me. 1775
Ye may hir gilt in othere bokes see;
And gladlier I wole wryten, if yow leste,
Penolopees trouthe and good Alceste.

Ne I sey not this al-only for these men,
But most for wommen that bitraysed be 1780
Through false folk; god yeve hem sorwe, amen!
That with hir grete wit and subtiltee
Bitrayse yow! And this commeveth me
To speke, and in effect yow alle I preye,
Beth war of men, and herkeneth what I seye! -- 1785

Go, litel book, go litel myn tragedie,
Ther god thy maker yet, er that he dye,
So sende might to make in som comedie!
But litel book, no making thou nenvye,
But subgit be to alle poesye; 1790
And kis the steppes, wher-as thou seest pace
Virgile, Ovyde, Omer, Lucan, and Stace.

And for ther is so greet diversitee
In English and in wryting of our tonge,
So preye I god that noon miswryte thee, 1795
Ne thee mismetre for defaute of tonge.
And red wher-so thou be, or elles songe,

That thou be understonde I god beseche!
But yet to purpos of my rather speche. --

The wraththe, as I began yow for to seye, 1800
Of Troilus, the Grekes boughten dere;
For thousandes his hondes maden deye,
As he that was with-outen any pere,
Save Ector, in his tyme, as I can here.
But weylawey, save only goddes wille, 1805
Dispitously him slough the fiers Achille.

And whan that he was slayn in this manere,
His lighte goost ful blisfully is went
Up to the holownesse of the seventh spere,
In convers letinge every element; 1810
And ther he saugh, with ful avysement,
The erratik sterres, herkeninge armonye
With sownes fulle of hevenish melodye.

And doun from thennes faste he gan avyse
This litel spot of erthe, that with the see 1815
Embraced is, and fully gan despyse
This wrecched world, and held al vanitee
To respect of the pleyn felicitee
That is in hevene above; and at the laste,
Ther he was slayn, his loking doun he caste; 1820

And in him-self he lough right at the wo
Of hem that wepten for his deeth so faste;
And dampned al our werk that folweth so
The blinde lust, the which that may not laste,
And sholden al our herte on hevene caste. 1825
And forth he wente, shortly for to telle,

Ther as Mercurie sorted him to dwelle. --

Swich fyn hath, lo, this Troilus for love,
Swich fyn hath al his grete worthinesse;
Swich fyn hath his estat real above, 1830
Swich fyn his lust, swich fyn hath his noblesse;
Swich fyn hath false worldes brotelnesse.
And thus bigan his lovinge of Criseyde,
As I have told, and in this wyse he deyde.

O yonge fresshe folkes, he or she, 1835
In which that love up groweth with your age,
Repeyreth hoom from worldly vanitee,
And of your herte up-casteth the visage
To thilke god that after his image
Yow made, and thinketh al nis but a fayre 1840
This world, that passeth sone as floures fayre.

And loveth him, the which that right for love
Upon a cros, our soules for to beye,
First starf, and roos, and sit in hevene a-bove;
For he nil falsen no wight, dar I seye, 1845
That wol his herte al hoolly on him leye.
And sin he best to love is, and most meke,
What nedeth feyned loves for to seke?

Lo here, of Payens corsed olde rytes,
Lo here, what alle hir goddes may availle; 1850
Lo here, these wrecched worldes appetytes;
Lo here, the fyn and guerdon for travaille
Of Iove, Appollo, of Mars, of swich rascaille!
Lo here, the forme of olde clerkes speche
In poetrye, if ye hir bokes seche. -- 1855

O moral Gower, this book I directe
To thee, and to the philosophical Strode,
To vouchen sauf, ther nede is, to corecte,
Of your benignitees and zeles gode.
And to that sothfast Crist, that starf on rode, 1860
With al myn herte of mercy ever I preye;
And to the lord right thus I speke and seye:

Thou oon, and two, and three, eterne on-lyve,
That regnest ay in three and two and oon,
Uncircumscript, and al mayst circumscryve, 1865
Us from visible and invisible foon
Defende; and to thy mercy, everichoon,
So make us, Iesus, for thy grace digne,
For love of mayde and moder thyn benigne! Amen.

Explicit Liber Troili et Criseydis.

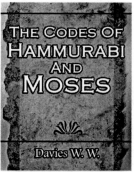

The Codes Of Hammurabi And Moses
W. W. Davies

QTY

The discovery of the Hammurabi Code is one of the greatest achievements of archaeology, and is of paramount interest, not only to the student of the Bible, but also to all those interested in ancient history...

Religion   ISBN: *1-59462-338-4*   **Pages:132**
MSRP *$12.95*

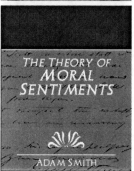

The Theory of Moral Sentiments
Adam Smith

QTY

This work from 1749. contains original theories of conscience amd moral judgment and it is the foundation for systemof morals.

Philosophy ISBN: *1-59462-777-0*   **Pages:536**
MSRP *$19.95*

Jessica's First Prayer
Hesba Stretton

QTY

In a screened and secluded corner of one of the many railway-bridges which span the streets of London there could be seen a few years ago, from five o'clock every morning until half past eight, a tidily set-out coffee-stall, consisting of a trestle and board, upon which stood two large tin cans, with a small fire of charcoal burning under each so as to keep the coffee boiling during the early hours of the morning when the work-people were thronging into the city on their way to their daily toil...

Pages:84

Childrens   ISBN: *1-59462-373-2*   MSRP *$9.95*

My Life and Work
Henry Ford

QTY

Henry Ford revolutionized the world with his implementation of mass production for the Model T automobile. Gain valuable business insight into his life and work with his own auto-biography... "We have only started on our development of our country we have not as yet, with all our talk of wonderful progress, done more than scratch the surface. The progress has been wonderful enough but..."

Pages:300

Biographies/   ISBN: *1-59462-198-5*   MSRP *$21.95*

www.bookjungle.com *email: sales@bookjungle.com fax: 630-214-0564 mail: Book Jungle PO Box 2226 Champaign, IL 61825*

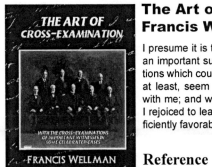

The Art of Cross-Examination
Francis Wellman

QTY

I presume it is the experience of every author, after his first book is published upon an important subject, to be almost overwhelmed with a wealth of ideas and illustrations which could readily have been included in his book, and which to his own mind, at least, seem to make a second edition inevitable. Such certainly was the case with me; and when the first edition had reached its sixth impression in five months, I rejoiced to learn that it seemed to my publishers that the book had met with a sufficiently favorable reception to justify a second and considerably enlarged edition. ..

Pages:412

Reference   **ISBN:** *1-59462-647-2*   *MSRP $19.95*

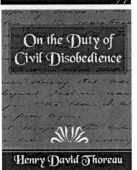

On the Duty of Civil Disobedience
Henry David Thoreau

QTY

Thoreau wrote his famous essay, On the Duty of Civil Disobedience, as a protest against an unjust but popular war and the immoral but popular institution of slave-owning. He did more than write—he declined to pay his taxes, and was hauled off to gaol in consequence. Who can say how much this refusal of his hastened the end of the war and of slavery ?

Law   **ISBN:** *1-59462-747-9*   **Pages:48**

MSRP $7.45

Dream Psychology Psychoanalysis for Beginners
Sigmund Freud

QTY

Sigmund Freud, born Sigismund Schlomo Freud (May 6, 1856 - September 23, 1939), was a Jewish-Austrian neurologist and psychiatrist who co-founded the psychoanalytic school of psychology. Freud is best known for his theories of the unconscious mind, especially involving the mechanism of repression; his redefinition of sexual desire as mobile and directed towards a wide variety of objects; and his therapeutic techniques, especially his understanding of transference in the therapeutic relationship and the presumed value of dreams as sources of insight into unconscious desires.

Dream Psychology
Psychoanalysis for Beginners

Sigmund Freud

Pages:196

Psychology   **ISBN:** *1-59462-905-6*   *MSRP $15.45*

The Miracle of Right Thought
Orison Swett Marden

QTY

Believe with all of your heart that you will do what you were made to do. When the mind has once formed the habit of holding cheerful, happy, prosperous pictures, it will not be easy to form the opposite habit. It does not matter how improbable or how far away this realization may see, or how dark the prospects may be, if we visualize them as best we can, as vividly as possible, hold tenaciously to them and vigorously struggle to attain them, they will gradually become actualized, realized in the life. But a desire, a longing without endeavor, a yearning abandoned or held indifferently will vanish without realization.

Pages:360

Self Help   **ISBN:** *1-59462-644-8*   *MSRP $25.45*

QTY

The Rosicrucian Cosmo-Conception Mystic Christianity *by Max Heindel*   ISBN: *1-59462-188-8*   **$38.95**
The Rosicrucian Cosmo-conception is not dogmatic, neither does it appeal to any other authority than the reason of the student. It is: not controversial, but is: sent forth in the, hope that it may help to clear...   *New Age/Religion Pages 646*

Abandonment To Divine Providence *by Jean-Pierre de Caussade*   ISBN: *1-59462-228-0*   **$25.95**
"The Rev. Jean Pierre de Caussade was one of the most remarkable spiritual writers of the Society of Jesus in France in the 18th Century. His death took place at Toulouse in 1751. His works have gone through many editions and have been republished...   *Inspirational/Religion Pages 400*

Mental Chemistry *by Charles Haanel*   ISBN: *1-59462-192-6*   **$23.95**
Mental Chemistry allows the change of material conditions by combining and appropriately utilizing the power of the mind. Much like applied chemistry creates something new and unique out of careful combinations of chemicals the mastery of mental chemistry...   *New Age Pages 354*

The Letters of Robert Browning and Elizabeth Barret Barrett 1845-1846 vol II   ISBN: *1-59462-193-4*   **$35.95**
by Robert Browning and Elizabeth Barrett   *Biographies Pages 596*

Gleanings In Genesis (volume I) *by Arthur W. Pink*   ISBN: *1-59462-130-6*   **$27.45**
Appropriately has Genesis been termed "the seed plot of the Bible" for in it we have, in germ form, almost all of the great doctrines which are afterwards fully developed in the books of Scripture which follow...   *Religion/Inspirational Pages 420*

The Master Key *by L. W. de Laurence*   ISBN: *1-59462-001-6*   **$30.95**
In no branch of human knowledge has there been a more lively increase of the spirit of research during the past few years than in the study of Psychology, Concentration and Mental Discipline. The requests for authentic lessons in Thought Control, Mental Discipline and...   *New Age/Business Pages 422*

The Lesser Key Of Solomon Goetia *by L. W. de Laurence*   ISBN: *1-59462-092-X*   **$9.95**
This translation of the first book of the "Lernegton" which is now for the first time made accessible to students of Talismanic Magic was done, after careful collation and edition, from numerous Ancient Manuscripts in Hebrew, Latin, and French...   *New Age/Occult Pages 92*

Rubaiyat Of Omar Khayyam *by Edward Fitzgerald*   ISBN: *1-59462-332-5*   **$13.95**
Edward Fitzgerald, whom the world has already learned, in spite of his own efforts to remain within the shadow of anonymity, to look upon as one of the rarest poets of the century, was born at Bredfield, in Suffolk, on the 31st of March, 1809. He was the third son of John Purcell...   *Music Pages 172*

Ancient Law *by Henry Maine*   ISBN: *1-59462-128-4*   **$29.95**
The chief object of the following pages is to indicate some of the earliest ideas of mankind, as they are reflected in Ancient Law, and to point out the relation of those ideas to modern thought.   *Religion/History Pages 452*

Far-Away Stories *by William J. Locke*   ISBN: *1-59462-129-2*   **$19.45**
"Good wine needs no bush, but a collection of mixed vintages does. And this book is just such a collection. Some of the stories I do not want to remain buried for ever in the museum files of dead magazine-numbers an author's not unpardonable vanity..."   *Fiction Pages 272*

Life of David Crockett *by David Crockett*   ISBN: *1-59462-250-7*   **$27.45**
"Colonel David Crockett was one of the most remarkable men of the times in which he lived. Born in humble life, but gifted with a strong will, an indomitable courage, and unremitting perseverance...   *Biographies/New Age Pages 424*

Lip-Reading *by Edward Nitchie*   ISBN: *1-59462-206-X*   **$25.95**
Edward B. Nitchie, founder of the New York School for the Hard of Hearing, now the Nitchie School of Lip-Reading, Inc, wrote "LIP-READING Principles and Practice". The development and perfecting of this meritorious work on lip-reading was an undertaking...   *How-to Pages 400*

A Handbook of Suggestive Therapeutics, Applied Hypnotism, Psychic Science   ISBN: *1-59462-214-0*   **$24.95**
by Henry Munro   *Health/New Age/Health/Self-help Pages 376*

A Doll's House: and Two Other Plays *by Henrik Ibsen*   ISBN: *1-59462-112-8*   **$19.95**
Henrik Ibsen created this classic when in revolutionary 1848 Rome. Introducing some striking concepts in playwriting for the realist genre, this play has been studied the world over.   *Fiction/Classics/Plays 308*

The Light of Asia *by sir Edwin Arnold*   ISBN: *1-59462-204-3*   **$13.95**
In this poetic masterpiece, Edwin Arnold describes the life and teachings of Buddha. The man who was to become known as Buddha to the world was born as Prince Gautama of India but he rejected the worldly riches and abandoned the reigns of power when... Religion/History/Biographies Pages 170

The Complete Works of Guy de Maupassant *by Guy de Maupassant*   ISBN: *1-59462-157-8*   **$16.95**
"For days and days, nights and nights, I had dreamed of that first kiss which was to consecrate our engagement, and I knew not on what spot I should put my lips..."   *Fiction/Classics Pages 240*

The Art of Cross-Examination *by Francis L. Wellman*   ISBN: *1-59462-309-0*   **$26.95**
Written by a renowned trial lawyer, Wellman imparts his experience and uses case studies to explain how to use psychology to extract desired information through questioning.   *How-to/Science/Reference Pages 408*

Answered or Unanswered? *by Louisa Vaughan*   ISBN: *1-59462-248-5*   **$10.95**
Miracles of Faith in China   *Religion Pages 112*

The Edinburgh Lectures on Mental Science (1909) *by Thomas*   ISBN: *1-59462-008-3*   **$11.95**
This book contains the substance of a course of lectures recently given by the writer in the Queen Street Hall, Edinburgh. Its purpose is to indicate the Natural Principles governing the relation between Mental Action and Material Conditions...   *New Age/Psychology Pages 148*

Ayesha *by H. Rider Haggard*   ISBN: *1-59462-301-5*   **$24.95**
Verily and indeed it is the unexpected that happens! Probably if there was one person upon the earth from whom the Editor of this, and of a certain previous history, did not expect to hear again...   *Classics Pages 380*

Ayala's Angel *by Anthony Trollope*   ISBN: *1-59462-352-X*   **$29.95**
The two girls were both pretty, but Lucy who was twenty-one who supposed to be simple and comparatively unattractive, whereas Ayala was credited, as her Bombwhat romantic name might show, with poetic charm and a taste for romance. Ayala when her father died was nineteen...   *Fiction Pages 484*

The American Commonwealth *by James Bryce*   ISBN: *1-59462-286-8*   **$34.45**
An interpretation of American democratic political theory. It examines political mechanics and society from the perspective of Scotsman James Bryce   *Politics Pages 572*

Stories of the Pilgrims *by Margaret P. Pumphrey*   ISBN: *1-59462-116-0*   **$17.95**
This book explores pilgrims religious oppression in England as well as their escape to Holland and eventual crossing to America on the Mayflower, and their early days in New England...   *History Pages 268*

www.bookjungle.com *email: sales@bookjungle.com fax: 630-214-0564 mail: Book Jungle PO Box 2226 Champaign, IL 61825*

QTY

The Fasting Cure *by Sinclair Upton*   ISBN: *1-59462-222-1* **$13.95**
In the Cosmopolitan Magazine for May, 1910, and in the Contemporary Review (London) for April, 1910, I published an article dealing with my experiences in fasting. I have written a great many magazine articles, but never one which attracted so much attention... New Age/Self Help/Health Pages 164

Hebrew Astrology *by Sepharial*   ISBN: *1-59462-308-2* **$13.45**
In these days of advanced thinking it is a matter of common observation that we have left many of the old landmarks behind and that we are now pressing forward to greater heights and to a wider horizon than that which represented the mind-content of our progenitors... Astrology Pages 144

Thought Vibration or The Law of Attraction in the Thought World   ISBN: *1-59462-127-6* **$12.95**
by William Walker Atkinson   *Psychology/Religion Pages 144*

Optimism *by Helen Keller*   ISBN: *1-59462-108-X* **$15.95**
Helen Keller was blind, deaf, and mute since 19 months old, yet famously learned how to overcome these handicaps, communicate with the world, and spread her lectures promoting optimism. An inspiring read for everyone... Biographies/Inspirational Pages 84

Sara Crewe *by Frances Burnett*   ISBN: *1-59462-360-0* **$9.45**
In the first place, Miss Minchin lived in London. Her home was a large, dull, tall one, in a large, dull square, where all the houses were alike, and all the sparrows were alike, and where all the door-knockers made the same heavy sound... Childrens/Classic Pages 88

The Autobiography of Benjamin Franklin *by Benjamin Franklin*   ISBN: *1-59462-135-7* **$24.95**
The Autobiography of Benjamin Franklin has probably been more extensively read than any other American historical work, and no other book of its kind has had such ups and downs of fortune. Franklin lived for many years in England, where he was agent... Biographies/History Pages 332

Name	
Email	
Telephone	
Address	
City, State ZIP	

☐ **Credit Card**   ☐ **Check / Money Order**

Credit Card Number	
Expiration Date	
Signature	

Please Mail to: *Book Jungle*
                                    PO Box 2226
                                    Champaign, IL 61825
or Fax to: *630-214-0564*

ORDERING INFORMATION
web*: www.bookjungle.com*
email*: sales@bookjungle.com*
fax*: 630-214-0564*
mail*: Book Jungle PO Box 2226 Champaign, IL 61825*
or PayPal *to sales@bookjungle.com*

Please contact us for bulk discounts

DIRECT-ORDER TERMS

**20% Discount if You Order
Two or More Books**
Free Domestic Shipping!
Accepted: Master Card, Visa,
Discover, American Express

CPSIA information can be obtained at www.ICGtesting.com
Printed in the USA
LVOW070203160512

281940LV00005B/100/P